The True Joy
of Positive Living

The True Joy of Positive Living

AN AUTOBIOGRAPHY BY

NORMAN VINCENT PEALE

This is the true joy in life,
the being used for a purpose
recognized by yourself as a mighty one . . .
—GEORGE BERNARD SHAW

QUILL
WILLIAM MORROW
NEW YORK

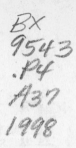
Copyright © 1984 by Norman Vincent Peale

All rights reserved. No part of this book may be reproduced
or utilized in any form or by any means, electronic or mechanical,
including photocopying, recording or by any information storage
and retrieval system, without permission in writing from the Publisher.
Inquiries should be addressed to Permissions Department, William Morrow
and Company, Inc., 1350 Avenue of the Americas, New York, N.Y. 10019.

It is the policy of William Morrow and Company, Inc., and its imprints and affiliates,
recognizing the importance of preserving what has been written, to print the books
we publish on acid-free paper, and we exert our best efforts to that end.

Library of Congress Cataloging in Publication Data

Peale, Norman Vincent, 1898–
The true joy of positive living.

1. Peale, Norman Vincent, 1898–
2. Reformed Church in America—Clergy—Biography.
I. Title.
BX9543.P4A37   1984   285.7'32'0924 [B]   84–8966
ISBN 0–688–16349–1

Printed in the United States of America

First Quill Edition 1998

2 3 4 5 6 7 8 9 10

BOOK DESIGN BY ROBERT FREESE

www.williammorrow.com

To my wife,

Ruth Stafford Peale,

partner in all our many activities,
with love, admiration, and gratitude

Acknowledgments

To Sybil Light
in appreciation of her help in
preparing this manuscript and to
Evelyn Yegella and Nancy Dakin
for their assistance

Contents

The True Joy
of Positive Living

CHAPTER ONE

Country Boy from Ohio

MANY PEOPLE WERE SURPRISED when I ended up a preacher, although I never got into too much devilment and was not what might be called a bad kid. In the small Ohio towns of the early 1900s, a preacher's kid was considered "different" and made to feel so. Every little thing he did that was a bit out of line marked him as a sinner. Preachers' kids' reputations generally were suspect.

But several influences conspired to make a minister out of an unlikely prospect for that profession. One was Father's preaching. The way he described Jesus Christ gave me, early in life, a profound admiration and enthusiasm for the Master. He had an incomparable way of making Christianity real and very exciting. He was a fascinating public speaker. I had enormous respect and affection for Father and always liked to hear him preach. So I was a regular churchgoer.

One summer Sunday in my boyhood, my mother was teaching a Sunday School class in the little Methodist church in Lynchburg, Ohio. Mother started out by commenting on the current status of the Cincinnati Reds, our baseball heroes. Then she launched into a description of Jesus, how He "set his face to go to Jerusalem," knowing very well what would happen to Him. What a man. What courage. Mother called it "guts." But He resolutely walked straight into the camp of His enemies because He loved me and was willing to die for me. That belief gripped me for life. It made me love Him forever. To me there has never been anyone like Him.

Although I tucked up this love and admiration for Jesus against my heart, had an accompanying love for the old hymns, liked to hear a good preacher, and was a believer, still I was what they called "not in the Kingdom." I was a vital, virile boy and attracted by the fleshpots, though I never did quite find out what they were all about.

I knew that my mother always wanted me to become a preacher. Father never pushed that idea, saying that I should learn from God what He wanted me to do in life and follow the divine will and guidance. Though I was drawn toward the ministry, I resisted it because, as a preacher's son in those small Ohio communities, I always seemed to be set apart as someone different from the other kids. If I did the slightest thing, like smoking corn silk behind the barn with the others, some would jeer: "Oh, you're a preacher's kid." This galled me, as it similarly troubled other sons and daughters of ministers, but such youthful trauma usually vanished as maturity advanced. However, I knew some ministers' children resented this attitude toward them so deeply that they repudiated the church altogether, though retaining personal veneration for their parents.

In one Ohio town we lived in, every Monday morning my father would go to the bank and the president would give him his salary check for the week. The banker would expect him to deposit the check forthwith in his bank. As he handed the check to Father, he would always ask, "Now, Brother Peale, do you think your sermon yesterday justifies this check?"

This riled me no end, for I usually accompanied Dad on this Monday morning ritual. But Father was urbane and responded in kind to this so-called witticism. It amazed me that my father and the banker were friends; I even found later that they actually loved and respected each other.

The banker lived in a big house down Main Street. It was set back, regally, among old trees, and a curving drive swept up to the door. Every morning a driver would take him in a spanking, shiny carriage, drawn by two beautiful black horses, down to the bank and back for lunch, and down and back in the afternoon. All as if he were some Roman conqueror; or at least that is how I resentfully thought of it. Who was this big shot to whom the servant of Almighty God had to come like a respectful suppliant?

But Father said, "One needs to know all about an individual, or at least all you can know, before a proper judgment may be formed. Now take this banker. He is the son of a poor farmer, a father who could never make a go of his few rocky acres. The family was poorer than we are. That boy came into town one day years ago and went up and down the street looking for a job, any kind of job. Finally he was hired by this bank as a janitor. He swept out, washed the windows, dusted the desks, ran errands, cleaned the toilet, and he did each lowly chore with cheerfulness and to the best of his ability. Years came and went, and finally he became bank president.

"He married a lovely girl and they lived together in happiness for twenty-five years or more. Then early one morning that team of horses and carriage you resent came to me and carried me to his big house where, for all his wealth and position, his lovely wife could not be saved. I was there when she died and sat with him in his grief. 'I'll never forget you and what you have done by being with me in the worst hour of my life,' he said, gripping my hand at the door.

"He has never spoken of it again, but it is his nature to conceal his feelings. But, you see, I know him and in his own way he loves me as one of his closest friends. So don't mind that we carry on that little ritual every Monday morning. It's just a way men have of showing the affection they have for each other."

Thereafter I saw the bank president as a man, rather than as a banker, which was what Father intended, I'm sure. And for this man I began to have compassion. Apparently it reached him because the last time I saw him, he put his arm around my shoulder and said, "Norman, you have a fine man for a father. Take good care of him always." So saying, he went back to his desk and waved me off. He had said all that he could. When some years later I heard of his death, I was saddened, but knew that a good man with clean hands had gone home to his Lord. To love people compassionately and to see the good in every man and woman was what my father taught his children by precept and example.

Then there is the lifetime memory of that Sunday night in winter when Father was holding the annual series of revival meetings in a little church in a small village in southern Ohio. In those days the two weeks of revival, with meetings every night, was the big event of the year in the country round about. There were no movies, no radio, no television to compete. The church had preeminence. It was not only the spiritual center but the enter-tainment center, the gathering place. And since Father was a powerful speaker, the church was always filled, and for the revival meetings it was standing room only.

In the little village, there was a man, Dave Henderson, a nice enough fellow when he was sober. But when drunk, he was by common consent "a holy terror." His drinking was periodic and he would be very much in his cups for several days.

Dave was a big man with hands like hams and fists having the driving power of pistons, so said those who had felt their impact in fights. Ordinarily genial, with liquor in him Dave would pick a fight at the slightest provocation. He also had the reputation of being the champion local cusser, and was quite foul-mouthed. Some said he was a wife beater, but his dignified and cultured wife would never admit to anything of the sort.

Curiously Dave was a fairly regular churchgoer, and he would sit in a back pew. He would always shake Father's hand on the way out afterward. "Good sermon, Reverend. I like to hear you talk." Father liked him, and often said that if old Dave ever got religion he would be a great man for the Lord. He worked on the big fellow spiritually, but with no apparent result. Until one night.

After preaching a strongly evangelistic sermon, it was Father's practice to invite any who wished their lives changed to come forward and kneel at the altar, and many did. His ministry re-sulted in conversions, and most remained faithful over the years. But this night after the revival sermon, no one had come forward, when suddenly there was a stir. Someone was walking down the aisle. The very floor seemed to shake with his tread. Mother looked around. "It's Dave!" she gasped. The big fellow knelt at the altar. He said something to Father. Afterward Father told us what Dave had said: "I don't want to be this way anymore, Rever-end. I want Jesus. I want Him to save me." Father prayed with him in a low voice and put his hand in blessing on the big fellow's unruly black hair.

Then Dave arose and faced the congregation. Boy though I was, I was awed by the look on his face, a look of wonder and inexpressible joy. It is printed on my memory to this day. Of course, some said the conversion wouldn't last. How could a renegade like that be changed in a minute of time? But it did last for over fifty years until he died. He became literally a saint, a new man in Christ, and for half a century he blessed the lives of everyone who knew him.

Then one day, only a few years ago, I heard that Dave's long and beautiful life was nearing its end. So I went to see him in his old home in the little Ohio village. I found him in bed, his hair as white as the pillow on which his great head rested. He was emaciated and frail. His hands on the coverlet were thin, the blue veins showing. I took his hand. It still had something of its former massive grip. Anyway, there was love in it. We talked of the old days and of the ways of the Lord Jesus, how He blesses all who love and follow Him.

"Your father was a great man, Norman, greatest man I ever knew. Who can be greater than a man who leads you to the Lord? And I love you, son. You were with me that wonderful night when my soul was cleansed, when the Lord came and saved me, one of His wandering sheep. I'll always love you, Norman."

"And I, you, Dave," I replied, choking up. "Let's have a prayer before I go," I said. "And I want you to pray." I knelt by the bed of the great old saint. He put his hand upon my head. His voice faded at times either through weakness or emotion, but every word is burned into my memory. His blessing is unforgettable. At the door I stood and waved at him. With a gentle smile he lifted his hand. I never saw him again.

As a little boy, awestruck by the mystery of change in a man's very nature, I asked Father to explain it. "All I can say is that it is the power of God." Then he added, "The Creator is also the re-creator." But the incident with Dave impressed my consciousness with the wonder and the glory of the ministry. I am certain that this, added to other experiences, overcame my resistance to becoming a minister.

* * *

I was born on May 31, 1898, in Bowersville, Greene County, Ohio, a charming village of some three hundred people, located on a dusty road running through lush pastureland. It was as peaceful and idyllic a spot as could be found anywhere in the Buckeye State, and it remains so today, even though it is only about a mile north of the Ohio Turnpike, halfway between Cincinnati and Columbus.

My father, Charles Clifford Peale, pastor of the local Methodist church, had been trained as a physician and had practiced medicine in Milwaukee, Wisconsin. He was the health commissioner in Milwaukee when he became very ill. His mother despaired of his life, and being intensely religious, she "promised the Lord" that if her son, Cliffy, was spared, she would endeavor to persuade him to abandon his medical career and become a preacher of the Gospel.

His return to health seemed a direct answer to prayer, and Clifford Peale, while in no way unduly subject to maternal domination, felt the influence of Providence and became convinced that his recovery did indicate that he was intended, by the Lord, to devote himself to full-time Christian service as a minister.

He had all the instincts of a physician, which he carried over into the ministry, and he became, I think, one of the first to demonstrate the working partnership in two healing disciplines: that of doctor of medicine and that of doctor of mind and spirit. As both an M.D. and a D.D., Father claimed whimsically that he was a paradox.

At any rate, my father turned out to be a very effective pastor and preacher. His first "charge," as it was termed in those days, was in 1895 at the village of Sugar Tree Ridge in southern Ohio. He and his bride, in a long one-day trip by horse-drawn wagon, a journey of some fifteen miles, transported their meager household goods from Lynchburg, Ohio, where they had grown up, to the little village to establish their first home. Three years later they moved to Bowersville, where I joined the family.

We were poor, but I never knew that we were. Later, sociologists wanted people like us to believe that somehow we had been mistreated by society. But we were good, clean, self-respecting, decent American poor, and we were not one bit ashamed of it.

At Bowersville my father was pastor of what was then called a

18

"circuit." He served three little churches scattered over an area of perhaps ten square miles. He would preach at one church on Sunday morning; at another, Sunday afternoon; and at the end of the Sabbath day he was in the third. From each church he might return home with a bushel of apples, a bag of potatoes, a basket of vegetables, sometimes a loaf or two of home-baked bread (I can almost smell its fragrance even now); and so we were able to get along famously.

He had to collect his own pay. I recall going with him once to a big brick farmhouse where the farmer gave him two round silver dollars. "That's all you've got coming to you, Reverend," explained the parishioner. "Due to the bad weather I've only been to church two times this winter." To which Father, who could always see humor in life, said, "Well, I'm glad to know that my sermons are increasing in value, for last time you only gave me fifty cents per sermon."

Mother's name was Anna DeLaney. She was the daughter of a native-born Irishman, Andrew DeLaney, and her mother, Margaret Potts, was a descendant of a member of George Washington's staff on the distaff side. Margaret Potts was a lady of English heritage. But somehow the Irish strain seemed to predominate in Mother's personality. She had a fair skin, blue eyes, and golden hair, and she walked with a charming, graceful carriage. I will always remember her hands as soft and gentle, but they were strong, too, with the effects of toil on them. She always did her own housework. At the same time she had an outstanding career in religious leadership. Everyone who knew Anna DeLaney in her youth, with one accord, told me that she was "the most beautiful girl in Lynchburg," some even going so far as to say "the loveliest young lady in Highland County."

Not long after my father returned from Milwaukee to Lynchburg, he was standing in the Peale Brothers store looking out at the passersby, when he saw a vision of loveliness walking up the main street of the village. Struck by her beauty and dignity, he asked his father, "Pa, who is that girl?"

"That is Anna DeLaney," replied Samuel Peale.

"Well, Pa, I'm going to marry that girl," announced Cliff Peale. And sure enough he did just that on October 25, 1895, in the

19

Methodist church in Lynchburg. Mother always said she held him off awhile so that he would not be conceited.

In all my growing-up days I thought she was the loveliest lady I had ever seen. I can remember her yet, always impeccable in her long white dress, a beautiful hat atop her golden hair, gracefully walking on a summer's day with a colorful parasol over her shoulder. And her beauty of face was matched by her beauty of character. I was always so proud of her. To me she always seemed everything that was good and fine. Mother was always a Christian woman of the old school, though not without a sense of humor and a happy delight in life.

The Irish in her nature would inevitably come out in the old Irish songs, which she sang in her sweet voice, and in poems about fairies on the lawn. She would recite traditional stories of the Emerald Isle that had been told her by her father and which she, in turn, passed on to her children. She possessed in full measure the proverbial Irish wit, romance, and tearful emotion. With misty eyes she would tell us romantically of old Erin, which she had never seen but which was very real to her nevertheless. But someday, some wonderful someday, she hoped to put her feet at last on the old sod of the Emerald Isle from whence her idolized father had come in the long ago.

Her mother, Margaret Potts DeLaney, was a dignified lady of the old ways. I remember her always in a rather formal black dress. She had the manners of an aristocrat, as befitted her background, but her humility and sweetness of nature endeared her to everyone, rich or poor. While she had the aristocratic manner, she was of that quality of character wherein she also had the common touch. I recall the delicious meals at Grandma DeLaney's house and the cultured character of her home; and even though she passed away when I was quite young, I can visualize her clearly over the mists of years as a great lady with a loving heart. My own mother took after her to a marked degree, blending her mother's dignity with her father's Irish wit and emotionalism, a remarkable and unforgettable combination.

Mother was fun, and she was always interesting. We would gather around her after dinner, and she would tell us in her charming and enthusiastic manner about what she had been reading, quoting from many authors. She was humorous, and if something struck her funny, which was a common occurrence, her laughter was irrepressible and infectious.

Once, something the preacher said at a funeral set her off. Sitting beside her, I could see that she was convulsed but desperately trying not to show it. Taking my hand, she whispered, "For heaven's sake, stop me from laughing." I gave her a stern look, which slowed her down somewhat, but I could still feel her shaking. Later I thought of this episode as I sat in the same pew at her funeral, and somehow the memory comforted me. Indeed, for me she never really died.

A few years ago I went back to Bowersville and called at the house where I was born. Mr. and Mrs. Roy Venard, kind and gracious people, live there now. Mrs. Venard asked me if I knew in which room I was born. Perhaps Mother had told me of that years before. I do recall a farm wagon that always stood in front of the house across the road and in which we neighbor children played. However, I have never been sure at what age memory begins, and perhaps I "remember" some events and incidents that were told me later.

Bowersville honored me by putting up historical signs at both outskirts of the village. Each sign is in the shape of the state of Ohio and reads: "Bowersville. Birthplace of the Reverend Norman Vincent Peale, minister and author."

I had heard about the signs, but had not seen them. So one day my wife, Ruth, our son, John, a professor of philosophy at Longwood College in Virginia, and I drove in a wide circuit from Dayton to Cincinnati in order to visit Bowersville. We saw one historical marker at the edge of town, and I was deeply touched and proud. We drove through the village to see if a corresponding marker was at the other end of town. John, who had made no comment at the first sign, now came up with the remark "Gee, Dad, they haven't got much to brag about around here, have they?"

Well, perhaps not, but I was invited back to speak some years ago at the celebration of the one hundredth anniversary of the village, and had one of the most curious experiences of my life.

I had developed a most excruciating earache. The strange part was that I had not had an earache since I was a young boy living in Cincinnati. At that time, my ailment had to be treated surgically. Now I was back at my birthplace to give an anniversary talk and suffering torments from my left ear.

Upon arrival in Bowersville, I said to Ruth, "You go in and tell the committee we are here but that I'm staying in the car until it's time for me to speak. Explain about the earache, but tell them nothing can stop me from making my speech. Have them keep the meeting going as long as possible. Maybe this ear will quiet down."

While I sat suffering in the car, a man came along and introduced himself as a local farmer. "The Lord has given me some healing power," he said. "Just why me, I do not know, but I would like to help you if I can." Then he continued, "It won't be me doing it. It will be the Lord who has, for His own reasons, worked at times through me, His humble servant."

So I said, "Please go ahead." Whereupon he put a big, rough, but gentle hand on my ear. "Now, Brother Peale, you just believe. That is all you have to do, just believe." Well, I liked this man, and I sat there affirming belief while he said a healing prayer aloud. Finally he removed his hand, and I did indeed feel much relieved and told him so gratefully. He left, and while I still had pain, it was much less than it had been.

Then another man appeared who was quite a bit younger than the farmer. He introduced himself as a doctor and said he had heard from Mrs. Peale about my ear. "Oh, it's much better," I said. "You don't need to bother, though I appreciate your kindness." And I told him about the faith healer.

He listened without comment, then said, "Well, tell you what let's do. In addition to that faith treatment, suppose I give you some antibiotic by injection." Being a believer in both methodologies, I replied, "O.K., why not?" And he proceeded to treat me.

I was so much improved when the time came for me to speak that I got through my talk without too much trouble. The next morning, after a good night's sleep, the earache was totally gone and to this date has never returned. Who healed me, the faith healer or the doctor of medicine? I am prepared to give credit to both. They were sincere Christian men. And does not God work through humble believers in all walks of life? Well, at any rate, this country boy from Ohio, who learned belief from a godly mother and a godly doctor-preacher, has long been convinced that spiritual power comes over many conduits.

One of Father's churches on the Bowersville circuit was called the Old Center Church. It still stands in a grove of great and aged trees, and in my boyhood it fronted on a dusty road. In the summertime, horses kicked up clouds of dust, and in the winter floundered through mud and ice and snow. Cornfields swept away on either side of the road, the corn knee-high by the Fourth of July, as the old saying goes, and tasseled out in the fullness of summer. After the corn was husked and stored in silos, the shucks were collected into sheaves. So characteristic is this of Ohio that those corn shucks in sheaves, silhouetted against the sky, are shown on the great seal of the state of Ohio.

Recently, on an autumn afternoon, I stood in the quiet sanctuary of Old Center Church with Wilbur Beard, a friend from boyhood. He recalled the names of devout people, household names of friends of the long ago, who used to sit in those pews when my father and mother were there. The pendulum of the old-fashioned clock on the wall, hung where the preacher could not fail to see it, was ticking off the minutes. Suddenly we were both silent, listening to the ticking of the clock.

"Wilbur, how long has the clock been on that wall?"

"Forever, I guess. At least as long as I can remember."

"My mother's pew?" I asked. He pointed to it, and I sat there for a few moments.

Then I walked into the pulpit and put my hands on the Bible where the hands of my father had often rested. "Same old Bible?" I asked. Wilbur nodded. "The clock ticked Dad's life away and Mother's and your parents and all those great people, those sturdy folk we knew."

"Time destroys at last," Wilbur said soberly.

"Yes," I replied, "but Lord Tweedsmuir once said, 'Time enshrines,' meaning, no doubt, the mystery of memory." We were two men growing older, sitting quietly in the understanding fellowship of long acquaintance. But Tweedsmuir was so right; time enshrines all those dear ones we have loved in life.

The long hold of Bowersville on my life was brought into focus years later when I needed to apply for a passport. I was twenty-five years old and decided that a trip to Europe would be an interesting project. Having no money for such an adventure, I organized a tour made up of about twenty of my church members in Brooklyn, New York. Thus I got a free trip and some two hundred dollars additional for expense money. Since I had no passport, I wrote to the registrar of births in Greene County, Ohio, at Xenia and asked for a birth certificate. In reply, I was told that there was no record of my birth, as births were not registered before the year 1900. The official suggested that I secure an affidavit of birth from the doctor who delivered me.

Not knowing the doctor's name, I wrote to my father for this information. He informed me that the doctor's name was Charles Clifford Peale. Fresh from big-city medical practice in Milwaukee, the doctor, recently turned preacher, felt he knew all about child delivery. The women of the town who knew him as preacher and not doctor "would have strung me up had anything gone wrong," he said with a grin. "I delivered you and put you in your mother's arms. Everyone in town came to see you."

I have spent most of my life in urban centers—Cincinnati, Detroit, Boston, Brooklyn, Syracuse, and over fifty years in New York City; but I thank God and Anna DeLaney and Charles Clifford Peale that I was honored by being born in a beautiful little American village where love of God and love of country and Christian morality were taught and practiced by sturdy people who were indeed the salt of the earth. To the last, at least in heart, I will always be a country boy from Ohio.

CHAPTER TWO

Steamboats on the River

IN EVERY PERSON'S LIFE, childhood memories are simple ones perhaps, but they are determinative influences in personality shaping. Life is not unlike a string of beads—a few memories, some unforgettable experiences strung together on a cord called routine. Perhaps we are largely made by memories and experiences of childhood.

My father's third church was in Highland, Ohio, some seventeen miles south of Bowersville, a small but charming village. My brother Bob was born there. In Highland I had one traumatic experience, which is still remembered locally. I was pushing a lawnmower and a neighbor girl was pulling it by the bar above the blades when one finger got out of position and it was suddenly severed. My father happened to be in the house, and I can see him yet as he replaced the finger, bandaging it in a proper manner until the girl could receive hospital attention. The lady is still able to use her finger normally, according to a friend of hers who visited me recently. Wonder if her memory of me is a pleasant one!

Old-timers in Highland still remind me of the Sunday in church when my young brother Bob was crying and being difficult to manage. Mother sent me home, to the parsonage next door, for a cracker. Soon I returned dragging down the aisle, to the amusement of the congregation, a five-pound bag of crackers, which is the way they were sold in those days.

In the years about which I am writing, the Methodist system of the bishop annually appointing pastors to churches, usually for a relatively short term, caused a feeling of uncertainty and some insecurity in a minister's family. As I recall, a pastor could not expect to remain at a church, no matter how well he was doing, for more than five or six years and usually not so long.

A family always "went to Conference" in September, the father not knowing for sure where he would be serving and the children troubled about where they would be going to school that fall. And generally schools had already started. The climactic moment of the conference was at the closing session when the bishop read off the appointments. Afterward families would sit back with either pleasure or disappointment.

From Highland we moved to the big city and were thrilled to be Cincinnatians. As a small boy living near downtown Cincinnati on a quiet, tree-shaded street, I recall lying in bed on summer nights and, when the wind was right, hearing the romantic whistles of steamboats on the river on their way up to Pittsburgh or down to New Orleans. A little boy's thoughts are long thoughts and they are mixed with dreams.

I would also hear train whistles, the long-drawn-out whistles of the old-fashioned steam locomotives as the trains sped through the night up Mill Creek, past East Norwood, the musical sound finally dying out in the distance. In my imagination I could see those brightly lighted trains flashing across the nighttime countryside through towns and villages on to Columbus, Cleveland, Buffalo; to New York or Boston. Would I ever ride those steamboats or trains to romantic cities? Then presently I would drift into sleepy childhood dreaming of steamboats on the river and speeding trains in the night. Perhaps it was then that I became a nomad. It may be why I now travel by air, over land and sea, approximately 200,000 miles a year.

Only once a year, on a long-anticipated and long-remembered day in summer, Mother and Father would take Bob and me on the old Island Queen up the Ohio River to Coney Island, which probably was named for the original in Brooklyn. Father's slim pocketbook was equal to only one such outing each summer. Of course, we went to the zoo, which was free. And at long intervals we would go to Chester Park, an amusement center, where Bob and I would ride the roller coaster once and stuff ourselves with one bag of popcorn between the two of us.

There were advantages to being minister's children, for occasionally the pastor would be given free seats to musical and athletic events. Naturally Bob and I were especially interested in the latter. We lived on Spencer Avenue in Norwood, a suburb of Cincinnati though an independent municipality. And our next-door neighbor was Frank Bancroft, a top official of the Cincinnati Reds National League baseball club.

Frank had a beautiful daughter named June, and not surprisingly the Reds flocked in considerable numbers to Mr. Bancroft's house. It was exciting for us kids to glimpse some of the most famous ballplayers in the country, and sometimes, in awe, we shook hands with them. Not infrequently Frank Bancroft would slip his neighbor, Pastor Peale, four tickets to the ball park. I still have a warm spot for the baseball club of my youth, the Cincinnati Reds. On moving to New York, I became a Brooklyn Dodgers fan and later rooted for the Mets.

Father was an excellent speaker, strong, positive, and persuasive; but Mother was, too. She was a raconteuse par excellence. She had the human touch and could weave a spell over an audience by her extraordinary ability to tell a story. Her narratives dealt with the old human things that every listener identified with. She would bring tears and heartthrobs one minute and laughter the next.

Mother had the most remarkable photographic memory I have ever known anyone to possess. I seem to have inherited it but not to the same extent. She could concentrate on a page of copy and repeat it nearly letter-perfect. Her talks were laced with apt quotations and literary passages; poetry fell from her lips in a flowing stream of inspired talk. Anna Peale was, in her time, what is now called a communicator. She could get a message across to her audience because she talked with complete sincerity in language and thought forms they understood.

I admired my father's he-man style of public speaking. I was charmed by Mother's lovely femininity coupled with her facility of mind and her skill in reaching the human heart. Both Mother and Father were ad-lib speakers who used neither manuscript nor notes. Both were avid readers and students of current events, eagerly participating mentally in everything that went on in religion, in public affairs, and in the thinking of their era.

Anna Peale was a natural-born leader. A diploma from the Lynchburg, Ohio, high school was the extent of her formal schooling, but the education she gave herself by reading, by listening, and by creative thinking added up, in my opinion, to the equivalent of Doctor of Philosophy and then some. There was no money to send her to college, which was a lifelong disappointment to her; but she made up for it many times over by constant self-education. She knew classic English literature more completely than anyone I ever knew.

Mother became interested in foreign missionary work and was soon put in charge of this activity for the National Foreign Missionary Society of the Methodist Church. She was assigned responsibility for the Methodists' work in South China, Sumatra, Singapore, and Taiwan. She made one very extended official trip to this area. And she spoke to many audiences abroad and at home. Her interest in public affairs was strong also. When she lived in Findlay, Ohio, she was the first woman to be elected to the city school board, and she served for several terms.

Had Anna Peale lived in a later era, she would very likely have run for Congress or some other form of public participation in citizenship. She would never have been considered a feminist. She was just an American, certainly not a pro-woman and anti-man individual. Mother was simply a human being who could easily hold her own in a very loving, outgoing way.

I went with her to the polls on the first election day that women could vote. It was my first vote, too, as I had just become twenty-one a few months earlier. We stood in line at the polling booth, she ahead of me. "Ladies first," I told her.

"Should have happened a long time ago," she muttered. "Imagine not letting women vote and that fellow over there has been voting for years," she said, pointing to the red-nosed town drunk.

When we emerged from voting, I asked, "Mother, how did you vote?"

"That is a private matter," she snapped, "but if you must know, of course I voted the only intelligent way—Democratic, for James M. Cox for President. And to show my impartiality, because I like him, I voted for Clint Cole for Congress, even if he is a Republican." Then curiosity got the better of her. "I suppose you voted Republican, like your father, for that old Warren G. Harding."

"Yes, I've got to admit I voted Republican. So I guess we cancelled out each other's vote."

"Not on your life," she declared. "I voted as an intelligent, thinking American solely on the issues, whereas you voted the Peale family men's tradition, unthinkingly." As we walked along, she put her arm through mine, lovingly, and said something about a black sheep in every family, politically, meaning me. Whereupon I reminded her that her father and grandfather had been Democrats.

Later we both became independent of political party labels, and at one time we both voted for the same presidential candidate.

My father loved people, all sorts and conditions of people, good or bad. To him there was no distinction. They were all God's children. He not only loved them, but he respected every person whether that individual was deserving of respect or not, for he never failed to see the better person within. He was one of the most genuine, big-hearted men I have ever known.

Once I encountered him on the street and to my astonishment and concern he was weeping. "Dad, what is the matter?" I asked.

"I have been calling on people as a pastor should, and the troubles and sorrows of humanity are enough to break your heart."

An event occurred one night that had a profound impact upon me and went far toward preparing me for my later work as a pastor. When I was perhaps nine or ten years old, a call came to my father from, of all people, the madam of a house of ill fame, called in those days by the explicit name of whorehouse, in the red-light district of Cincinnati.

Mother took the call, which shocked her some, but she reported that in that house a young woman, only nineteen years old, was dying and wanted to see a pastor. Would my father come and talk with her and offer a prayer? Father was never one to turn down a person in need. "Norman," he said, "you come with me and we will do what we can to help this poor soul through the gates of death."

"Clifford," exclaimed Mother, "you are not actually going to take your young son into such a place?"

"I am," he replied firmly. "Norman might as well start learning about the evil of this world. And besides, Anna, don't you think it will prevent misinterpretation if I go to that house with my own son rather than alone?" Father asked sagely.

Grudgingly Mother assented and we went on this unusual pastoral errand. We found the young woman, her face as white as the sheet, her slender hands lying limply on the coverlet. The madam and other women stood around the room against the wall. Father sat by the bed and asked the woman her name and where her family lived. His doctor's knowledge and instinct told him that she was indeed near death's door.

She told him that she came from a little country town in Kentucky where her family still lived. She described them as "honorable and upright Christians. But I am a bad girl. I started down a wrong path and have ended up a harlot. I'm a very bad girl. Is there any hope for me? Will the Lord forgive me?"

Father took her little, frail hand in his big, strong hands and said, "Not a bad girl, just a good girl who has acted badly. Do you love Jesus, honey?" he asked in his gentle, fatherly voice.

"Oh, yes, sir. But I've been unfaithful to Him."

"But don't you remember how He went out to find the lost sheep, Good Shepherd that He is?" She nodded and he continued, "Are you contrite and sorry for your sins?"

"Yes," she whispered. "Oh, yes."

"And do you here and now accept Jesus Christ as your Savior and ask His mercy and forgiveness?"

"I do," she said.

Then Father said impressively, "The Lord has forgiven you all your sins and will take you this day to be with Him in paradise." Then Father said a prayer, one of the most tender and beautiful in all my Christian experience. I opened my eyes as he prayed and saw tears running down the faces of the other women. But upon the girl's face was a look of peace. Even though I was still so young, the experience awed me by its beauty. This unholy place of evil became holy because, for a fact, the Lord was there. In that moment I saw the wonder and glory of the ministry, the majesty and power of the work of the pastor. That night the poor broken girl died, but the divine love accompanied her across the river.

When I was a young boy, I attended the old Williams Avenue school in Norwood, Ohio. The teacher of the fifth grade was Professor George Reeves. In those days, teachers, even those below university rank, were referred to with a dignity regretfully absent today. Mr. Reeves is stamped indelibly upon my memory. He was a large man, weighing over 220 pounds and of good height. He had a stern look, which covered up a kind heart. He was, in a sense, a character, which seems to be a term applied to any "different" type of person. But Mr. Reeves would do things that were unforgettable. For example, occasionally he would write on the blackboard in large letters the word "CAN'T." Then, dusting the chalk off his fingers, he would look at the class and ask, "What shall I do now?"

We knew what he wanted and chanted back, "Knock the 't' off the 'can't,' " which he proceeded to do forthwith with a sweeping gesture. Then he would say, "Let that be a lesson to you—you can if you think you can." Following this, he would point his big forefinger and growl, "And don't you ever forget it either."

Doubtless some modern instructors would lift an eyebrow at such pedagogy. But it must have had some teaching effect, for one student at least remembers the lesson after more than half a century. I bless the name of George Reeves, for he started a trend of thought working in the mind of a shy little boy. I am sure he had an influence upon my development of the positive thinking principle. He lodged in my mind the essence of an idea: The way one thinks has a powerful effect upon one's ability to perform effectively. Of course, I did not realize it at the time, but since the incident never faded from memory it follows that it had a pervasive and continuing influence in my growing experience.

I have a clear memory of the incredible night when Halley's comet, in all its glory, hovered over our very house on Spencer Avenue in Cincinnati. As we watched it, Father told us that so exact is the universe that this comet came on the dot every 76.1

years. "Dad, do you think I will be here when it comes again 76.1 years from now?" I asked.

His answer was characteristic. "I don't know; but length of life is not nearly as important as quality of life. I really do not care so much whether you will be here, but I do hope you will amount to something before Halley's comet comes back."

Our parents were always telling Bob and me to work and study hard, to be honest and of good character, to "be somebody." And along with it, we were adjured to serve the Lord and help people. We were to be true to the Christian religion and follow Jesus Christ in all things.

The current generation of young people can hardly know the intensity of the old-time Americans' wish to rise out of poverty. Mother often told us how the mother of Abraham Lincoln said to her son even though they lived in poverty, "Abe, be somebody." The same entreaty was given by succeeding generations of American mothers and fathers to their children, at least those we knew. These parents hated poverty, and mediocrity. Their consuming desire was that their children should amount to something in life, do more than they had done.

But this emphasis on achievement was accompanied by another one that apparently arose from the same desire to improve human nature and everyone's lot in life. It stressed the worth, even the sacredness, of personality. It was a concept that is indeed inherent in democracy itself, and that can be traced back to an even older literature, one basic to an American's faith: "Thou shalt love your neighbor as thyself." (Leviticus 19:18) From this derives compassion, respect for all men and women, and the urge to motivate everyone to be what, by God's grace, they can be.

This ideal was so ingrained in the heritage of my parents that they were forever indoctrinating their children with it. At one time we lived in a hillside section of Cincinnati, up which street cars growled, finally screeching around a curve at the top. A man was employed to grease the tracks to reduce the screeching noise. We children called him "Greasy Dick," shouting this at him frequently. Our parents told us to stop annoying the old man, but to no effect.

Then we missed him for several days, and one afternoon Father said, "Norman, I want you to go with me to the hospital to call on a friend of mine who is ill." Imagine my surprise when the patient turned out to be "Greasy Dick." But he was introduced to me as Mr.——, formerly a businessman who had fallen on hard times. Courteously Mr.—— said, "I have had the pleasure of meeting Master Norman." (In those days boys were often referred to politely as "Master.")

"You see," said Father as we left the hospital, "your 'Greasy Dick' is a fine man. Treat him that way."

But the greatest lesson came one Christmas Eve. Father and I were late Christmas shoppers, a habit which carries over into today. We were on Fourth Street in Cincinnati. A dirty, ragged old man approached me, put his filthy hand, which was like a claw, on my arm, and asked for a handout. I shook him off and wearily he continued on his way.

"Never treat a man like that, Norman. Besides, it's Christmas Eve," said Father. He reached for his thin wallet, extracting a dollar bill. "Here, take this," he ordered. "Go after that man and say to him just what I tell you. 'Sir, I give you this Christmas gift in the name of our blessed Lord Jesus Christ,' and watch what happens to him."

I recoiled. "Oh, Dad, I don't want to do that."

"You do as I tell you. Go on."

Thus prodded, I ran up the block and said, "Sir, I give you this Christmas gift in the name of our blessed Lord Jesus Christ."

A look of complete surprise came over his face. He swept off his battered hat, and with a courtly bow he replied, "And young sir, I am honored to accept your kind gift in the name of our blessed Lord Jesus Christ." As he said these words, he became transfigured. A wonderful smile illuminated his face and dignity seemed to possess him. In him, I saw the man he once was and could be again.

On our way home on the street car rumbling up Gilbert Avenue, Father asked, "What did you see when you gave the dollar to that man on the street?"

I did not need to fumble with words. I knew the answer. "I saw the man he really is," I said.

And Dad, ever the preacher, added, "Always remember and never forget it. Jesus Christ can make men and women what they can be."

When I was a boy, every Christmas was wonderful, but one stands out in memory. To begin with, Mother started making candy. There wasn't much "boughten" candy in those days except maybe the licorice, lemon, and chocolate drops that you bought at the grocery store. Fancy boxed candies were hardly available. So most families made their own, and I fondly remember the aroma that filled the house.

Mother laid out the pieces of freshly made candy. Then we all helped dip them in melted chocolate, maybe dropping a nut on top of each. Some pieces were green, others yellow, and so delicious that even now I find myself longing for a taste satisfaction that no modern machine-made packaged candy can supply.

But such is adult life that the thrills of childhood are elusive in recovery. I once read a letter written by an old man to the editor of a newspaper. He stated that in his childhood he had eaten peaches from a tree that grew by a brick wall in the yard of his family home in Troy, New York. He had never forgotten the taste of those peaches, and now in old age he would love to have one of them again. Did the editor perhaps know where such a peach could be found?

The editor replied in an editorial that speaks to all who wistfully look back on childhood's exquisite joys. "Better enjoy those peaches in memory, for even if you could go back and pick a peach from the very tree, something would have gone out of the taste that it had when life was fresh and new. Just keep it enshrined in the sweet taste of memory."

So it is with the aromatic candy my mother made in childhood's happy hour. What fun we had at Christmas with all the neighbors in for a taffy pull. Plenty of candy disappeared right then and there, but lots of rich-looking pieces were cut off with household scissors and laid out on the cleanly scrubbed table. No taffy I've eaten since compares with Mother's Christmas taffy.

For months before that never-to-be-forgotten Christmas, my brother Bob and I had dreamed of a bicycle. We haunted the stores looking at "wheels," as we called them in those days. We argued long on what color we would like, and about the virtues of the new ball bearings. We wanted a light on the front and a loud musical bell.

But our father was a preacher on a small salary and it wasn't easy to make ends meet. So the bicycle remained in the land of dreams.

Every year that Christmas did not fall on a Saturday or Sunday the family went to Lynchburg, Ohio, to the home of Grandpa and Grandma Peale. When Christmas Eve came, we all gathered in the parlor after supper. There we trimmed the tree that had been freshly cut in the woods nearby. On went the ornaments, a few of which still hold honored places on our Christmas tree today. Then followed the candles, not electric ones as now, but made of tallow. Surely not even in fairyland could there be any tree so beautiful as ours when, with room lights off, it stood in all its glory, and the combined aroma of pine and tallow candles filled the air.

We noticed whispered conferences between our parents and worried looks after the evening train had arrived from Cincinnati. But they put on a good front. Christmas morning came, and before daylight we crept downstairs. Mother and Father were already there, the tree was alight, and they greeted us with a kiss. There were gifts under the tree and what a happy time we had! However, there was a note of disappointment, though it was not mentioned. Then Mother said hopefully, "Let's all go down to meet the morning train from Cincinnati. Maybe Santa Claus forgot to send something, and perhaps it will come on the train."

So through the snow, the sound of sleigh bells filling the crisp, cold air, we went to the old B. & O. station. We heard the chattering telegraph instruments, watched the stationmaster come out looking important, heard the long whistle of the steam locomotive in the hills south of town. With a surge of power and much escaping steam, the train pulled into the station.

I could see Mother and Dad holding their breath as they looked toward the baggage car. And then there it was—a red bicycle with a light on the front. It was a secondhand bicycle, to be sure, and the two brothers had to share it, but to this day and forever that scene is etched in my memory. Bob and I were happy, but this was as nothing compared with our parents. Joy and love were shining in their faces.

Long afterward I learned that Mother had made her old coat last another season, and Dad had made do with a shiny blue serge suit so that we might have our dreamed-of bicycle. But you see,

35

ours was a home full of love and joy. And this is the reason why that Christmas will forever be enshrined in memory.

It was in my youthful learning process that I encountered the first direct emphasis on the positive thinking principle I was to develop later in several books and in many speeches and articles. I was impressed with the positive American way that produced an economic system providing more goods and services for the average person than any other system in man's history on earth. The system was not free of periodic depressions, nor did it eliminate poverty, but it raised the standard of living for millions.

I happen to have grown up and to have formed my life philosophy in a period when the Horatio Alger "strive and succeed" work ethic was universally believed in; when individual study and effort were honored; when to make something of your potential was highly regarded. Having been born and raised so close to poverty as to feel it breathing down my neck, I felt a strong desire to escape its control. Not that money in and of itself ever meant anything, for by nature I am of plain people. But still I have always resented poverty for myself or for anyone else.

I believed that by my own efforts in a free society, I could move up to a better level of existence for my family and perhaps help others to do the same. Hence, I have written and spoken on this subject constantly, urging people to believe in their own worth, to understand their God-given potential; and, therefore, by right thinking, decency, creative work, and God's guidance to make something really worthwhile of their lives.

Whenever I spend a night, as I do occasionally, in Cincinnati, I open my hotel room window and try to hear from out of the past the whistles of trains in the night and steamboats on the river.

CHAPTER THREE

Aluminum Salesman

LOWELL THOMAS AND I both lived for a time in Greenville, Darke County, Ohio. Lowell's father was a physician in Greenville, when my father was the Methodist pastor there.

Lowell attended high school in that town, several years before my time; he was expelled for some infraction, later considered minor. Many years afterward, when he returned as an honored guest, he buzzed the school in an airplane. I fared better, for when, with a couple of other boys, we painted the class numerals '16 on the walks leading to the school building, all we received was an order to wash them out plus a good licking from John Martz, superintendent of schools. Years later Mrs. Martz told me, "John hated to do that." To which I replied, "He didn't hate it as much as I did."

When one remembers incidents of a long life, the exact times and dates of early years become a bit of a problem unless a daily diary was kept. That I did not do. I was always much too busy or perhaps not sufficiently well organized. But I do know precisely the dates of our sojourn in Greenville.

One day a few years ago, on a Greenville stopover, I walked up the street where our family had lived and tried to recognize the house. The one at 222 West Fourth Street seemed most likely, though it looked different; certainly there had been some architectural changes in the property. At any rate, I took a chance and rang the doorbell. A pleasant-looking young man answered. "Is this, by any chance, the Methodist parsonage?" I asked.

"It was at one time, but the church built a new house. What can I do for you?"

"Once upon a time I lived here . . ." I began.

"What's your name?" he interrupted. When I told him he became sort of enthusiastic. "Hey, honey," he called back into the house, "here's the man whose name is carved in the attic." Whereupon a lovely young woman came to the door and invited me in. "Look around all you like," she said hospitably.

"What do you mean 'my name carved in the attic'?"

"Well, come along and we'll show you one of your boyhood enterprises." So, we mounted to the attic and, sure enough, there, carved deeply into a big beam, was "Norman Peale, Jan. 1, 1912." It appeared that on a New Year's Day long ago a thirteen-year-old boy wanted to be sure he would be remembered, or else he just had nothing better to do at the moment. I was glad to get to know Mr. and Mrs. Robert Marchal, who now own my boyhood home.

Another certainty as to the date of our stay in Greenville comes from a shocking memory. As the local newsboy for the *Cincinnati Enquirer,* a morning newspaper, I got up early every day to collect my papers at the railroad depot. One day after picking up the bundle, I started on my delivery route, then I opened the package. To this day I can remember exactly where I was standing, rooted to the spot, as I read perhaps the most dramatic headline of the era: "EIGHTEEN HUNDRED LIVES ARE LOST IN ATLANTIC OCEAN WHEN LEVIATHAN TITANIC PLUNGES INTO THE DEPTHS: WORLD-FAMOUS PERSONAGES ARE AMONG THE DEAD." That was on April 16, 1912.

Some of my most exciting boyhood memories have to do with my uncle William Fulton Peale, who graduated from the University of Tennessee and became a high-school teacher in Knoxville. Then he went into the oil business with a successful man named Edgar Davis and made a substantial fortune in Texas. But at the time that I was in high school, he was in the real-estate business in Iowa.

For the first time in my young life, I traveled alone on what seemed a long and complex journey to visit my uncle Will. My father told me that if I felt lost or confused to ask questions, and he suggested a policeman, a railroad employee, or an elderly lady as being the safest to approach. "Anyway," he said, "just use your head."

I found that using my head worked all right. The folks saw me off as I left home. I had to transfer in Chicago to take a Rock Island train to Des Moines, Iowa, where Uncle Will was to meet me.

The conductor told me to take a Parmalee bus to transfer between stations. So, clutching my suitcase—it was called a valise in those days—I pushed wonderingly through the milling crowds in the huge depot. At a driveway within the station portico, I waited for the bus, which proved to be an old-fashioned conveyance entered by a step up at the rear. Inside upholstered seats ran along the sides and accommodated probably ten persons. Passengers sat looking at others on the opposite seat as the bus rolled along the crowded streets. Overhead, elevated trains thundered. It was all terribly exciting to a half-scared country boy who was trying to appear nonchalant and sophisticated. I have a feeling through the mists of memory that this bus was double-horse-drawn. I also recall that to open a window you pulled up on a strap that let the window down, and tassels hung along the inside.

Upon arrival at Union Station, the driver clambered down from his high seat and turned a handle to open the rear door. The step came down and we all piled out. Some passengers stood waiting for the driver to hand down baggage where it was held in place on the roof by a brass railing.

I entered the station and found the big arrival and departure board where my train to Des Moines was listed. I was thrilled that I was going away out west beyond the Mississippi. I felt like a pioneer pushing on to the vast prairies. Perhaps I would even see some Indians. A tall, blue-uniformed conductor, whose cap read Rock Island above the peak, stood watch in hand. The watch was attached to his vest by a big gold chain. "Train to Des Moines and West," he announced. The engine was breathing steam. "All aboard," came the cry. Clutching my valise, I mounted the steps, entered the coach, found a seat, put the suitcase on the rack above, and sat back proudly. I had made the transfer in the big city.

The train moved out, bell ringing, and clattered across the points to its own track. Interminably, it seemed, street after street flashed by. But finally the city was left behind and we were traversing the farmland, towns, and villages of Illinois.

A vendor came through, and I bought a ham sandwich and a glass of lemonade. It was a hot day in summer and cinders from the engine up front blew in the open window.

Finally the train came onto a long bridge spanning the great Mississippi, father of waters. Across it we rolled to Iowa. I was out where the West begins, a long, long, long way from Greenville, Ohio. I was a man of the world. I was an adventurer, a descendant of all those intrepid souls who had traversed these prairies in covered wagons. Still, I was relieved when the train pulled into Des Moines Union Depot to see standing among the waiting crowd my uncle Will, straw-hatted and smoking a big cigar. He greeted me affectionately, "You made it, Norman, all by yourself. I'm proud of you." One of the most exciting memories of anyone's youth has to be that first big trip all alone.

My uncle conducted sales of building lots in various towns, Corydon and Clear Lake being two places I remember in particular. A local banker, for example, would make a deal with him to sell lots at auction on a piece of land taken over on a mortgage default. Uncle Will took me along with him on several such sales during summer vacation periods. This was a most exciting experience for a fourteen-year-old boy. We would map out streets on the plot and mark the lots with stakes I had painted. Then I would walk along the streets of the little town and give ladies boxes of candy and hand out an occasional five-dollar gold piece, merely saying to the surprised recipient that more candy and gold would be given at an auction to be held daily at a specified place.

Each day everyone present could put his or her name on a numbered card for a later grand drawing when a Model T Ford would be given free to the holder of the right number. But the winner would have to be present at the grand drawing in order to receive the car. This was designed to keep people coming daily to the auction.

So I was the advertising man, the painter of stakes, the street layout man, and the general flunky. It so happened that Uncle Will was a powerful speaker. In that pre-microphone era, it was claimed by admirers that the one prized voice that could be heard clearly by thirty thousand people at an outdoor meeting belonged to the silver-tongued orator William Jennings Bryan.

Before an auction, which was usually attended by thousands from the surrounding countryside, my uncle would test his own voice by having me go farther and farther away and signal at what distance I could still hear him clearly. He always claimed that he could do better than Bryan; and having heard both, I was prepared to accept Uncle Will's claim.

His speeches would move a heart of stone as he described how the lots would have homesteads on them in future years. First, little children would play under little trees; but in the evening time of life, the owners would be walking under giant oaks and maples.

The prices at which those lots went would be bargains at present values, and he did cause the development of some fine subdivisions. Traveling with Uncle Will and working with him provided a growing experience. "If you want to be a public speaker," he said, "rule number one is to be heard clearly. Rule number two is to articulate so people will know what you are saying. Rule number three is to have something worth saying. Rule number four is to be honest—completely honest. Rule number five is to give good value in what you are selling or advocating. Rule number six is to appeal to the mind, the heart, common sense, reason, and emotion. If you are going to be a preacher," he added, "stick around with me awhile and you'll know how to keep your church filled up." I protested his assumption that I would be a preacher, but he waved it off. "I know you," he would say.

Uncle Will was one of those simple, kind-hearted men who wanted to appear quite the contrary. But his assumed toughness was a phony effort, for always his big, loving heart showed through. I idolized him.

Uncle Will had to undergo an operation for cancer of the tongue when he was sixty-eight years old. He came to New York's Memorial Sloan-Kettering Institute for Cancer Research, and I was with him constantly. On the night before the operation, which would result in his being unable to speak, sadly I contemplated the fact that I would never again hear that great voice and the melodic tone that distinguished it.

"Uncle Will," I said, "I am sorry that you must undergo this suffering. The way you stand up uncomplainingly to this crisis and with such great peace impresses me greatly. You are a true Christian in the face of this adversity."

"Well, isn't that what we are supposed to do?" he asked. "To meet life's hardships like men? And besides," he added simply, "Jesus will see me through."

After a period of silence he said, "Norman, do you remember how Ma [his mother, my grandmother] used to pray for each of us when we all were little children? She made Jesus seem so near. Would you pray for me now? Not one of the high-faluting, Fifth Avenue prayers," and he grinned rather pathetically. "Just pray like Ma prayed. You remember how she prayed, don't you?"

"I'll try to do it her way," I said. So we closed our eyes and I prayed. "Dear Lord Jesus, bless my little lamb this night. Take little Willie in Your loving arms and watch over him throughout this night. Bring him safely to morning light. He is just our little boy, dear Jesus, and we love him so. Keep him always in Your watchful care that he may be a good boy always.

"Put him to sleep now, dear Lord. And may the everlasting arms shield him from all harm. Take care of our dear little Willie, always. Thank You, Heavenly Father. Amen."

Uncle Will opened his eyes, which were wet with tears. "I could almost hear her beautiful voice as you prayed," he said. "Don't you worry about me, Norman. With the help of Jesus I'll get through it."

I kissed him on the cheek and ran my hand over his head as Grandma would have done. I had never done so before, but things were different now. He pressed my hand and I went away. On this earth he lived only a short time, but I expect to meet him again in that heavenly land where there is no separation.

Perhaps the most difficult problem I ever faced as a youth was my consummate inferiority complex. I was shy and filled with self-doubt. In fact, I lived like a scared rabbit. I constantly told myself that I had no brains, no ability, that I didn't amount to anything and never would. I lived in a miserable world of self-deprecation. Then I became aware that people were agreeing with me, for it is a fact that others will unconsciously take you at your own self-appraisal.

One summer Sunday afternoon, my father said he wanted to call on a family living a couple of miles out of town in the country near Greenville, and he asked me to accompany him. We went on foot, our little fox terrier, Tip, running along with us. It was a rich countryside we traveled—Darke County, Ohio—and we passed prosperous-looking farms and waved to the people, since of course we knew them all. I recall that one family persuaded us to stop for a drink of cold lemonade, it being a warm day, then the farmer's wife served us a heaping dish of homemade vanilla ice cream with cookies. I have eaten ice cream all around the world, but this homemade dish remains in my memory as the most delectable ever—it was unforgettable.

We reached the family my father wanted to visit. There was some kind of trouble there to which he brought his caring spirit and practical skills. Then we started home, and he got me to talking about myself. I unloaded my problem about my inferiority feelings, which I had discussed with him on previous occasions.

My father's experience as a doctor and his genius as a pastor made him an acute curer of souls. His perception that abnormal guilt from bad thoughts, or wrong thinking about personality traits, could be harmful made him adept in dealing with my inferiority complex.

Finally we came to a place where several trees had been cut down, and we sat on convenient stumps. Father described the mechanism of inferiority and self-doubt feelings in a manner that would do credit to a modern psychiatrist. He stated that scientific treatment could probably cure me, but that such treatment was not available in our little village and besides, it was quite expensive.

"But," he continued, "there is a Doctor right here who can cure any disease of the mental and emotional life. He has a rare and amazing power to curette our unhealthy thought patterns. And He can heal the sensitive self-centeredness that lies at the root of inferiority-inadequacy feelings."

Finally Father asked me, "Norman, are you willing to let this

43

great Doctor, Jesus Christ, treat you for that inferiority complex? If you will let Jesus take charge of your mind, indeed your whole life, you can be freed of this misery which, if it continues, can destroy your effectiveness." I was profoundly impressed and said I would give my life into the hands of Jesus. Father told me to kneel down by the stump and he, too, knelt. I remember that Tip came up and licked my ear, then sat beside me. Father committed me to Christ in a moving prayer.

He then asked me to tell Jesus that I was giving myself into His hands and letting go, by an act of affirmation, all my inferiority feelings. As we walked home in the gathering twilight, I felt a strange sense of peace and happiness, as though I were really on top of my problems. Although I had another bout with inferiority feelings during my college days later, the same remedy was applied again, with the result that this self-defeating thought pattern was healed through the positive power of Jesus Christ.

I suppose I have spoken at just about as many sales rallies and conventions as most anyone, and I have had a lifelong interest in salesmanship and an appreciation of people in sales. In all likelihood this interest began with another sales experience during the summer vacation period at Greenville. In *The Youth's Companion*, a magazine long since defunct but widely popular among boys and girls of my generation, I read a very persuasive advertisement. It told enticingly of the profits that could be made in selling aluminum cooking utensils, house to house. The ad emphasized that this was an easy job that any enterprising boy could do. "It is a cinch," it assured.

I showed the advertisement to my father, who encouraged me to respond to it, perhaps because he thought it would be good for me, and he loaned me the fifteen dollars necessary to purchase the kit. Along with this kit came a suggested sales talk, a sure-fire spiel that would get results every time. After a few days, I felt I had mastered the sales talk; so one morning, blithely swinging my kit, I boarded the streetcar for Union City, a town just over the line in Indiana. I didn't quite have the nerve to sell in my own town of Greenville.

Arriving at the outskirts of Union City, I let a couple of streets go by as I mustered up a faltering nerve. Disembarking finally, I started up a street. The first house was unpainted and somewhat dilapidated, which gave me an excuse to pass it by. "They aren't progressive people and wouldn't buy this new aluminum ware," I reasoned. The next house was quite the contrary, well painted and neat, the grass closely cut, flowers along the walk. "These people are really up-to-date," I said to myself. "They know the best and already have aluminum ware. No use trying this place."

Then I realized I was afraid and looking for an out. So, resolutely I took myself in hand and, with a good old positive spirit, marched straight up to the door of the third house. Praying that no one would respond, I pressed the doorbell tentatively. The door swung open violently, and to my fear-struck eyes the biggest and most ferocious woman I'd ever seen stood before me, glaring. In a weak voice I mumbled, "You don't want any aluminum ware, do you?"

"Of course not," she barked and slammed the door in my face.

By this time I was tired. Telling myself that I had done a day's work, I boarded the streetcar for home, realizing I had failed completely. But I wasn't about to settle for failure, so I went to see my friend Harry. "Harry," I said, "have you ever been in the aluminum business?" When he said he hadn't, I turned my full potential sales power on him. "What," I thundered, "you've never sold aluminum ware? Boy, you are really missing the experience of your life and really good profits, too." I ended up by selling Harry a half interest in my business for $7.50. Giving him the sales talk to study, I said, "I'll meet you at the corner tomorrow morning at eight o'clock sharp. Don't be late. And we'll go back to Union City and have a terrific day selling."

Thus admonished, Harry showed up on time carrying his share of the merchandise. At Union City we passed the street of my abject failure of the day before. "That looks like good territory," said Harry. "Let's get off."

"No. We'll go on to the next street. I worked that one yesterday," I explained. At the street selected I said, "Now, Harry, get this straight. You must believe you are serving the needs of housewives and you must believe in yourself. Walk right up to the door firmly, put on a big smile, and never take no for an answer. You take that side, I'll take this one."

Harry walked up his walk; I walked up mine. Harry approached

45

his door; I approached mine. Harry rang his bell; I rang mine. And, believe me, I was fortified, for I had a partner.

After my strong and vigorous ring, the door opened slowly, and before my now-confident eyes appeared the most inoffensive little woman I had ever seen. "Madam," I said in a firm, clear voice, "I've come to do you a great favor. I have come to supply you with aluminum ware."

Weakly and very politely she asked me in and ended by signing one of the best orders I sold all summer long. Years later when I spoke in Indianapolis, an aged lady took me by the hand. "You sold me some cooking utensils long ago in Union City. I liked you, for you were young and confident and enthusiastic; and what a good salesman! Now you 'sell' the Gospel with the same enthusiasm, if you don't mind my using that expression." As she turned away, she said with a smile, "Would you believe it? I still have a couple of those pots and pans." A footnote—Harry also made a sale.

I have one painful memory of our life in Greenville, and it has to do with the time William Jennings Bryan came to town to deliver a speech. From the standpoint of public speaking, no politician could compare with Bryan, so great were his voice, musical flow of words, and dramatic gestures. Once during a speech, I saw him lift a water pitcher high above the table, at least three feet, pour a long stream of water into the glass held in his left hand, then empty the glass into his mouth, placing both pitcher and glass back on the table without missing a syllable in the entire process. The vast audience watched this procedure in rapt fascination. Great crowds would always turn out to sit spellbound as this three-time candidate for President spoke.

Greenville had less than ten thousand population, and perhaps the appearance of William Jennings Bryan may have been at the summer Chautauqua program, in those days a vastly popular institution and a speaker's circuit that brought the greatest artists and orators to small towns. The meetings were held out of doors or in a huge circus-type tent to accommodate the crowds that came in horse-drawn buggies from miles around. Another boy and I, excited by the great occasion, surreptitiously secured a cigar and cut it in half. Crawling under the roughhewn speaker's stand, we lit up and sat puffing away while Bryan stamped about on the platform above us. Soon we both began to turn green, and then we both were deathly sick, retching and vomiting while Bryan thundered on. Perhaps this experience was not without value, as it started me on my way to becoming a lifetime non-smoker.

I heard Mr. Bryan many times after that, and to this day I remember the matchless quality of his inspired delivery and his impressive presence. Perhaps his most famous speech in a political context was the one which swept him into nomination for President at the Democratic national convention in 1896 when he declared dramatically, "You shall not press down upon the brow of labor this crown of thorns. You shall not crucify mankind upon a cross of gold." But I believe his masterpiece was not a political speech at all, but a religious one entitled "The Prince of Peace," which he gave countless times over many years. To me and to the thousands listening, that address was the speaking event of a lifetime.

I heard Mr. Bryan deliver that speech two or three times. The first time was when I was a very small boy and I distinctly recall going with my father on a train to the old Lancaster Ohio Camp Grounds where the address was to be given.

Bryan rode, like everyone else, in the day coach. En route he was surrounded by men, including Father and me. The great man said, "Son, come and sit on my knee." And for a little while on that train journey, I perched on the Great Commoner's knee.

Although Father was a Republican, he often said that Bryan was one of the greatest orators of the era.

Father had a great belief in people. For example, take the case of the minister whom I shall call Bill. Brother Bill, as he was affectionately called, was a happy, dedicated pastor. He was an inspiring preacher who loved and served his people, partaking with them in all their joys, successes, troubles, and sorrows. A caring and unselfish man, he was considered to be truly a saint. He was content with the little crossroads church he served. As superintendent of churches in that area, my father was Bill's ecclesiastical superior.

Then, sudden tragedy descended. Bill's always peaceful existence was shaken to its foundations, and apparently he was unprepared for it, not having developed a faith for personal adversity and a philosophy to cushion the shock. He tramped the roads unceasingly, no longer the man he had been. He would absent himself, but always provided a good substitute so that the work of his church went on after a fashion.

One day Brother Bill appeared at our home. He was obviously under great strain. "Dr. Peale," he said, "I can't stand it anymore. My life is ruined. I've come today to resign from my ministry and from the church. And I'm going away somewhere never to be heard of again. You see, I'm ashamed to look you in the face, you've been so good to me. But I have become a drunk, a plain no-account drunk. I can't carry on as a preacher when my conscience accuses me as a liar and a cheat."

Father hadn't been a doctor and a pastor for nothing, and he knew how to receive a confession and explore a personality to apply healing. He showed no sense of shock, certainly expressed no condemnation. Father had the dispassionate objectivity of a scientist, together with love for this poor broken man.

"Bill," he said, "I want you to do as I say." He reached in his pocket and pressed some money into the minister's hands. "I want you to go up to Lakeside, Ohio. They are having a revival meeting there and you just get converted all over again. If you can't handle alcohol, the Lord can; and I'm going to pray for victory. There are better days ahead. Stay at Lakeside until I send for you." Though he protested, Bill docilely followed orders.

Then Father called a meeting of the members of Bill's little church. He told them about their pastor, and the additional fact that Bill's father had been an alcoholic. He gave them a little talk on his idea of the nature of Christian fellowship. He stated that with the help of church members he wanted to work out a plan of salvation and understanding for their pastor and he asked them not to expel him from the fellowship until every effort had been made to restore him by the grace of God.

He was speaking to a group of men and women, farm people, the sort of folk the tongue-in-cheek, supposedly sophisticated, and holier-than-thou media often write off as stiff-necked and narrow-minded.

A long silence ensued until a rugged, middle-aged farmer spoke: "It might have been any one of us. It might have been me."

One said, "Some of you know that I was anything but a saint. And I backslid after I was converted and joined the church. But you didn't turn your backs on me. Let's do the same for Brother Bill."

Father was surprised by the turn of the meeting, but it was as if everyone wanted to stand by Bill's side. True, some were tight-lipped, and Father expected some denunciation. But it did not happen, for the atmosphere was understanding and forgiving.

Father made the situation clear. Bill could not serve as pastor until and unless he gained victory over his problem, until the Holy Spirit had reorganized him. Meanwhile, all would pray for their leader, for his redemption and renewal.

When he told us about it later, Father said, "Perhaps some might criticize me as being lenient and careless of the integrity of the church. But I believe it is our duty to go out after the lost sheep, even if it is the pastor himself. For the first time, in this small country church I saw the glory of Christianity, the brotherhood of humility and love in action. It was wonderful."

Brother Bill, supported by the prayers and affection of the people, found the Lord in the power of the Holy Spirit. He became a new man in Christ, old things passed away, all things became new. The validity of his change was attested by the fact that he never again fell away and continued faithful until his death, a walking, living sermon on the power of Christ to change a person and the effect of Christian fellowship in action.

Never have I forgotten the saga of Brother Bill, his tragedy and his falling away followed by his recovery. But more than that, I saw early in life that through faith in Christ and by living in His spirit, Christians can attain stature in compassion, in understanding, and in brotherhood. In Christ the humble believer becomes great.

While living in Greenville, our family became complete with the birth of my brother Leonard DeLaney Peale on April 20, 1912. He was born in Christ Hospital in Cincinnati, and Bob and I were playing ball with other boys in the backyard at home in Greenville when a neighbor woman came running across the lawn to tell us we had a baby brother. To celebrate, Bob and I went that evening to the "picture show" (the term "movie" would

49

come later). But we were summoned from the theater and told that we must go to Cincinnati by the early train next morning if we were to see the baby alive. I recall how, hand in hand, we two young boys were led in to see the baby brother whose little life hung in the balance. Happily, he survived.

CHAPTER FOUR

Chapel Steps

THE LEADING MEN'S CLOTHING STORE in Bellefontaine, Ohio, where we lived after Greenville, was run by Emil Geiger. Emil's outstanding characteristics were a gracious and lovable personality and strict honesty. I know, for I used to work for him after school, on Saturdays, and occasionally on some special project.

In those days men and boys in our low economic level had only two suits, one worn every day and one called our "Sunday suit," worn only to church or other special occasions, and both had to be long lasting. Accordingly, Emil's turnover of inventory was slow, and now and then he had to unload merchandise that was perfectly good but had gone a bit out of style.

One day he said, "Norman, I want you to take some trips out into the country and sell these leftover suits to farmers, house to house." He had displayed them neatly in a covered wagon. "These are perfectly good suits, splendid English cloth, and well made. They will make fine 'Sunday suits.' And if the customer takes good care of the garment and keeps it awhile, it will eventually come back into style. Emphasize this and don't sell a suit unless it fits or can be altered satisfactorily. And I'm putting a fair price on each suit. Always remember, son, the secret of salesmanship is to have good merchandise that you can honestly recommend. And when your product is something the customer needs and will serve him well, be a good persuader."

After Emil talked to me along these lines, I picked up the reins, clucked to the horse, and off we went into the farmlands of Logan County. There was one advantage to this job which I had not realized. The only leisure a farmer had was at noontime or in the early evening. So I planned to arrive at a farmhouse at dinnertime, which was always at noon, or at suppertime. As a result, my selling job got me some of the most delectable and filling meals I ever had in my life. Always it was good old Ohio cooking, which I still believe is the finest in the world—meat or chicken, mashed potatoes, gravy, vegetables, and closing off with big wedges of pie topped with ice cream. My lifelong waistline problem began, I do believe, during my clothes-selling campaign for Emil Geiger. It required only a few days to sell out my goods completely, and was Emil pleased! He gave me a couple of dollars as a bonus and put his arm around my shoulder. "Son, you have the makings of a real salesman. You liked those people and well you should, for they are the salt of the earth. You dealt honestly with them and you are a genuine good persuader."

The years passed, and one day from my pulpit in New York I noticed a familiar face in the congregation. It was my dear friend, Emil Geiger. He grinned at me, and I was so pleased to see him that I smiled back. Later in my study we talked over old times. Emil said, "Remember when you sold our excess inventory by peddling suits in an old wagon? Well, you are just the same in this job. You love the people, you have merchandise we all need, you are honest in your belief in what you are offering, and you are a good persuader." Then he added his highest Jewish compliment, "Only, you should have been a rabbi." As he left my study, we embraced affectionately. I never saw him again but shall remember him forever gratefully.

Over the mist of years, fond memories of Bellefontaine flood my mind: the courthouse in the center of town surrounded by what was claimed to be the oldest paved street in Ohio; the high school with its great teachers, especially Professor Guy Dietrick, later a member of the Ohio legislature, who made the drama of history come alive; the boys and girls whom I knew, some now gone on to a higher school beyond, some still the fine people they have always been: Bob Cooke, Vincent Castle, "Hike" Newell, Garton Churchill, Glenn Hill, Sammy Kaufman. Wish I could remember all the names, but I can still see their happy faces as they were then in the morning of our lives.

And then there was "Sport" Dietrick, no relation to the professor. Sport pressed clothes to work his way through high school and college. After college he worked in a bank in Worthington, Ohio, and was a rocklike man of character in that community. Came the dark days of the Great Depression when there was a panicky run on the banks. To the line of worried people outside his bank, Sport, now its president, made a simple statement: "I assure you of the safety of your deposits." That was enough. Sport Dietrick's assurance was as good as gold; or better still, as good as his character.

Sport took me to Delaware, Ohio, one day and pledged me to his fraternity, Phi Gamma Delta, at Ohio Wesleyan University, himself placing the white star on my lapel. Sport was a saint of sorts, but he would laugh that big old laugh of his if he were to read these lines written by his boyhood friend. However, one thing is sure, he is with the saints over there today because of what he was here.

I think of my lifelong friend, Sammy Kaufman. The Kaufmans and the Geigers were the only Jewish families in a community of mostly Methodists, Presbyterians, and Baptists. But in those good old days of the early twentieth century, no one seemed to give any thought to distinctions of race or religion, at least not in our little town. Sammy and I went to school and high school together, inseparable companions. He was always an honorable and upright man. He worked for community development and was a constructive influence. Sammy lived out his life, never seeking acclaim but earning the love of all who knew him. He was a great American and deserves love and honor.

My old shyness followed me to college, though I had better control of it after that never-to-be-forgotten spiritual experience with my father at Greenville. But it was always there: an inferiority feeling, a sense of inadequacy. It was especially evident in social contacts beyond my own close personal friends. I was tongue-tied with new people of any age. But strangely enough I wanted to be a public speaker, though the mere thought of appearing before people terrified me.

As though it were yesterday, I recall the time in school when my assignment was to make some brief remarks at a special assembly of all the students. Starting fairly well, imagine my chagrin to hear a girl in a front seat say in a stage whisper, "Oh, look at his knees shake." They were indeed shaking, but how diabolical to mention the fact publicly. This angered me, so doggedly I persisted if for no other reason than to show her. I can see her impish and derisive face to this very day.

Yet an extra force always seemed to emerge when I prayed earnestly about my problem. Thus, I prayed myself onto a debating team in high school. There was real elation when we actually won a debate on a subject then on the public mind: "Resolved that the primary system of selecting candidates for office is superior to the old convention system." Enthusiastically I spoke on the positive side of this question, becoming so interested that I forgot myself and therefore had an exciting and satisfying experience in public speaking. This clearly showed me that the problem was my consciousness of self, but it wasn't all that easy to correct.

One night a while later my father sent me to the church on an errand. I walked into the darkened auditorium where the only light in the large sanctuary came from the streetlamps on the corner as it filtered through the stained-glass windows. The encircling balcony was filled with shadows.

Still excited by the experience of the debate, I went into the pulpit and started speaking to the empty church. If I say so myself, it was a powerful sermon, probably my best; and sadly, no one heard it. But without my knowledge I did have an audience. Father had thought of something else he wanted, and on entering the church had heard his son declaiming from the pulpit. Sitting in the far shadows, he listened. Later, he said, "You have it in you to be a speaker, better than your father," he added modestly and with the self-effacing pride fathers take in their sons. "But you must get yourself out of the picture. And the best way to do that is to put Jesus at the center. If you love the people to whom you speak and forget yourself, you will eventually find yourself. Anyway, congratulations from one who, tonight, heard the real Norman Peale. Always be real, son," he admonished as we walked home to the parsonage on North Detroit Street.

On a September day in 1916, Father drove me to Delaware to enter Ohio Wesleyan University as a freshman. The choice was Wesleyan because the children of ministers got a generous discount. As we approached the beautiful college town where I was to spend four years, I grew more and more shy and I was already homesick. The Phi Gamma Delta fraternity house would be my home, so Father took me there and together we carried my belongings to my room. Then he said, "Well, Norman, it's time for me to go." Sadly I followed him to his car. Standing there, he said, "Aside from vacations, you are today leaving your home for good. Mother and I have tried to raise you as an upright, Christian boy. We love you and believe in you. I hope you will never fall into sin, for the temptations to which a boy away from home is subjected are many. I only want to say this: If you ever get mixed up with liquor or women or anything, don't lie to me. Always level with me and I'll help you work through it." Then he choked up. "Just remember this—always stick to Jesus. I love you."

So saying, he got in the car and with a wave of his hand, turned the corner and was gone. Standing there with tears in my eyes and feeling very forlorn, I thought, "I love him—what a guy." He knew precisely what to say to a boy under the circumstances and how to say it. And what he said and the way he said it remain clear and loving to me as I write these lines more than sixty years later.

In the Phi Gam house, I roomed the first year with Cecil J. Wilkinson, "Scoop," as he was called because he was editor of *The Transcript,* the college paper. Later Scoop became editor of the Phi Gamma Delta magazine and general secretary of the national fraternity, and was always an influence in the life of college youth. In our room was a double-decker bed. Naturally he, being president of the fraternity and a senior, occupied the lower bunk and I, a lowly freshman, the upper.

One of my memories is of putting up the window on bitter-cold winter nights, climbing up to my bunk, and snuggling under warm blankets only to hear Scoop say, "Freshman, get up and turn on the lights. I want to take a last look at Nell's picture before I go to sleep." Painfully, teeth chattering, I struggled out of my upper deck, the cold wind whipping at my bare feet, and turned on the light so that Scoop could gaze again fondly upon the face of Nell Herbert, a lovely girl whom he subsequently married.

Scoop Wilkinson was the acknowledged Mr. Phi Gamma Delta of his time, as the present national secretary, Bill Zerman, is of his era. He became the undisputed leader of the college fraternity system in the United States, and did much to hold it to the high standards and objectives for which it had been organized a hundred years earlier.

I was most fortunate in the type of boys who were my fraternity brothers. A later roommate was Charles B. Mills of Marysville, Ohio, the son of a country doctor. "Chid," as he was called, started his working life as an after-school and vacation office boy in the O. M. Scott Seed Company. He never worked for any other employer, continuing after college to become president and finally chairman of the board. He built the company into one of the largest and most respected in the country. Chid was always a leader in this industry, and became one of the most influential people in Ohio, a friend to governors and senators.

But primarily Chid's service was as a Christian layman. He, too, was a saint, a humorous, rugged one who had a good time being a Christian. He was the acknowledged Mr. Ohio Wesleyan. I owe much to these, my college roommates, and to their continuing lifelong friendship.

My closest friends in college were John J. Joseph, later vice-president and legal officer of the Ohio Bell Telephone Company; Belford P. Atkinson, executive vice-president of the Ohio Bankers Association; Charles H. Eichorn, an Ohio insurance executive; Gardner H. Townsley, a newspaper editor in that state; Doug Torrence, a Marion, Ohio, businessman; and Leo Wilson, an Ohio clothier.

Though I had these intimate associations with campus leaders and enjoyed an interesting and exciting life generally, still I continued to struggle with inferiority feelings and my miserable self-consciousness. Then one day occurred the supreme event of my college career. Although I did not know it at the time, later it proved to be one of the most important turning points in my life.

One day after a class with Professor Ben Arneson (who taught economics), he said, "Peale, wait a moment. I want to have a little talk with you." When all the others had departed, this kindly man was really tough with me; that is, as tough as he could get. "What's the matter with you?" he asked sternly. "I know that you are proficient in this course, that you know the stuff. But you are so terribly shy, so embarrassed when I call upon you, that you get tongue-tied, red in the face, and your inferiority feelings stick out all over. No wonder students snicker. Don't you know that shyness actually is a form of egotism and extreme self-awareness? In the name of heaven, be a man! Stop being a worm, or a scared rabbit. You are a minister's son and ought to know something of our Savior Jesus Christ. Let Him help you, for He will." He had given me the plain, unvarnished truth about myself. He had described me, and I didn't like what I heard at all.

Stomping out of the classroom, I was filled with anger and vowed I would leave the university forthwith. But by the time I had reached the outside, my anger had cooled a bit and I stopped, for some reason, on the steps of Gray Chapel, on the fourth step from the bottom. I remember it well. Professor Arneson was right and he was interested in my welfare. What should I do about it? I prayed, really prayed from my heart, from the deep place inside. "Lord Jesus," I said, "I need help and I need it now. You can change a drunk into a sober person, a thief into an honest man, a harlot into a good woman. Can't You change a poor soul like me into a normal person? Please, dear Lord, work Your transformation in my life." And I thanked Him, for the feeling was overwhelming that my prayer was going to receive an affirmative answer.

Nothing happened at the moment except that I felt strangely peaceful. I wanted to cry and to laugh at the same time. And there was a warm and happy feeling inside me. A sense of Presence came to me, as if Jesus were right there. And I am sure that He was.

There may have been some collusion between teachers, but I never thought so. A few days later our professor of English literature, William E. Smyser, stopped me after class. "Norman," he said, "there is a book in the library edited by Bliss Perry on the works of Emerson. You might find it helpful. And while you are at it, look into *The Meditations of Marcus Aurelius*. These two writers suggest the great possibilities in the control and use of the human mind. They outline how our thinking can be increased in effectiveness." And so Emerson and Marcus Aurelius became my lifelong teachers.

Then another day some weeks later, our professor of English Bible, Roland Walker, told me I needed another degree credit in Bible. Still resisting the ministry, I was trying to short-cut the Bible requirements. The professor said, "My suggestion is that I give you a special course on Paul's Epistle to the Romans. Doing it privately will take a much shorter time than in a semester of class work. Also, you should seriously bring your mind up against one of the few greatest minds in history, the mind of St. Paul. What you learn about the Bible will be secondary to what this study will do for you as a thinker." That study project became one of the most determinative influences in my total learning process.

Gradually my shyness lessened and the old inadequacy feelings became more normalized. They have never entirely disappeared and probably never will. Even now, when I am being introduced as a speaker to some large crowd in a hall or at a dinner, or even before a small group, that old inferiority tries to reach me. But I know what to do. I pray to Him who released me back on the chapel steps long ago, and He gives me, once again, power over myself.

When World War I broke out in 1914, our family was spending a month at Lakeside, Ohio, a Methodist camp meeting center on Lake Erie. As though it were yesterday, I can remember stopping in my tracks, caught by the headlines in *The Cleveland Plain Dealer* telling us that the Kaiser's helmeted goose-stepping troops had invaded Belgium. Europe was at war. I was sixteen years old. Though it was all far away and remote from our peaceful lives, the drama had an unforgettable impact.

When I entered Ohio Wesleyan in the fall of 1916, the war fever was rising and the United States' entry into hostilities was imminent. Seniors and juniors were already enlisting in the Rainbow Division, and on April 2, 1917, when President Woodrow Wilson sent the declaration of war to Congress, the upper classes were soon practically denuded of male students.

This, in effect, put sophomores, of which I was one, into student leadership positions. The Student Army Training Corps

(S.A.T.C.) was inaugurated on campus. We were inducted into the U.S. Army and put in Army uniform. The campus, in fact, resembled an Army camp. We moved into barracks. The gymnasium was one, and it was filled with cots. Another barracks, the local Y.M.C.A. building, was where I was quartered. A rather tough old Army captain became our commanding officer, displacing our genial president as top campus authority.

While we all ranked as privates, some were appointed student officers, and I was made a second lieutenant. None of us, of course, had any military training, but we soon became fairly knowledgable about "attention," "squads right and left," and the rudimentary orders. There was much bungling by the untrained student S.A.T.C. officers. I'm sure the worst incident of all happened on the crisp autumn day when our hard-boiled Captain Loman mustered Company A outside the Y.M.C.A. and marched us to the university gymnasium. The route was through a side street and on down to the campus.

To my surprise and consternation, when the company was formed the captain bawled out in stentorian tones, "Lieutenant Peale, take command." We discovered later this was one of his tricks or tactics to train us to be ever alert and ready. But I was neither. I could only salute and say, "Yes, sir."

I must point out that in those days Ohio Wesleyan was a thoroughgoing dry institution that frowned upon any use of alcoholic beverages. And saloons were completely off limits. One of the saloons was operated by a man named George Buchman. He had an expansive waistline across which spread a golden watch chain, from which dangled a resplendent fob. His green tie always sported a bulldog stickpin. We were never supposed to have any association with George, but he was a gregarious person and spoke in friendly fashion to all of us on the street.

Well, as temporary commanding officer I yelled, "Attention," and with much heel-clicking the company responded. "Forward march," I thundered and could hear the troops behind me marching in orderly style. Then we came to the corner. Directly ahead was Mr. Buchman's saloon, the swinging doors already opened for business and George by the doorway. For the life of me, I could not remember at the moment whether the command should be "columns left," or "squads left," or "to the left, march." My schoolmates, upon whom military discipline rested lightly and moved by a diabolical impishness, marched on relentlessly, piling up in disorder inside the saloon to the great delight of all including George.

Forgetting all about anything military and overwhelmed by confusion, I reverted to prewar type, yelling at the top of my voice, "Come on, you guys, get out of here!" They pretended not to hear and continued to mill around in the saloon. Finally they took pity on their frustrated lieutenant. I got them into some kind of order, but I could hear them chuckling all the way down the street. All of which may explain why I never moved up in the military establishment.

Despite this faux pas, I was slated to go with others to officers' training camp. But then came the armistice. The war ended and the campus returned to the quieter pursuits of peace. We were mustered out of the U.S. Army. The world was "saved for democracy" and there would be no more war, or so we innocently thought.

Of my unhappy memories of the First World War period two stand out. One was the great flu epidemic. It was a veritable worldwide plague that killed 21,000,000 people, more than twice the number killed in the war. The medical profession was hard put to it to cope with this scourge. Apparently it was a new sort of infection, originating in China, whose virulence resulted in an extraordinary death toll. However, our doctors finally found answers, and subsequent influenza epidemics have never had the potency of that of 1917–1918, which entered so many households and took the lives of more than 500,000 Americans.

The second memory is also tinged with sadness. It was the attitude developed toward our German American population. Suddenly these loyal citizens became suspect. Some people of non-Germanic ancestry turned against lifelong friends whose parents or grandparents had come from Germany years before to the United States. To this day, I recall my parents telling of the hurt experienced by these good people whose only "misfortune" was to have had German names. They were sturdy, moral, and upright churchgoing men, women, and little children who suddenly became outcasts. But native-born Americans, while likely to be swept up occasionally by irrational feelings, are still good at heart. At war's end, they tried to make up for their unkind super-patriotism and unthinking actions. And it is to the credit of our German citizenry that they put their hurt aside.

I could never understand this anti–German-American attitude for I was reared in Cincinnati among an almost totally German population. They were my classmates, my closest friends. I knew them well, never doubted them, and always loved them. This hate tendency in human nature manifested itself again in World War II, this time toward loyal Japanese American citizens. It is to be hoped that such attitudes will never again have currency.

Dr. John W. Hoffman, president of Ohio Wesleyan University during my time there, was a man of gracious and charming personality. He was a former football player, and helped innumerable students by his caring spirit, keen insights, and loving concern. President Hoffman, "Prexy" as he was called, was a member of our fraternity of Phi Gamma Delta at Washington and Jefferson College, so naturally he was invited to a special dinner at our chapter house, Fairbanks Lodge, the night before commencement. As president of the fraternity in my senior year, I asked him to make an after-dinner talk, which he did with his usual charm, humor, and nonpreachy appeal. He challenged us to live great lives, and the boys listened to him with affection, a genuine response in their eyes and on their young faces.

As the dinner broke up, Prexy Hoffman said, "Norman, can you spare the time to walk home with me? You are graduating tomorrow and this may be our last chance for a talk." Since I could "spare" the time to talk with my college president whenever asked, we walked together up to the president's house on Oak Hill Avenue. We sat on his front steps in the moonlight and talked. It was June and the night air was filled with the fragrance of flowers. The next day I would leave college and go into the world. The future beckoned. Dreams filled my mind. And there I was, sitting alone for a few moments with my president, a man I loved and respected. It was an incredibly precious experience.

"I asked you to walk home with me tonight, Norman," he said, "because I wanted a chance to tell you how much I like and admire you. But more importantly, to tell you that I believe in you. You have great ability and potential. If you will completely let Jesus take charge of your life, if you believe with all your heart in Him, you will learn to have a humble but valid belief in yourself, and you will do great things in your lifetime." Then he continued, saying things I have never related heretofore. "You have a bell-like carrying voice and a clear, strong enunciation. You can be an outstanding speaker. God has given to you remarkable gifts of personality and ability. I know you will use them well. I shall always believe in you and be proud of you as one of my boys." He arose. "It's going to be a privilege to hand you your diploma tomorrow morning."

He took my hand and said, "God bless you every day all the long way you will go in life." I was too choked up to make any kind of adequate response, but I went down Oak Hill Avenue that June night walking on air. This great man actually believed that I could be somebody, could amount to something. He really did. So it came to me that these professors and Dr. Hoffman were trying to get over their final message to me; namely, to shed my self-doubt and let Jesus Christ make me a normal, effective man. What kindhearted people they were!

So time passed and I became a minister, always trying as best I could to live up to their hopes for me. Then I heard that Dr. Hoffman had cancer of the throat and was not expected to live long. He could no longer speak above a whisper. It shook me to think I would hear that golden voice no more, the voice that could move great audiences with such eloquence. So I made a special trip to see him in his home in Pasadena, California. His face lighted up with the same old smile when I walked in.

As he greeted me from his chair, the handclasp was still strong, though the great, old athletic form was shrunken. We talked, by writing our questions and replies. "How are all the old boys?" he asked, naming them one by one: Slick Burgess, John Joseph, Chid Mills, one after the other. We laughed much and cried a bit. Then I knew that I must go. But I hesitated for I realized I would never see him again on earth. I took his hand and saw that he wanted to say something. So, leaning down near his lips, I heard, "I am very proud of you. I have always believed in you. I love you. God bless you always." I was unable to speak, so I just put my hand on his head for a moment and moved to the door. Turning around, I saw for the last time his smile and old-time gesture of farewell. The memory of this inspiring man I shall carry to the end, for he wanted to make me have more faith in myself and in what God might do with me, one of His humblest servants. It is a wonderful blessing to have some people believe in you.

To live through two world wars, the most severe economic depression in history, and other major crises along with all others of my day and generation has been to experience tragedy and sorrow, but also to be part of one of the most exciting periods of human history.

CHAPTER FIVE

Ink on the Fingers

THERE IS AN OLD SAYING in the newspaper and publishing trade that once you get printer's ink on your fingers you can never entirely wash it off. I have had a pen in hand for the greater part of my life, nor do I want to wash the ink from my fingers. For though I am only a practical sort of writer, as distinguished from a literary one, I have found that it is possible, by writing, to reach more people and in a more lasting way than can ever be done by public speaking or by radio or television.

A speech, however effective and compelling, is gone with the wind when it is over; but the printed word lingers on, in some cases for many years. And that same printed word has a strange authority. "I saw it in the paper, I read it in a book," seems to say it must be so. Therefore, I have stayed with writing in preference to television or radio, though I have used both. As to radio, it is said that since the death of Lowell Thomas, my radio broadcasting has been the longest continuous national voice on radio, having started in 1933. As to speeches, I have made many, but only as a supplement to books. I have always had ink, lots of it, on my fingers.

Actually I wanted to be a newspaperman, a writer. Always I was fascinated by the smells, the clatter, and the air of excitement in a paper's newsroom. It seemed to be the center of events. I was thrilled by the power of words to convey an idea, and to move to action. The beauty of a word, standing out clear and sharp, and its sweep when used in combination with other words, always charmed me. Emerson refers to a word as being alive. When properly used, words can move irresistibly on people's minds to change them, for when thoughts change, a person changes. And when it is *the* Word, the Word of God with which you are working, the power increases measurably with the belief held. To convey *the* Word through one's own words is the highest skill in communication, and so it is ever the most challenging of activities.

Perhaps no one has better expressed the power of words than Arthur Gordon in "Those Little Black Marks."

Isn't it amazing how we take them for granted, those little black marks on paper! Twenty-six different shapes known as letters, arranged in endless combinations known as words. Lifeless, until someone's eye falls on them . . .

But then a miracle happens. Along the optic nerve, almost at the speed of light, these tiny symbols are flashed to the brain where they are instantly decoded into ideas, images, concepts, *meanings*.

The owner of the eye is changed, too. The little black marks can make him love or hate, laugh or cry, fight or run away. And what do we call this incredible chain of events?

We call it reading.

Partly because it is such a complex process, reading is not just a habit or a skill, it's a deeply satisfying emotional experience. Something in us knows that the soundest insights, the truest wisdom, the most enduring knowledge come through this channel. The spoken word rushes by and is gone, but the written word remains. It endures. It can be consulted over and over again. Forever.

How wise then to surround oneself with books and magazines.

How wise to love them, and teach one's children to love them.

How wise to *read!*

From my youngest days I was in and out of newspaper offices, first as a paper carrier. Then as a freshman in college I hung around the office of *The Transcript* and ultimately got on the editorial staff. During summer vacations I was a reporter on *The Morning Republican,* as it was called then, in Findlay, Ohio (the name of the paper was changed later to *The Courier*). I worked under the city editor, Anson Hardman, a fine newspaperman who gave me valuable guidance and instruction.

The head of the newspaper at the time was the late I. N. Heminger, a Christian gentleman of the old school. He was succeeded by his son Lowell, also an outstanding editor and leader in the church. Lowell's son Ed, a third-generation head of "our" paper, as I like to think of it, carries on the family tradition in high order. On my office wall is a photograph of Lowell Heminger on which he wrote: "With kindest regards to a former *Republican* staffer," an inscription I prize highly.

My first job on *The Morning Republican* was to make daily rounds of funeral parlors, ascertain any deaths, then write an obituary notice. To accomplish this assignment it was necessary to visit the bereaved families for information and photographs. This moved me so deeply that often it affected my obituary stories, which sometimes were flowery and even poetic. So much so that one prominent citizen of Findlay asked me to promise to write his obituary. "The only trouble is," he said sadly, "I won't be around to read it."

The kindness with which Anson Hardman and Lowell Heminger received my amateurish efforts and the skillful way in which they edited my reports were highly instructional. I owe them a debt of gratitude for improving my writing style. They also taught me that much can be said in a few words, provided those words are well chosen. The art of economy in words, the crisp, short sentence, the unbroken flow of ideas were all valuable skills I learned on my newspaper job, and I have striven ever since to perfect them.

At length, the scope of my work was widened and I reported police news and city-council procedures. My extreme youth apparently rubbed the tough police sergeant the wrong way, and he proved very difficult, clamming up and perfunctorily dismissing me as just a know-nothing kid. Naturally this troubled me, for the other paper, the afternoon *Courier,* was getting news which I also should have had.

At the city-council sessions, I sat at the same table with Irwin Geffs, chief reporter of *The Courier,* a man more than twice my age and one of the best writers I have ever read in any newspaper anywhere. He was a kindly man and would give me helpful hints, so I felt free to open up and tell him of my difficulty with the police sergeant. "He isn't as tough as he acts," said Mr. Geffs. "He's got a big heart under that exterior and he tries to conceal it. Tell you what, Norman, use a little strategy on him and you'll win him over."

He explained that the police sergeant had a little granddaughter, the apple of his eye, and suggested that if I contrived to see the little girl and then talk to the "old bear" about her, I would worm my way into his good graces. So the next day I rode my bicycle along the street where the child lived and saw her playing in the yard of her home. I went at once to the police station, where the sergeant grunted, as usual, in answer to my bright "good morning."

"Sergeant," I said, "I happened to see that little granddaughter of yours. She is by all odds one of the most beautiful children I have ever seen."

"That," he replied, "is the most sensible thing I have ever heard you say." He didn't melt overnight, but this glimpse into the heart of a rugged man gave me a genuine liking for him, and in time this transmitted itself and we became friendly. When I reported this to Mr. Geffs, he said, "I have found that when you look for good in people you'll find it and in turn they will do good to you." Irwin Geffs was one of my teachers along life's way and I hold him in affectionate memory.

My work on the paper was enjoyable and fascinating even though since it was a morning publication, I had to work all night. I felt sure that I had found my lifework until, in church on Sunday, listening to my father preach great sermons I would feel stirrings within. But I resolutely put them down and enthusiastically received a suggestion from my college classmate Gardner Townsley that we buy a small-town paper at Troy, Ohio, as partners. He would run the business side and I, the editorial. "With what do we buy this paper?" I asked.

"With O.P.M.," he replied, which was the first time I had ever heard of using other people's money. "We will borrow a down payment and work hard; and as we make money, we will pay off our borrowing, thus establishing ourselves as a good credit risk and go on from there."

While this made sense, for the economy was going strong just then, still, for a boy who had hardly two nickels to rub together, it seemed like a wild dream. Besides, a little voice inside seemed to caution that this wasn't for me.

Just about that time I was offered a reporter's job on a big paper in Detroit, the *Journal,* and I figured that represented a safer O.P.M. I took the job. But Gardner continued on his course, as was the sturdy nature of the man. He acquired the oldest daily newspaper in Ohio, *The Western Star,* at Lebanon, a beautiful town near Cincinnati. He edited this paper successfully for years and became one of the most distinguished men in his profession in the Middle West.

So I went to Detroit, where I worked for a great newspaperman, Grove Patterson. The first day on the job Mr. Patterson called me into his office. "What do you know about newspaper work?" he asked.

"Well, to begin with I was an editor of my college paper." This did not seem to impress him, and I went on. "I have just come from being a reporter on the Findlay *Morning Republican.*"

"Now you are saying something," he declared. "That is a great newspaper, one of the very best, and the Hemingers are fine men. You were fortunate to have started on their paper."

In a conversation with Grove Patterson I learned one of the most valuable lessons of my humble "career." I put quotation marks around that word, for I do not believe a minister has a career in the same sense that it is used about a movie star, an athlete, or a politician. Career indicates, I believe, some aspect of stellar material achievement and therefore is not properly used in connection with a pastor. The pastorate is a humble service occupation in the name of the greatest Servant of all, Jesus Christ. So I have never used the word career in connection with my own life.

I mention it here in passing because recently I received a letter from an obviously nice young man living on the West Coast who said he had been helped by my ministry and wanted suggestions on how he might emulate my "career." In replying to his letter I pointed out that I personally had no career, giving the reasons outlined above. I am pleased that he admitted the word was picked up from the less than spiritually minded media, and he agreed that we in the ministry would be better advised to conduct ourselves after the fashion of St. Francis of Assisi, as nonpublic persons who try to represent the Savior of mankind.

Well, to get back to Grove Patterson and his "lesson." It was on how to write a newspaper story. He took a pencil and put a dot on a sheet of paper. "What is that?" he asked.

"A dot," I replied.

"No, it's a period, the greatest literary device known to man. Never write over one. And use as many as you can. Write in short, fast-paced sentences." Then he posed a question. "Up at the university is an erudite professor, while down in the street is an uneducated but literate ditchdigger. To which of them will you write?"

"To the ditchdigger," I replied, "for then they will both understand what I'm saying."

"Right, go to the head of the class! And always make your story interesting, truthful, and don't editorialize in a news story. Put the basic facts in the first paragraph, amplify sufficiently to tell the whole story, put down a period, and stop. Use simple language, such as the word 'get' instead of 'procure.' Always use good old understandable American English all the way. And keep the human touch."

Grove Patterson subsequently wrote a daily column, "The Way of the Word," for *The Toledo Blade*. One of his pieces especially impressed me as an example of how profound truth can be written in a simple, moving way and in such a manner as to be unforgettable. It had the human touch. I have kept this editorial and reread it for years; it has helped me immeasurably. I think it is a classic.

A boy a long time ago leaned against the railing of an old-fashioned bridge and watched the current of the river below. A log, a bit of driftwood, a chip, all floated past. Again the surface of the river was smooth. But always, as it had for a hundred, perhaps a thousand years, the waters slipped by—under the bridge. At seasons the current went more swiftly, and again quite slowly, but always the river flowed on—under the bridge.

Watching the river that day, the boy made a discovery. It was not the discovery of a material thing, something he might put his hands upon. He could not even see it. He had discovered a great idea. Quite suddenly, and yet quickly, he knew that everything in his life would some day pass under the bridge and be gone, like water. And the boy came to like those words, "under the bridge."

All his life thereafter the idea served him well and carried him through, although there were days and ways that were dark and not easy. Always, when he made a mistake that couldn't be helped, or lost something that could never come again, the boy, now a man, said, "It's water under the bridge."

And he didn't worry about mistakes so much after that and he didn't let trouble get him down—because it was "water under the bridge."

My most interesting experience on the *Detroit Journal* concerned a fire in a six-story building. A big crowd had gathered when I came up, showed my press pass, and stepped up to the fire line. I noticed the crowd looking up in anxious concern. There a young girl, maybe twelve or thirteen years of age, was trying to muster up nerve to crawl over an eight-foot space on a one-foot-wide plank that someone had shoved across. She would try to move out, but on looking down became terrified and drew back. People in the crowd were shouting encouragement to her, but she was frozen with fear.

Breathing a prayer and unconscious of the crowd, I called up, "Honey, do you believe in God?" Down on all fours, she nodded. "Do you believe that God is up there with you, that He loves you and will take care of you?" Again the nod. "Then look straight ahead, see Him, and He will lead you across to safety in no time. And I and everyone down here will be praying for you."

The girl hesitated, then slowly lifted her eyes and looked straight ahead. She crawled out slowly onto the plank. Halfway across she seemed to hesitate, and I called out, "Don't stop, honey, God is helping you. Keep on straight ahead." She did so, to the cheers of the crowd, and soon friendly hands received her in safety. A big burly policeman standing by said, "Good job, son. You sound like a preacher."

"Oh, I'm no preacher," I protested.

"The hell you are not," he replied.

I walked around in excitement for two or three hours; then, though late at night, I telephoned my parents telling them what had happened.

"The man said that I sounded like a preacher. What did he mean?"

"He meant you have faith and communicated it to the girl. That's preaching," said Dad. "Wait a moment until I tell your mother." There was no telephone extension in our home. "She says you were born to be a preacher," he reported.

"But how can I know?" I asked, disturbed and perplexed.

"Only through prayer and by the willingness to do what God wants, not insisting on what you think you want." And my wise father added, "Good-night, son. We will pray also."

My struggle between a strong liking for newspaper work and a persistent pull toward the ministry kept me in an unsettled state. Continuing to work hard at my job, I was soon handling a murder case in the courthouse at Windsor, Ontario, across the river in Canada. The details of this trial, quite interesting at the time, have faded except for the memory of two opposing attorneys, both of whom were copious chewers of tobacco. During argument, both jury and spectators (and, I felt, even the judge) became fascinated by which of the attorneys, as they walked up and down, could expectorate the farthest, hitting the brass spittoon and causing it to ring like a bell. I seem to remember that this spitting contest found a place in my reports of the trial and got by the blue pencil of my hard-boiled city editor.

Came early September, and the Methodist conference, a great annual event in small Ohio towns, was scheduled to be held in Delaware, my old college town. I decided to attend. Mother and Father would be there, affording me a chance for a visit. And besides, I always found inspiration in the great talks and sermons given there. During the sessions one sermon moved me so deeply that I left the church and wandered the streets, finally sitting on

71

the steps of the Delaware county jail just opposite the church. I could hear the beautiful old hymn music from the meeting. I realized full well that I had been running from the Lord. So finally I said, "Lord, what is Your Will for me? Whatever it is I will follow. I really do not believe I am what You want for Your ministry, but I know You give calls to the most unlikely people. If You want me, I am Yours to command." At several times in my life I have had certain experiences of the Presence, and this was one of them.

But, perhaps, still wanting an out, I began to hedge. "It's late September, Lord," I explained, "and it may be too late to be admitted to Boston University. That is where all the ministerial students I know seem to be going for their training. I will send a telegram; and if they turn me down, that will be a sign You don't want me quite yet (reserving an "in" for possibly later). If they say, 'Come,' I will go."

The telegraph office was closed for the day, so I trudged down to the railroad yards and climbed to the tower to send the message. Next day I received the answer: "HAVE A PLACE FOR YOU STOP COME AS SOON AS POSSIBLE STOP." But still I equivocated, and it's a wonder the Lord did not lose all patience or decide I was too vacillating and chuck me altogether. For I wired back that I would enter the graduate course for a Master of Arts degree, meanwhile taking a couple of courses in the theological college to test the waters. I wanted to see how I liked other ministers and whether I was in any sense qualified to be a pastor and preacher.

On Monday, as usual, I went to the old *Detroit Journal* building on Jefferson Avenue. I must have gone further in the decision process than I thought, for that day I went to see my boss, Grove Patterson, to tell him the earth-shaking news that hereafter his paper would have to get along as best it could without my valued services. I thought he bore up right well. I explained that I was passing through a valley of decision. Great Christian layman that he was, he understood perfectly. He was kind enough to say that I was doing a satisfactory job as a reporter on his paper and would in time make a good newspaperman. But he added: "The ministry of the Lord Jesus Christ is the greatest work on earth; and if the Lord has called you to preach, then you can only follow the call and my prayers will go with you all the way."

But, seeming to have a bit of doubt, he said with a grin, "Norman, if you don't like the ministry or you don't do very well at it, I want you to know that your old job will always be here waiting for you."

This assurance was tucked away in my heart as a kind of security. Years later, from the pulpit in Marble Collegiate Church in New York City where I was preaching, I looked down into the congregation and was pleased to see Grove Patterson. Being human, I wanted him to feel that his erstwhile reporter wasn't too bad in the role of minister. I pulled out all the stops and produced the best possible sermon of which I was capable at the time. Then I sat down, thinking that while of course it was nothing great, still it wasn't too bad. Speaking with people after the service, I saw my old editor in the line approaching to speak to me. I was sure that, even if he had to stretch the point, he would say something of an appreciative nature. But instead, upon reaching me, he put out his hand and, with a dour look on his face, said, "Well, Norman, your old job is still waiting for you."

·

CHAPTER SIX

South Station

WHEN A YOUNG PERSON moves into a new phase of life, a fresh and exciting adventure begins. On that September afternoon in 1921 when Mother and Father took me to the Toledo railroad station, we did not have much to say to each other as we stood on the platform awaiting the train that would take me to Boston and into the Christian ministry. We just stood there loving one another in a family experience that was too deep for words.

Came the long, low whistle in the distance; then the sleek train pulled into the station—Pullman coaches and dining car; a kiss from Mother, a firm clasp of the hand from Dad, then the conductor called, "All aboard." I stood in the vestibule as the train moved out, the three of us waving until the train rounded a curve and my two dear ones faded from sight. I sat looking out the window into deepening twilight descending over the Ohio landscape, a bit homesick but already excited. I was on my way to the future.

I opened the lunch Mother had packed for me. Dining cars were too expensive. Then, beginning to feel lonely, I walked through the cars in the hope of seeing someone I knew and ran into Bill Stewart, a classmate from college. He told me he, too, was on his way to the same school, also to study to be a minister. Bill was always a sensitive boy. He was homesick already. "We're all alone in the world," he said, and I thought he was going to cry.

"Don't feel badly, Bill," I sympathized. "We at least have each other. We are going to have a great time."

Shyly he asked, "Got anyone to room with, Norman?"

"Yes, you if you can stand having me around."

It was early in the morning when the train puffed into South Station and the two country boys from Ohio stepped down to the platform, each clutching his one suitcase, looking about wonderingly. It was the morning rush hour and we were jostled by seeming thousands of commuters. After many inquiries, we found our way to Mt. Vernon Street, where Lafe, a genial black man, ushered us to our assigned dormitory room as he had been doing for theological students for years. "Hope you like it here and become good preachers. Believe me, we need them," he said as he left us.

At Boston University I enrolled in courses leading to both the Master of Arts degree and to the degree of Bachelor of Sacred Theology (S.T.B.). The professors were obviously scholars of note in their fields of interest. Each in his own way was outstanding as a personality. A few were memorable. Professors Leslie, Knudson, Vaughan, Lowstutter, Brightman, and Cell were my favorites. They combined high intellectual stature with attractive human qualities. For example, Dr. Cell one spring day opened his class in church history by saying, "Gentlemen, you have worked faithfully all semester in this course and since this is opening day for the Boston Red Sox, how would you feel about adjourning to Fenway Park to support the team? We can get seats in the bleachers for four bits [two quarters]." That the ayes had it unanimously was not surprising.

The challenge to become an objective thinker, an intellectual of sorts, became a daily and exciting experience at Boston University School of Theology. True, I was a bit troubled by the greater emphasis upon Christianity as a social gospel rather than as an evangelical, life-changing way of life, and I could not see why both emphases were not germane. But I had confidence in the professors who were training us for Christian service.

On Sundays, until I had my own student church, I went with classmates to hear the great preachers then serving in Boston: George A. Gordon, the masterful preacher at South Church in

75

Copley Square, and the Reverend Dr. A. Z. Conrad at Tremont Temple. In the latter church one Sunday night, I heard Dr. Emil Coué, the famous teacher of "Every day, in every way, I am getting better and better." I was impressed by the obvious popularity of his theories and was fascinated by the believers who thronged there for healing. It was very evident that there was power present and this manifestation interested and intrigued me.

My meager funds were running lower each day, and I knew I had to generate some income or this halcyon existence would come to a close. Finally a classmate and I secured a two-man job handling the dumbwaiter at the Y.W.C.A. on Beacon Street. Indeed, we were described by a cynical classmate as two of the dumbest waiters the Y.W.C.A. ever had. My friend manned the dumbwaiter in the basement kitchen sending up food to me in the dining room on the fourth floor. "Take 'er up," he would yell from the kitchen. And then, after loading the device with dirty dishes, I would yell, "Take 'er down," and the dishes would disappear into the depths. For this arduous service my friend and I received the colossal wage of two dollars a day for five days, and two meals, lunch and dinner. This continued for my first year.

Breakfast of coffee and rolls was on our own at the New England Kitchen at the corner of Mt. Vernon and Charles streets. It was there one historic morning that I read in the *Boston Herald* of the death of President Warren G. Harding and the midnight swearing-in of Vice-President Calvin Coolidge as President of the United States. This was done by his justice of the peace father by kerosene lamplight in the old Coolidge homestead in Vermont. Those were interesting days.

Later I heard Coolidge give a speech in the old North Church in his own dry Yankee twang and unimpassioned, down-to-earth commonsense manner. Still later, we arranged to visit Washington, D.C., en route back to Boston after Christmas vacation. With the help of Clint Cole, our congressman, a classmate and I got tickets to President Coolidge's Wednesday noon public reception. We were both members of the college fraternity of Phi Gamma Delta. We knew that the President was also a Phi Gam. Accordingly we each brashly gave him the fraternity secret grip

76

when we shook his hand. He immediately recognized the grip and stated, "I, too, am a member of Phi Gamma Delta, the Amherst chapter."

"We know that, 'Brother Coolidge,' " we said, moving on, leaving the President both astonished and amused.

During my last two years at the school of theology, my brother Bob was a student at the Harvard University medical school. It became our habit to have dinner together once a week. He would join me and a group of student ministers in Boston, and the next week I would go to Harvard and join him and his medical-student friends. The interchange of ideas resulting from this contact of the two disciplines, medicine and religion, proved most interesting and rewarding.

At least, it so affected me. Even then I was working out in my own mind the combination of medical-psychological therapy with the pastoral office that later marked my work at Marble Collegiate Church in New York.

Some of the young ministerial students at Boston University School of Theology had student pastorates. There were many small churches in the Boston and Providence areas, and the ministerial students served in them on weekends. When time came for my second year, I applied to the Methodist bishop in charge of the Boston territory, Edwin H. Hughes, for a church when one became vacant.

A few days later the bishop asked me to come to his office. "Norman, I have two churches for you to consider. They are totally different in location, in membership, and in problems. One is located in a picture-postcard type of Massachusetts town. The church is old New England in architecture, located across the village green, and the parsonage is down a quiet, tree-shaded street. The church has no problems, though the congregation is not large. The salary is fifteen hundred dollars per year."

Then he described the other church. It was located in a Rhode Island cotton-mill town, where a prolonged strike had embittered the community and caused great hardship. The town lay alongside a busy highway on which huge trucks sped noisily, night and day. The membership of the church was largely composed of people fresh from Lancashire, England, good solid folk, most of whom worked in the Berkeley and Lonsdale mills where the famous Berkeley and Lonsdale cloth was manufactured. "So you see," said Bishop Hughes, "there are emotional and economic problems facing you if you take on this church.

"But that isn't the worst of it. For the past two years there has been a student pastor there who is a 'bull in a china shop' sort of fellow. He is a crusader type, not yet quite dry behind the ears in his method of advancing new sociological ideas to conservative people loyal to biblical Christianity. He has caused a cleavage right down the middle and engendered about the worst, deplorable, inner-church fight I have ever known. The salary offered is nine hundred dollars per year. Whoever goes to this church will break or grow. If he goes with love and human understanding, it can make a great minister of him.

"I will appoint you to either of the two churches I have described. What is your choice?" he asked with a smile. Young though I was and not very wise in the ways of the world, I knew instinctively that I was being tested. Did I have what it takes to decline an apparently easy job and opt for an obviously tough one? Here was an idyllically beautiful place in contrast to a church in the middle of industrial dispute and torn asunder by a well-meaning but blunderbuss type of pastoral administration. I knew there could be only one answer.

"If you approve, Bishop Hughes, I will take the church in Rhode Island." He put his hand on my shoulder. "That's the boy," he said. "I knew you had good stuff in you. Just go down there and love those people and you will have a great ministry."

Arriving at Berkeley, Rhode Island, the next Saturday, I went at once to the parsonage, down Mendon Road from the church. It was a two-family house, the minister's apartment being upstairs. The key was to be obtained from Mr. and Mrs. Arthur Morris who lived downstairs. I knocked on that door and it was opened by a kind-looking lady. "Are you Mrs. Morris?" I asked.

"Indeed I am, lad. And who are you?" All in a British accent.

"I'm the new minister," I announced.

At once a compassionate look came over her face. "Ah, you poor fellow. Come in and have a cup of tea." Soon afterward Arthur Morris came in and joined us. I learned that he was the organist of the church. Two better friends I never had, and I fell in love with them at once. "You go on up and look over your church. Get the key from Mrs. Follett next door. She's got a sharp tongue, but don't mind her. She has a good heart. And while you are gone I will make up your bed. You will have dinner and breakfast with us until I find out whether you can take care of yourself," said Mrs. Morris and shooed me out in motherly fashion.

"Are you Mrs. Follett?" I asked with as big a smile as I could work up. "My name is Norman Peale and I'm your new minister."

I thought a bit of a glare came into her eyes. "I suppose you want the church keys. Here's one for you. The other I'll keep myself. You've got a hard time coming. God have mercy on you." She said this with not too much mercy in the tone. I sensed she might be the chief partisan of the faction supporting the ex-pastor whom I was replacing. Later I heard that Mrs. Follett was telling around town that the new minister had arrived and in her opinion, "He doesn't look as if he had sense enough to come in out of the rain."

I stood in front of the little church looking at it with pride. Emotion welled up in me. Someone had tacked a piece of light wood over the name of the last pastor and had lettered in my name so that it read: "Berkeley Methodist Church, Norman Vincent Peale, Pastor." It was mine, my very own church! Thrusting hands in pockets, with shoulders back, head up, I read it again out loud. "Norman Vincent Peale, Pastor. Let them bring on difficulty. The Lord will help me and all of us. We will have a great church here." I was excited and happy and could hardly wait for the morrow to preach about Jesus Christ to these people, all of whom I was going to love.

The sermon the next day was not my first. I had given that a few months earlier at the Methodist church at Walpole, Massachusetts, where I substituted one Sunday for Eugene McKinley Pierce, the student pastor who later—and for twenty-five years—was my associate pastor at Marble Collegiate Church. Mac gave me the opportunity to preach my first sermon in his church, and it was for me, if not for his congregation, an unforgettable experience.

Early that week I had wired my father: PREACHING NEXT SUNDAY

79

STOP PLEASE SEND SERMON STOP, to which panicky message he wired back: SUGGEST TEXT JOHN 10:10 STOP PREACH YOUR OWN SERMON STOP GOOD LUCK, DAD STOP. I didn't need to look up John 10:10, for I knew it well, having heard Father preach on that, his favorite text, so many times. "I am come that they might have life, and that they might have it more abundantly." So at Walpole I went early to the church, and in a little study in the church tower, I watched the congregation assembling.

I was nervous, frightened, and self-doubting. The old problem of inferiority and shyness faced me again. Then I saw a tall, stately old gentleman among those coming up the walk to the church door. "What could I possibly say to him?" Then he chanced to lift his face, and I read sadness and trouble on it. I went into the pulpit, conducted the service, and gave a short sermon, simply telling what Jesus Christ meant to me, the greatest mind in the history of the world, the great lover of all mankind, the One who can change us from every defeat to victory and save us to eternal salvation. Afterward at the door, people said kindly things. Then stood before me the stately old gentleman. "You must have read my mind," he said. "I needed help and you gave me that help in your sermon."

I had preached two or three times during the winter in the Congregational church at Hancock, New Hampshire, and once in Ohio during the summer. I had returned home to Findlay, where my father was superintendent of churches. One Saturday morning he told me that one of his ministers was ill, nothing serious but enough to prevent his presence at church the next day. Would I go out and preach in his stead? I worked all day on a sermon which I wrote out, word for word, entitled "The Kinetic Theory of the Atonement." This topic I had heard discussed in class at the seminary.

Late that hot July Saturday, Dad and I were sitting on the front porch. He was in a rocking chair, one foot on the porch railing, eating peanuts, which he loved. "What are you doing?" he asked.

"I've written a sermon for tomorrow on 'The Kinetic Theory of the Atonement.'"

"What's that?" he asked. I wasn't too sure myself, so I asked him if he would like to read the sermon. He took it, still popping peanuts into his mouth, and read it carefully.

"What do you think?" I asked anxiously.

"Really want me to tell you?" he asked.

I nodded. "Well, I would tear it up and put it in the stove. In the first place, never read a sermon or a speech. Speak it straight out like you mean it, looking the people straight in the eyes as you preach. And you've far too many big words in this sermon. Have you forgotten Grove Patterson's advice? It applies to preaching as well as to newspaper writing. Use simple, strong, meaningful words that everyone understands, even the least literate. And as for that, what do you call it, kinetic, just remind the people that the Lord Jesus shed His blood on Calvary's cross to atone for their sins. In fact, make your sermon a witness to what Jesus has done for you, like you did at Walpole."

Though somewhat deflated, I knew my sophomoric attitude was wrong and my father's mature one was right. The next day, Sunday, I drove out alone to this little country church, which stood at the corner of two dusty roads. It was a beautiful summer day, sunny and brisk, overhead a cloudless blue sky, beneath the feet a carpet of green in the churchyard. Horses tethered at hitching racks stomped their feet and swished their tails. People crowded in, filling every seat. All were in their Sunday best. Little girls looking sweet in their prim dresses and boys uncomfortable in collars and squeaky shoes. In each family group the father sat at the end of the pew on the aisle, the mother at the other end to better police the kids in between.

As I, the preacher, entered the pulpit, all talking and rustling stopped. A hush came over the congregation. The choir had preceded me and rose to lead in the opening hymn, "Holy, Holy, Holy, Lord God Almighty!" As the old hymn was sung lustily and with feeling, I looked at the people, old and young, and thought how fine they were. Out the windows I saw ripening corn waving in a gentle breeze. How wonderful it all seemed.

And then in the sermon I talked about the love of God and about Jesus Christ His son. I told about Jesus healing the sick, turning sinners into good men and women, bringing out the best in boys and girls. Suddenly I was conscious of a deep stillness, a hush. It seemed that eternity, the infinite, was for a suspended moment impinging on the finite. The Holy Presence brushed every person. So quiet it was that the buzzing of a bee which flew in the window seemed loud. In that moment I felt the power of preaching.

The service ended with the hymn "What a Friend We Have in Jesus." And as we sang I noted several brushing a tear away. After the service a big middle-aged farmer invited me to his house for dinner. "You look skinny and underfed," he said. "We'll have to fatten you up." I sat on the front porch with the men while the womenfolk were in the kitchen preparing dinner, the enticing odors of which floated to us on the summer air as we sat in rocking chairs just talking. The host farmer was shaking hands with guests who, like me, had been invited to his home. He sat in a chair next to me and brought down his big hand on my bony knee. "I like you, boy. You're my style. But you've got a lot to learn about preaching; you know that, don't you?"

"Yes, sir, I know that," I replied.

"But you're on the right track," he continued, "for you love Jesus and you tell the folks what Jesus has done for you and can do for them. That is right, son, just stick with Jesus always." Whereupon he blew his nose and seemed to choke up.

Suddenly he arose and went around the corner of the house, leaving me a bit mystified by the suddenness of his departure. The other men rocked in silence until one explained, "He was converted from a pretty bad life and he can't talk about Jesus without getting all broken up."

I have always been impressed and deeply moved by the effect of Jesus on people. He draws them like no one else and there is profound truth in the Scripture "I, if I be lifted up from the earth, will draw all men unto me." He does, indeed. And for that reason, and because I love Him personally, I've preached about Him all my ministerial life.

That first Sunday at Berkeley, Rhode Island, when I walked into the pulpit, it was evident that the unhappy instigator of the church fight had left a congregation divided, for one half sat on one side of the aisle, figuratively making faces at the other half across the aisle. I walked into the pulpit. Looking out over the full church, I said, "Friends, I'm just a young fellow studying to be a minister and I have lots to learn. I'm going to ask you to help me learn to be a good preacher and minister of Jesus Christ. I was sent here by our Bishop who tells me you are kindhearted people. And I can tell that you are by just looking at you." So saying, I gave them a big smile. And a few smiled back.

Again, as at Walpole and at the country church, I talked to them simply about what Jesus meant to me personally, how I had experienced conversion, and how the love of God and Christ had come into my life. I did not worry about myself in trying to be completely true to Christ. After the service a man introduced himself as Rob Rowbottom and said, "Keep going that way and one of these days you will have them all loving you, and Jesus, and each other." Obviously I had in my church one Christian of stature who could rise above small things.

At once, I began calling on the people. And because I was single, with no wife to cook for me, the church members began having me to meals. Never have I found such a great congregation of superior cooks at one time and place. After dining at one house I would accept a dinner invitation with someone from the other faction, and I would tell the lady there what a great meal I'd had at Mrs. So-and-So's. And after that dinner I would brag about hers to others of the across-the-aisle crowd. I really and valiantly ate a church into unity.

Once I went into Mrs. Follett's kitchen and noticed a batch of just-baked luscious-looking cookies laid out on waxed paper. They smelled too great for words and I told her so. She only grunted. I kept coming back to the cookies until finally she was badgered into offering me one. After finishing it I took another, meanwhile saying, "Bessie Smith said something about you when I was eating her pie the other day."

"Humph," she snapped. "What did that old gossip say about me?"

"When I told her how good her pie was and that she was a marvelous baker she said, 'Well, there's one woman in town who is better at baking and it's Mrs. Follett.'"

"She did, eh! She actually said that? Well, I always did say that Bessie Smith was a pretty nice woman. Next time you see her . . ."

"Hold it," I said. "I'm going to tell her that you are the best cookie baker since my grandmother and she was the best in

Ohio." Mrs. Follett actually kissed me as I left. "You're a nice boy," she said.

"And you are nice, too," I replied, and she was.

So it went. Preaching love on Sunday, living a loving life among the people, and weaving strands of love daily until they crossed and crisscrossed into an unbroken pattern of affection. The church became, once again, a caring community of Christ's people. I have great respect and love for human beings. They may, or shall I say *we* may, act badly at times. But such actions do not truly represent us as we really are. Under the touch of Christ's love and esteem, all of us show our real nature as children of God.

As a student pastor, it was my practice to take a train from South Station, Boston, for the forty-mile-or-so trip to Providence or Pawtucket, there to be met by a church member and transported by car to Berkeley or go by bus. Every Friday evening I would conduct a prayer meeting and it was always well attended. In these meetings I gave talks on the great principles or teachings of Jesus and their applicability to the common problems of life. This would be followed by a question-and-answer period and a general discussion in which the people participated with interest. Though the church members for the most part were workers in the cotton mills, only a few being college-educated, they were thoughtful and perceptive.

On Saturday I spent all day calling upon church members in their homes and also stopped by to get acquainted with prospective members who attended services or had been otherwise called to my attention. Never could I endure empty pews. I had become a minister to communicate with people and intended those pews to be filled. And soon they were filled, for the members came regularly, as did also many persons in the community who had not previously been connected with a church.

On Sunday I had two services, one in the morning and the other in the evening. I sat up late Saturday night burning the midnight oil to put two different sermons together. This last-minute sermon preparation was necessitated by heavy schoolwork from Monday to Friday together with my daily job running the dumbwaiter for meals at the Boston Y.W.C.A.

An incident of my student pastoral days in Berkeley got me an immortality of sorts. At least, it was still remembered when my son, Dr. John Stafford Peale, also served the church as a student pastor. The church had a kitchen but, incredibly, no toilet. It was suggested that something be done about this. It so happened that the superintendent of the Berkeley mill and I were friends, so I sought his counsel. He came to me one day saying that a closing of one section of the mill made available a three-holer privy in good repair, and the church could have it without charge if we would move it to its new location behind the church building. Just how this was accomplished I hardly remember over so many years, but I do recall that some forty willing and hardy men turned out one Saturday morning to join their pastor in the removal of the privy from the mill grounds to those of the church. Before nightfall the privy was set in place and ready to go into service for Sunday morning.

It was suggested by some wag that the first hymn at the Sunday service should be "Holy, Holy, Holy." But the pastor's, shall we say, Puritan sense of dignified propriety could not quite countenance such an element in the order of service. But even so, for years Peale's Privy Project was referred to by succeeding generations as one of my greatest contributions to the Berkeley church!

During much of the time that I served the church at Berkeley, the mill workers were on strike. Many of these good, solid British people lived in mill houses, long rows of squat brick structures all looking the same. These houses had no inside toilet facilities, only old wooden outhouses or privies. Wages were as low as possible and working conditions were anything but good. A large number of the strikers were members of my church.

I endeavored to help their cause, for I felt their complaints were justified, and on several occasions I represented them in negotiations with the millowners in Providence. The owners were obviously cultured persons, but, to say the least, socially unenlightened and even politely arrogant.

Among the benefits I asked for the strikers was an inside bathroom in each company-supplied house as an amenity to which every American at that time was entitled. "Why those people wouldn't know what to do with a bathtub. They would probably fill it with coal for their stoves," one said.

"I'll take on the job of preaching them a sermon on 'How to Use a Bathtub.'"

"You win," they finally said grudgingly. The people got their bathtubs. I do not think the milling industry in Rhode Island was ever the same after that prolonged strike.

As to the sermons themselves, at least they were delivered enthusiastically. I have always been enthusiastic about the Gospel. I know that the Gospel works when one believes and follows the teachings. So Sunday after Sunday I told what faith in and commitment to Jesus Christ could do for those who would believe.

All my sermons were evangelistic. They were designed to persuade and to win people to acceptance of Jesus Christ as Lord and Savior. Following the sermon I invited people who wanted their lives changed to come forward and kneel at the altar. There they were to confess to God their sins and weaknesses and truly ask for salvation and life changing. Never shall I forget the first Sunday night that I "gave the invitation." To my surprise five persons came and knelt at the altar, three men and two women. I knew them to be quite non-Christian in their attitudes and life-styles. Now that they humbly knelt before the altar, accepting my assurances that their lives could change, I hardly knew what to do with them. So I appealed straight to the Lord in whose name I had promised them newness of life.

"Dear Lord," I prayed aloud, "You know what I promised these people. You know it is the truth. Please change them now by Your power." One man, Henry G. I will call him, was generally referred to as "the meanest devil in town." He himself confessed as he knelt there that "a devil is in me filling me with hate and anger. I've been this way from my youth. I hated my father."

"Henry," I said, "do you want to be changed? Do you mean it one hundred percent?"

"I do, I do," he said and his voice broke.

"And do you believe that Jesus Christ can change you here and now?"

Again he replied with deep feeling, "I do."

I told him to say to the Lord, "What I can't do for myself You, Lord, please do for me now."

Then in my believing enthusiasm I declared, "Henry, you have been changed. You are a new creature. Old things have passed away. You are a new man. All that old hate stuff is gone."

When I told some of the students at the school of theology about this, they shook their heads. "What if it had not worked?" But I remonstrated that Henry had met all the qualifications for life changing: confession, witnessing to his faith, appeal to the grace of God, commitment. Furthermore, I believed that if the faith is in depth, the change is so powerful as to be immediate. Whatever the reasoning, the operation of spiritual power swept this man's personality totally clean. He became calm, quiet, controlled, a loving and lovable person from that minute in time, and continued so until his death over thirty years later.

But learning to be a preacher is no easy process. After all these years, I still think that public speaking is one of the most difficult of all human occupations to master. Just when one begins to think he is getting fairly good at it, will come an embarrassing and humiliating experience. In public speaking, for sure, "pride goeth before a fall." And the falls are many, at least so it has been in my experience.

How well I recall the Sunday at Berkeley when I just couldn't get going at all in my sermon. Everything seemed to go wrong. I left out the best ideas I had intended to present and came out with pretty poor material. Coming down from the pulpit, I told a retired and distinguished minister, who was in church that day, about my discomfiture.

"Tell you what, Norman," he said. "When you are in the pulpit just do the best you can. And when it's over come down and forget it. The congregation will and you might as well make it unanimous."

My ordination as a minister was performed in what was then called the Methodist Episcopal Church, later renamed the United Methodist Church. The ordination ceremony took place in a Sunday morning service at the annual session of the West Ohio Conference in September 1922. I was ordained by Bishop William F. Anderson.

I came to this significant point in life through a hard decision process, but when I was actually made an ordained minister, an unforgettable sense of peace and rightness came upon me. Though there have been some difficult times across the years, I have never for one minute regretted the decision to become a preacher and pastor. The Lord has blessed my ministry beyond all expectations and, of course, always beyond all deserving.

While pastor of the Berkeley church, I baptized my first baby, Kenneth Rowbottom, son of Rob and Sadie; conducted my first funeral; married my first couple. At that church I learned lessons that would guide me for a lifetime.

My years at Boston University School of Theology were deeply meaningful and inspiring, though I had some painful experiences. One was the class in preaching where we received instruction in how to construct a sermon and deliver it. Our professor of homiletics, as it is called, was Dr. George S. Butters, one of the kindliest men I have ever known. A distinguished pastor and preacher, he was also an approachable, down-to-earth, lovable, and compassionate person.

In his class each student in turn was required to preach a sermon before the other students. This filled me with self-consciousness and fright. I stood in awe of other students, especially the presumptuous ones who, to me at least, acted as if they knew it all. And added to that was an awe of preachers, especially when I had to perform before them. Curiously this feeling bothers me even today.

So when my turn came to preach before my peers, I was tense and nervous. I felt tied up and horribly self-conscious and, of course, did poorly. Later, sitting miserably in my fifth-floor room, I heard a tap on the door. It was my preaching professor, "Daddy" Butters. He had a game leg and limped somewhat. Puffing a bit from the walk up five floors, he sat, resting. "I could run up these steps at your age just as you do. It's great to be young but," he added, "it can be pretty painful also. Son," he continued, "I just came up here to tell you that I know you are going to be a good preacher. Just learn to forget yourself and love the poor souls in your congregation who suffer so many hurts and sorrows and troubles. Just love them and talk to them out of your heart. Tell them God loves them." Rising from his chair, he continued, "I'm taking a couple of boys to lunch down at the New England Kitchen. Please join us." As we sat around the table, Dr. Butters told stories with the rare facility of a raconteur. We roared with laughter. Suddenly it dawned upon me that the professor and the other fellows were trying to show love to me. I went up steep Beacon Hill to my room with tears in my eyes but with happiness in my heart. How kind they all were.

Intellectual brilliance, Christian commitment, and kindliness seemed to mark the professors at Boston University School of Theology. They were mentally and spiritually challenging, well fitted to prepare men for Christian leadership in the new era that came in with the 1920s. One later incident in which I figured lingers in my memories of the school. Some ten years after graduation, I was invited to speak in Boston at a gathering connected with the school. Professors, students, and alumni would be present.

It fell on a date, I recall, when I had asked Captain Eddie Rickenbacker to speak at a big dinner at Marble Collegiate. But Eddie in his kindness urged me to go to Boston. "Nobody ever invited me back to my old school. They must think you're pretty good. Go on. I'll handle it here."

But when I started my speech before the large crowd of alumni, preachers, faculty, and students, suddenly I sensed a chilly atmosphere. The feeling came over me that they did not like me. What right did I, of all people, have to be preaching in a Fifth Avenue church and at so young an age? Still, I tried to surmount my feelings and get through the talk as best I could. I have had some speaking disasters over the years, but that speech at Boston University School of Theology is at the head of the list. A few generous men came up to shake my hand, but I only wanted to get away. (Actually I have never been back there since.) As I was leaving, the professor who was perhaps the most intellectual person on the faculty, Dr. Knudson, intercepted me. He was never a demonstrative man, but kindness shone in his eyes. "Peale," he said, "you are quite a man. Keep it going." He put his hand on my shoulder affectionately. I have never forgotten him.

A gracious gentleman, Dr. David Vaughn, taught the one course in psychology that was offered while I was in graduate school, as I recall. He opened up for me a whole new concept that would be applicable to my future ministry. I think I became aware for the first time of the powerful effect of thought processes upon the totality of a person's life. When I began to apply this new-found knowledge to my own problems, I saw with increasing clarity that much of my self-doubt and self-consciousness was related to my manner of thinking about myself and other people. Through Dr. Vaughn's course I learned that a deeper commitment to the mind of Christ could turn my habits of thought from negative to positive, from self-centered to outgoing in nature, and would therefore increase both my well-being and my effectiveness.

As I look back now all these years later, I think perhaps I was going through the last stages of finding myself while at Boston University. This may account for the bittersweet mixture of memories of this period in my life. The artificially created dualism of the individual and social concept of the Gospel which seemed to prevail at the time at Boston University School of Theology disturbed me. I also acquired the reputation that I was against the social application of the teachings of Jesus because I insisted upon advocation of the personal life change. However, always I have considered both points of view as of profound importance.

CHAPTER SEVEN

Brooklyn in the Roaring Twenties

IN MY SENIOR YEAR at the seminary, before returning to Boston after the Christmas vacation, a classmate and I were walking on Fifth Avenue in New York. It was the first week in January 1924. Suddenly I felt strongly motivated to take an action. The feeling was so intense that, as I think of it now, it demonstrates one way in which God guides those who follow Him.

"My father knows the bishop of the Methodist Church here in New York," I said, "and I'm going to his office right now at one fifty Fifth Avenue and see him. New York City is where I want to serve, and I'm going to ask him to consider me for some small church under his jurisdiction."

My friend was aghast. "You can't just walk into a bishop's office like that."

"Why not? All he can do is say no; and he might say yes. Anyway, you never get anywhere without trying. Besides I feel the compulsion so strongly that I'm going to go to his office right now." My friend trailed along.

The bishop's secretary received me in kindly fashion. She told me the bishop was in, that he was busy as always, but perhaps he could see me briefly. In a moment she returned and ushered me into the office of Bishop Luther B. Wilson. He greeted me pleasantly, asked after my father, and what could he do for me? I explained that in June I was graduating from the seminary in Boston and felt strongly drawn to the challenge of serving in New York under his leadership. Did he, perhaps, have a little church somewhere for a beginner? He smiled, leaned back in his big office chair, and said, "I sort of like you for walking in here this way and humbly asking for a church for a beginner. What prompted you to do that?"

"It suddenly came over me, Bishop Wilson, that here in New York is where I'm intended to work."

He nodded understandingly. "Can you come back this afternoon at two-thirty?"

"Certainly," I replied, though my friend and I had intended to take the noon train for Boston. But this was an opportunity I was not about to pass up. My friend did take the twelve o'clock train, but at two-fifteen I was sitting in the bishop's outer office with his genial and, I thought, slightly amused secretary.

Presently she ushered me into the bishop's office where he introduced me to the Reverend Doctor Abram S. Kavanagh, district superintendent of the Brooklyn south district, whom I liked instantly. "Still want to work with us, Norman?" asked the bishop.

"Yes, sir, very much so."

"Well, we have a nice little church, small but strong in the quality of its membership, a beautiful church building with a nice parsonage. But then, you are not married, are you?"

"No, I'm not, sir."

"Oh well, time will take care of that. The church is about one hundred miles down on Long Island."

Then he proceeded to offer an alternative, much as Bishop Hughes had done when I went to Berkeley! "We have an altogether different church in Dr. Kavanagh's district at Flatlands in Brooklyn. It is not doing well, which puzzles us, for there is a tremendous growth there in the community. Still, the church remains as it has been for years, just a few loyal families hanging on. The attendance at services is sparse and the membership is down to about forty persons. We cannot send a married man to this little church, for there is no way in which he could be supported by the small and dwindling income of the church. But we can send you to St. Mark's Methodist Church on Ocean Avenue as an assistant pastor. St. Mark's has generously agreed to take this faltering little church under its wing. It will be your job to work with it as well as to help out at St. Mark's in any way you can. It's a tough job we are offering you, but so many people are moving into the Flatlands community that there is potential for the future if you are willing to work hard and keep that enthusiasm of yours going."

"Thank you, Bishop Wilson," I said. "I will be glad to accept the Flatlands church with your approval."

Dr. Kavanagh said, "Son, I like the cut of your jib. You are willing to take on a hard job instead of an easy one." In this experience I learned for the second time to take a church that was down and bring it up, rather than one that was already up and struggle to keep it at that level.

Dr. Robert M. Moore, pastor of St. Mark's Methodist Church at Ocean Avenue and Beverly Road in Brooklyn, a gracious gentleman and a gifted preacher, was interested in developing the little church in Flatlands that his own church had agreed to sponsor. And he seemed to take a liking to me, for he treated me with every consideration. A lot was purchased at Kings Highway and East Thirty-seventh Street, in anticipation of a future building program. Dr. Moore suggested that the name of the church be changed to the Kings Highway Church. "If we change the name we will just have to build on that site," he said. "It will be the church of the future; the name Flatlands belongs to the past."

The congregation continued to worship in the hundred-year-old frame building, but so many people came that in the warm weather we pitched a large tent on the new corner lot, and crowds thronged there to worship every Sunday morning and evening. People were pouring into the area as quickly as new houses were ready for occupancy, and the church became a popular center for the community. A great program of music by volunteer singers was offered at every service and often instrumentalists were added to the evening service. The enthusiastic singing of old favorite hymns by the large congregation was helpful in attracting people, who seemed hungry for friendly Christian fellowship. We tried to present a message related to human need and the problems of people.

As every new home was sold and newcomers moved in, I went to welcome them to the community, introducing myself as pastor of the church in the tent on Kings Highway. My approach was that the church was as new as their house, and that I was a new resident, too. Scores responded to my invitation, and the membership and attendance grew rapidly, especially the Sunday School. Young families had moved in and there were many children. I think Kings Highway may have had the largest Sunday School in Brooklyn at the time.

If in calling on new residents I found that they were Roman Catholic or members of some Protestant denomination with which they wished to maintain affiliation or if they were Jewish, I would give their names to the priest, minister, or rabbi in the area, thereby trying to help foster the ecumenical spirit that developed locally. I had an especially close relationship with Pastor Roeder of the nearby historic Flatlands Dutch Reformed Church.

Other friendships formed in Brooklyn which in later years would mature into helpful relationships were with Mr. and Mrs. Frank C. Goodman, their niece, Ethel Rich, and Mr. and Mrs. Wesley Goodman, Frank's son and daughter-in-law. They lived around the corner on East Thirty-eighth Street and were attracted by the tent services, which they attended regularly.

Frank had been a well-known gambler in New York City but became converted in depth during an evangelistic meeting where the famous evangelist Billy Sunday preached and prayed him into the Lord's Kingdom. He was always a dapper dresser, and his hands seemed to be like those of a man given to the clever shuffling of cards. But never have I known a more deeply committed Christian than Frank Goodman.

Frank and his wife would invite me to their home for dinner, after which he would make me stand before a full-length mirror and speak as if to a congregation, meanwhile watching my facial expression, stance, and gestures. "You are a preacher bringing the greatest message, indeed the supreme message of all time, and you must give it all you have of spirit, mind, and even body. You must throw your entire self into the process of persuading people to give their lives to the Savior."

Though at first this procedure was embarrassing, I soon sensed Frank's sincerity and his regard for me. Besides, he knew some of the arts of theater from his previous experience.

Dr. Robert M. Moore, the pastor of St. Mark's Church, appointed a Kings Highway committee to work with me in developing the new church. I cannot imagine any church committee having a membership of more distinguished and committed laymen. Though I am writing of events that took place over fifty-eight years ago, their names come out of the mists of memory: Thomas E. Cisney, the overall chairman, a Brooklyn real-estate leader; Anthony Krayer; Charles R. Gay, president of the New York Stock Exchange; and Paul Ihrig, a commission merchant in downtown Manhattan. These men of experience in finance and the building trades taught me much about the way in which a committed man can dedicate his talents and experience to the advancement of the church. The St. Mark's men were matched by representatives from Kings Highway Church, notably Robert P. Brand and Clarence G. Neese.

The problem they faced was not lack of interest or enthusiasm or people. The old building was no longer adequate and the tent was not usable in winter. Therefore, the new church had to be rushed to completion and, as usual, the problem was money. Being cautious men, they felt that a custom, somewhat in vogue among churches at the time, of roofing over a basement until such time as it became possible to add the upper structure perhaps should be considered. But they had little enthusiasm for the idea. One night very late, Paul Ihrig, who was chairman of the building committee, telephoned me with the surprising question: "What time do you get up in the morning?"

"At whatever time you say," I replied.

"Well, how about meeting me at four A.M. at my place in downtown Manhattan? You know where it is." Mr. Ihrig supplied melons and similar merchandise to clubs and big hotels in New York City. He was said to have an extraordinary sense of touch by which he could invariably determine the quality of a melon. This meant he had to be on hand, personally, to sort the deliveries for breakfast.

When I reported at 4:00 A.M. he was seated on a crate, taking melons out of boxes, rapidly feeling each one and making the decision as to quality and ripeness. "Sit down, Norman," he said, hardly looking up and without interrupting the flow of melons through his hands. "I've done a lot of praying. Don't believe the house of God should be a roofed-over basement. I believe the Lord will provide according to our faith. You and I and the others can raise the money if we believe that we can. I just want you to know that, acting on my own, as chairman of the building committee, I've ordered the whole church to be built before snow flies. Will you and the boys go along? Anyway, you'll have to, for I've signed the contract."

I watched him admiringly and listened with deep feeling, for I was looking at the very personification of the faith of Christian laymen. "Paul," I said, "stop throwing those melons for one minute while I pray to Almighty God, thanking Him for a great Christian named Paul Ihrig." On the day of dedication, he handed me the key to the completed new church and gave me a conspiratorial wink as he did so.

A by-product of this incident was that I learned something about raising money. Namely, the most important principle is that, if the need exists and you believe with God's help the money can be raised, then for sure it can be done. Tom Cisney, the committee chairman, always my loyal friend, gave me a small car, to help bring in new members and collect the funds to finish the construction job.

When the first Easter in the new church was coming up, our head usher, Bob Mirrilees, said, "Look, Norman, even if we have half a dozen services on Easter, our new church cannot handle the crowds of people wanting to worship with us. We are pretty popular as a church in this area and we can get hundreds to come on this one day, at least. I want to rent the Marine Theater for Easter."

"That big place!" I exclaimed. "How many does it seat?"

"Oh, I don't know, maybe three thousand. Just think of getting that many people all fired up about the Gospel."

"O.K., go ahead. Only be sure it's not a rainy or even a snowy day. Easter is early this year, late March; remember that." When Easter Day dawned, I sprang to the window to see what the weather was. Thankfully it was not snowing, but it was raining.

Bob Mirrilees phoned me. "Thank God for this great day," he

said. "And never mind the rain. It won't matter. Only faith matters."

When I drove to the theater, crowds were milling around outside, for the auditorium was already packed to capacity. As I entered by the stage entrance, Bob was getting everything organized. With tears on his cheeks, he grabbed my hand. "The Lord is marching on," he declared, voice breaking. "Just tell this crowd about Jesus. Keep it simple and straight. I've prayed my head off about today." Bob was an average everyday salesman, but he reflected the spirit of those wonderful people in Brooklyn during the exciting days of the twenties.

Despite that unforgettable Easter service and the new church and all our progress, the street in front of the church was still unpaved. On rainy days it was a sea of mud. Actually the stupendous growth of the Flatlands area made it very difficult for the borough of Brooklyn to keep up with street construction. Some who hoped they had influence at Borough Hall tried to get the street paved, but their efforts had no results. By this time our church enjoyed a not-inconsiderable impact upon Brooklyn generally. So I got in touch with the borough president, inviting him to be the speaker at our first annual dinner, letting him know that he would be the first in a series of our most distinguished citizens to speak on each anniversary occasion. He was a kindly man, a believer, and accepted the invitation.

The night of the dinner when the borough president arose to speak, he said, "The fine young man who came to drive me here tonight did the best he could for my comfort, but the potholes in this unpaved street out in front have all but broken my bones. I wonder, could this be the real reason your enterprising pastor invited me to speak in your church?" Interestingly enough, the street was paved within a month, all of which shows that things can happen speedily under the proper circumstances.

From the very beginning of my ministry, my object has always been to get people to come to church. My desire has been to preach the Gospel to them, to outline the plan of salvation, to convict them of their sins, and to effect a change of life through the cleansing power of the blood of Christ shed upon Calvary. This I have said in differing form and expression, but never with a variation or watering down of the content. It has resulted in

97

many conversions and changed lives across the years, not through any power of my own, but solely through the power of God through His Divine Son Jesus Christ.

A fourteen-year-old boy came one day to my office in Kings Highway Church. Sitting on the edge of the chair, he nervously twisted his cap. He was disturbed about something and that it was a painful matter was very clear. I tried to put him at ease.

"What is your given name?" I asked.

"It's Robert and you know my father. I don't know what to do," he stammered.

"Why don't you talk to your father?"

"I can't; I just can't. That's why I've come to you."

"Well, tell me about it and I will help all I can. And remember that as a pastor you can tell me anything in confidence."

"Reverend Peale, is my father straight? Is he a good man?" He seemed to choke up as he put this question.

"Robert, I am not very well acquainted with your father, but to me he seems a fine man and I've never heard anything bad about him. Why do you ask this question?"

"Well, you see, I love my father very much and I've always looked up to him. I think he is great, the finest man in the world." As he made this statement, tears ran down his face.

"I'm sure he is just that, Robert."

"Oh, I hope so. But the other kids have been whispering things so I can hear them about Dad and some woman. Oh, it can't be true, it just can't," he sobbed.

"Now look here, Robert, you must not let your faith in your father be shaken by some stupid whispers by a bunch of kids. You and I are going to believe in your father. But just to give you peace of mind I'll check up a bit."

Next day I telephoned Robert's father for an appointment. "What is it about?" he asked. I told him I had a matter to take up with him. As I sat across the desk from him, I felt that he was somewhat uneasy. I noted the strong resemblance between father and son. "In the job of being a minister we get all kinds of cases and problems," I explained, "and some of them are quite delicate and personal. But we have to do the best we can with each one. We are in the people-helping business."

"Yeah, I get you," he responded impatiently. "But what has this got to do with me? I don't need any help."

"Maybe not, but your son Robert does."

"Robert," he echoed. "What possible trouble could he have that he wouldn't talk to me about?"

I let the matter hang in the air for a few seconds. "You," I said.

He flushed angrily. "What do you mean by that, Reverend? I don't like what you are saying."

"I don't blame you for that, and you may think it is none of my business. I assure you that what must be said to you is most unpleasant for me. But I have to keep faith with your son who loves, no, idolizes you." Then I told him of my conversation with Robert. "I've gone out on a limb in urging him to have faith in you and not to believe those whispers. But in my opinion you are on the edge of absolutely devastating this boy and ruining your relationship with him. What shall I say to Robert; or how do you want me to handle it with him?"

He sat quite still as though in shock, face white. The silence continued until I became concerned about him. Finally he said, "Let me think. May I see you later?" I left him with his thoughts and his problem, and my heart ached not only for the boy but also for his father.

That night, after a meeting at the church, I found the boy's father waiting for me outside. We went back and sat in my office.

"I want to level with you, Reverend. I am involved with a woman. I'm a dirty, low-down no-good. My wife is the finest woman in the world. I've done this because I'm dirty in my mind, in my thoughts. I see clearly what I'm doing and it just isn't worth it. I'm a damned fool. But how can I get out of it?"

"Just tell her you're through. And then be through." He didn't say anything, so I continued. "But that is only the start. You not only must get out of it but, more importantly, you have to get it out of you. It is just plain old sin that got you into this mess. And now we need to get sin out of your mind, out of your heart. That is done by your becoming a new person through faith in Christ. Do you want this change to happen in you?"

Suddenly all the pretense dropped from him. "Oh, my God, Reverend, I can't live unless you get me out of this and get me

99

changed. I've got to control my evil thoughts. Lust, that's what it is. It's the evil in me. I'm no good."

This was healthy, the way he was talking, for it was conviction of sins. He made no excuses. He was honest about what he was and what he had done. And that was basic to becoming what he could be. He was also taking another important step: confession. He emptied out all his sneaking and lying and dishonesty and infidelity. He portrayed graphically his inner warfare between good and evil. He saw what he was and the sight was decidedly unpleasant.

Then, it was important to have him see what he could be. "Telephone the woman now and break it up."

"You mean right now, here with you?"

I shoved the telephone over to him. "Tell her you are with your pastor, in confession, and you are changing your life, beginning now."

Red of face, with a shaking hand holding the receiver, he told her exactly that. Slowly he replaced the receiver. "Know what she said?"

"What?"

" 'You're a good man. Better be that.' "

"She is right," I commented. "It's very hard for a good man to be a bad man. Now ask the Lord Jesus Christ to forgive and cleanse you from all sin. Tell Him that you believe in Him with all your heart and accept Him now as your Savior."

He did this with deep sincerity and with tears. I repeated that great old verse: " 'Though your sins be as scarlet, they shall be as white as snow,' " and the glorious words of Jesus to the woman taken in adultery: " 'Go, and sin no more.' "

When he arose from prayer, on his face there was an unforgettable smile mixed with tears, like sunshine after rain. He grasped my hand with a grip like steel. "How can I ever thank you?" he asked.

"Just by keeping the faith with the Lord and being a wonderful father to that terrific boy of yours. And," I added, "by being true to your real self, your good self."

Some weeks later father, mother, and son stood at the altar of the church as I received them into membership in Christ's Holy Church, into the society of the redeemed. But it was the look on the boy's face that got me. The whispers ceased and the father kept the faith to the end, so powerful was the change that Christ made in him.

I had an exciting three years in Brooklyn. Being young and enthusiastic with boundless energy, full of ideas, I was into everything that would in any way help to build up the church. I joined the Masonic fraternity, one of the first to be raised in the newly formed Midwood Lodge No. 310, of which I am still a member. Subsequently I passed through all the degrees of Masonry, Scottish Rite and York Rite, becoming a Thirty-third-degree member and recipient of the Gorgas Medal. I am Grand Chaplain of the Grand Lodge of New York, Past Grand Prelate of the Knights Templar and of the Shrine. I also became a member of the Kings County American Legion, of which I was the Protestant chaplain. The latter got me into one of the most memorable and creative experiences of my life.

It happened on a Sunday afternoon, Memorial Day, May 30, 1926. The community service that day was in memory of those who had died and in tribute to the Gold Star Mothers, so called because they had given sons for their country. As chaplain of the Legion, I received an invitation to give the invocation, or brief opening prayer, at the service, which would be held at the bandstand in Prospect Park. Upon arriving, I noted the huge crowd; a policeman told me it numbered at least fifty thousand people. Looking out from the platform, I could see that all available space was filled, and seated in the section immediately in front was a large number of the Gold Star Mothers of Brooklyn.

I reported to the chairman of the meeting, found my seat on the platform, and scanned the program. I couldn't believe my eyes, for there was my name listed, not for the invocation but for an address—As plain as day it read: "Address—Norman Vincent Peale." And to make matters worse, I was scheduled to speak just before the orator of the day, General Theodore Roosevelt, Jr., famous son of the late President of the United States. Never had I faced so large an assembly.

Aghast, all but petrified by fear, I rushed up to the chairman. "It's all a mistake, sir. I'm listed here for an address. It was only to be the invocation. I just can't do it."

General Roosevelt, overhearing my protestation, entered into the discussion. "Son," he said, "you are a minister of our Lord. As such, surely you have something to say to these women." He pointed at the Gold Star Mothers. "Every one of them is even now thinking of a little boy she reared, only to have him go off to war and die in Flanders fields. And all these people love our country just like you and I do. Talk to all of us out of your heart. Put your trust in God, love these people, and you will do a fine job." So saying, he slapped me on the back.

Fortunately I had given a Memorial Day sermon that morning at the church. So, calmed by the general's words, I readjusted a brief version of it to suit this occasion, at least enough to get by. I gave my little speech, received kind applause from the vast multitude, and resumed my seat. General Roosevelt seemed genuinely pleased, patting me approvingly on the knee. "You rang the bell. That was great," he enthused.

It was a feeble ringing of the bell, I well know, but the general added, "I knew you could do it. All you needed was to *know* you could do it. When we forget ourselves, think of others, and try to be of help to them, we can surpass ourselves. Always remember that," he concluded.

Well, I have tried to remember this advice. But there was never any trouble in remembering General Roosevelt, for he did help a young preacher confronted by a multitude. I always think of him with abiding gratitude and affection.

A Christian pastor may be defined, I think, as a person who loves people and tried to help them in the name of Jesus Christ. This, of course, may be an oversimplified definition. But then I have always had an uncomplicated approach to life. Anyway, I have always loved human beings, those who are lovable by nature, and have tried to love those who are not. As a result, I've ended up by more or less loving everyone; in many cases, even those who certainly do not love me.

One Christmas Eve in Brooklyn, I had dinner at the home of friends and upon emerging into the clear cold night, noticed a strange contradiction. Across the street were two wreaths on a house: One, as might be expected, was a Christmas wreath, the other was a funeral wreath. "What does that mean?" I asked the friends to whom I was saying good-night.

"The people living there have lost a child," they replied. "They have only recently moved into that house and we have not as yet had opportunity to get acquainted. Now we hesitate to intrude under the circumstances."

On the street I walked up and down. Wasn't it, perhaps, my duty as a pastor to offer solace and help, even though I had no knowledge of their religious faith or indeed if they had any at all? Finally, deciding that the offer of love and sympathy was never amiss, I rang the bell. A very pleasant young man opened the door. "My name is Norman Peale and I am pastor of the Kings Highway Methodist Church. If I can be of any service to you in your sorrow. I will be glad to help in any way that I can," I said.

He invited me in, explained that they had two children, one, a little boy, was downstairs and he was reading the Christmas story from the Bible to him. "My wife is upstairs helping watch over the body of our little girl." He took me upstairs to meet his wife, a sweet-faced, calm young woman. "We thank God we had her for nearly five years. She was so sweet and wonderful. Then God took her. Our hearts are breaking, but our Lord knows best, though we wonder why. But we accept His holy will." This family later became members of my church and lifelong friends. As I walked down the frosty street that Christmas Eve, I reflected on the birth of the Christ Child and the passing of a little innocent one.

Only a few weeks earlier I had had my first funeral service for a child. A little girl had died, the daughter of my friends John and Mary. In their home I stood by the small casket looking on her sweet face. She was in a white dress and had ribbons in her hair. She seemed almost able to rise and speak. I myself was devastated, for she had been a favorite of mine. Yet I knew I must speak, not of death, but of life and the immortality in which we believed. I read scriptural passages: "Though I walk through the valley of the shadow of death, I will fear no evil . . ." And again: "I am the resurrection, and the life, sayeth the Lord. He that believeth in me, though he were dead, yet shall he live."

Then it was time for my remarks, but I did not yet have my emotions under control. I looked at the two young parents, sitting huddled together, holding hands, heads bowed, he in a dark suit, she in a dark dress. Finally after a long silence, I walked over to them, put an arm around them both, hugging them to me. "John . . . Mary," I said brokenly, "God loves her. God loves you both. And . . . and . . . I loved her and I love you." I held them like that for a moment longer, then pronounced the benediction. I well know that it was not the proper way for a minister to conduct such a service; but long afterward, John told me that he had often heard about the love of God, but not until that moment did he really know what it meant.

Certainly our Christian faith deals with the hard things, the pain and suffering of the Savior and of His followers, but since it is "the victory that overcometh the world," it contains laughter as well as tears and sorrow. There were many funny, even riotous, things that happened during my years at Kings Highway. There is a lot of fun in the life of a minister. Why not? for Christianity is a joyful religion. "These things have I spoken unto you," said Jesus, "that your joy might be full." "Rejoice . . . I say, Rejoice," and "Ye rejoice with joy unspeakable."

Clarence G. Neese, himself a minister's son and one of my most able helpers, was the song leader on Sunday evenings. One night the church was packed to capacity, every pew filled. Since people continued to come, extra chairs were brought in and arranged in front of the pews. Then appeared a fat family. This is no exaggeration. The father and mother were huge, as were all three children, though to a lesser degree. The aggregate weight of the family must have approached eight hundred pounds. Suddenly the chair holding the enormous mother gave way and with a terrific crash fell to the floor, carrying the lady with it in quite an undignified sprawl. This created some uproar and Brother Neese called out a hymn number to cover the excitement. To the astonishment and amusement of all, it proved to be the old Gospel hymn, "Rescue the Perishing."

I cannot recall what songbook was used in those days, but one hymn figures in memory that I've never heard since. On another evening while Brother Neese was leading the song service, a family of twelve, known to everyone, came in late. And as they marched down the aisle, the congregation burst into a hymn, "Here Come the Reinforcements."

One day in early spring of 1927, I received a letter from Bishop Adna Wright Leonard of the Buffalo, New York, area, asking if I would preach on a certain Sunday at the University Methodist Church in Syracuse. I appreciated the opportunity to preach in this great church, just off the campus of Syracuse University, and had a pleasant experience there. Subsequently came another message from Bishop Leonard stating that the church board had unanimously requested him to appoint me pastor of the University church and asking if I would accept the appointment.

I was enjoying my work in Brooklyn and loved the people there so much that I hesitated to leave, as attractive as was the opportunity at Syracuse. My brother Bob happened to be visiting me at the time. Upon occasion he could be a very forthright character, and in this instance he declared, "You have got to move forward to new opportunity. You have finished your job here. You have built a new church, established a strong and growing congregation. You thrive on problems and from what I hear there are plenty at Syracuse." It was my turn to have a telephone placed before me. "Call the bishop and ask him when you start at your new church."

So an exciting three years in old Flatlands, Brooklyn, New York, in the Roaring Twenties came to an end.

CHAPTER EIGHT

·

Upstate on a May Day

IT WAS A MORNING in May 1927 when I said farewell to Brooklyn. My father would have described the day with his characteristic phrase: "bright as a May morning." Storing my meager worldly goods in my small car, I turned down Flatbush Avenue, went over the Brooklyn Bridge, up Broadway, then onto Route 9 to Poughkeepsie. Continuing through Albany, I drove west on old Route 5 through the ever-beautiful Mohawk Valley to Utica, and my lonely and sad feelings gradually gave way to a mounting excitement. I was on my way to the future. It was May, I was young, the sky was blue, the noble landscape of upstate New York swept away to the far horizon.

Stopping for lunch at the old Hotel Utica, I bought a newspaper and read the thrilling story of the historic landing of Lindbergh in Paris after flying the *Spirit of St. Louis* all alone across the Atlantic.

Arriving in Syracuse, I arranged to live at the Hotel Syracuse and was assigned to room 648. Being a bachelor, I required only one room for there was a commodious office in the church. I remained at the hotel until Ruth and I were married three years later.

The room was on a courtyard, but it was comfortable, and a middle-aged motherly sort of maid, whose name I seem to recall

106

was Grace, pampered me. Indeed, all the hotel personnel, including the general manager, looked out for my welfare and helped make me feel at home. I recall the rate was approximately forty dollars a week, hardly half a day's cost today. Of course, meals were extra, but the church members took pity on me and invited me to their homes much of the time.

Notable among these kind and generous friends were Geoff and Elsie Brown. They often took me into their home when I needed to get away to quietness. This became a special necessity on the nights before and after the traditional Colgate football game when alumni swamped the hotel and made it a bedlam of noise.

One winter evening I stopped at a very small lunch-counter eating place. A friendly, courteous Armenian came over to wait on me as I perched on a stool. "Reverend Peale," he exclaimed with a big smile. "Welcome, welcome. My whole family are members of your church, and here you are in my humble place. I'm going to fix you a nice steak." It was memorable, except he wouldn't let me pay. "I owe you a lot, your sermons have helped me." It became almost a running battle about the bill—one I could not win by staying away at the risk of losing a friend. This went on for forty years because Joe Edison moved to Los Angeles, and almost every trip I made there, I had dinner in his palatial home, where he would personally "fix a steak" in the same loving manner as he had in the hole-in-the-wall restaurant back in Syracuse.

Mother came from Ohio to be with me my first Sunday at University Church. It was and is a beautiful stone structure with huge stained-glass windows on each side of the sanctuary. On any day when the light was right, it was a place of glory. On that first Sunday morning, I faced a congregation that did not quite half fill the seats, and no one was seated in the large balcony. Instead an extra-tall ladder, evidently designed for reaching high lights, lay across the empty seats. "That ladder is going to come out of the balcony and people take its place," I promised myself.

A layman, a man of large proportions and obviously a distinguished person, presided at the service, sitting beside me in the pulpit. "When you speak," he advised, "aim your voice at the bottom of the balcony, in the middle, and you'll manage the acoustical eccentricities of this auditorium." As he introduced me, he said, "The members of this congregation have a great responsibility. We have a very young minister, younger than we have ever had. We can make him either an ordinary or a great preacher. Our congregation is composed of outstanding people in the field of education, the sciences, medicine, business, and industry. Let us make a great preacher of him by praying for him, helping him, teaching him, loving him, and this to the glory of God and the advancement of Christ's Kingdom."

I was overwhelmed and deeply touched as I looked at the intelligent and friendly faces looking up at me. After expressing appreciation for the kindly introduction, I said, "Together let us make this a great church, truly a place where all may learn to walk in newness of life through Christ."

As the closing hymn was being sung, I leaned over and asked the man who had welcomed me so graciously, "Professor, what subject do you teach at the university?"

I nearly collapsed when he answered, "I am Dean of the School of Speech and Drama." This remarkable man, Hugh M. Tilroe, became one of the great influences in my life. He was an outstanding public speaker. He was also a hunter and invited me often to eat game he had shot. He was a valiant outdoorsman, a fisherman of skill, and I often visited his lodge on Oneida Lake.

Some three years after I had come to Syracuse, Mrs. Tilroe called me to say that her husband had suffered a stroke and would I come? I sat by his bed, looking sadly at the great, immobilized figure, his speech somewhat slurred but still intelligible. He lay like a great tree felled by lightning. "Norman, just look at me. I'm laid low. Can't hunt anymore or fish anymore or speak anymore. I want you to take a speaking engagement for me tomorrow night."

"Oh, Professor, no man can take Hugh Tilroe's place."

"Listen, son, you just go there and take Norman Peale's place. Remember that your old friend says you are a great man on the platform. Don't ever forget that."

What a man he was. There was a preacher in a little town upstate married to an extraordinarily beautiful woman whom he worshiped. But she went bad, and presently it became generally known. Yet the preacher lived on happily in ignorance until one stormy night he came home, calling out endearments to his wife as he always did. There was no response. Then he found a note on the table.

Dear —
    I cannot stand it anymore. You think I am a pure, good woman and wife, an angel. But I am not. I'm a bad woman and cannot help being so. God knows I've tried.
    But not to be what you think I am and, instead, to be what I really am is breaking me apart. So I am leaving tonight with [naming a man of low character in the community].
    Don't ever try to find me. I will love you and revere you always. You are a saint. But, God help me, I cannot live with your goodness.

The note fell from his fingers, his head dropped to his arms as he sat numbed and shocked. Presently he stumbled to the telephone and fortunately reached Dean Tilroe at his lodge on Oneida Lake. Between sobs he told the story.

In his gruff voice Tilroe said, "You stay right where you are. I will be there in a couple of hours. Just do nothing. I'm leaving for your place immediately."

It was a wild night, as it can be at times upstate. But eventually the professor arrived, went into the bedroom, put the minister's clothes in a suitcase, helped him on with his coat, and said, "Come on, old fellow, get in the car." For two hours they drove through rain and snow. Tilroe said nothing at all; but the stricken pastor told me how comforted he was seeing his friend's strong profile lit by the light on the dashboard.

Reaching the lodge, Tilroe built up the fire in the big fireplace, then cooked some bacon and eggs, made coffee, and forced the man to eat. "Now," he said, "you get into bed." Obediently, the pastor did so. Standing by the bed, Tilroe said, "Let's pray. 'O God, put Your great big loving and everlasting arms around my friend and give him peace. Amen.' Now go to sleep. I'll sit up and be right here if you need me."

Later the minister told me that his sleep was troubled and broken. During the night, when he would wake up, there was

Tilroe still sitting by the fire. In the early morning he saw that Tilroe had wrapped a blanket around himself, but he was still awake and watchful. And, said the pastor, "Peace began to come, for watching that man made me realize what God is like. A line from Scripture came to mind: 'For He shall give his angels charge over thee, to keep thee in all thy ways.' "

Bishop Leonard's reason for sending me to Syracuse was, in part at least, aimed at trying to get the big student population of Syracuse University more involved in the church. He seemed to feel that possibly I might be able to reach the young people. Only a very few students had any interest at all in the church at that point. I organized a committee of the ones who were, and after services one brilliant October Sunday we held a meeting in a front pew.

Suddenly the doors at the rear of the sanctuary opened, and a girl stood framed in the golden light. I looked up and forgot everything. I stood transfixed. That was the girl. I had never seen her before, did not know her name. But I did know who she was; she was for me. From that minute, when she stood in that effulgent light, I fell in love with Ruth Stafford. She was waiting for one of the girls in my committee meeting, but actually it was I who was waiting for her. And I had been waiting for a long time.

I was introduced to her later by her roommate, Phyllis Leonard, the bishop's daughter, who had persuaded Ruth to come to the church for a social function for students. Ruth says that at the time of the introduction I held her hand just a fraction of a second longer than was necessary, and she thought, "This is going to be interesting!"

I asked if she would serve as chairman of a committee to arrange a large student dinner. Being a good Christian girl and a natural-born leader, she not only had a sense of responsibility for work among students, but she loved to organize things. So she agreed to take on the job. I said, "We will work closely together." I must admit that this possibility took precedence in my mind over the student dinner.

I told Ruth it was only occasionally that a meeting of the whole committee would be required and that she and I could do most of the work, perhaps over dinner. Of course, the best places were charming restaurants in the country. When finally the night of the dinner came and she was placing the seating cards , she modestly put herself at the end of the head table. Naturally I changed her place to right by me.

When I met Ruth, it was in the fall of her senior year, and as the months passed I suddenly realized that in June she would be graduating. Then she would go home to Detroit, and the prospect of no longer being able to see her was just too painful to contemplate. Carl Alverson, a close friend of mine, was superintendent of schools in Syracuse at the time. He had casually mentioned something about a shortage of teachers. Remembering this, I said, "Carl, there is a young lady in our church who would make a fine teacher. Why don't you look into her qualifications?"

He did, and Ruth was hired as a teacher of mathematics in Central High School. "She was," as Alverson later told me and others, "an outstanding mathematics teacher and made a splendid contribution to the life of the school." However that may have been, one thing is sure, she made a great contribution to the life of Norman Peale; so much so that I called on Bob Pond one day. Bob was head of a famous firm of jewelers and an active member of our church. "What's the situation about rings nowadays, Bob?" I asked, as offhandedly as possible.

"Well, jewelry is a bit high at the moment, but it looks like a depression is coming and, if so, prices will drop. I hope not too much. How come you are interested in rings?"

"Oh, just a general economic interest." I shrugged it off.

But I didn't fool him any, for as I was leaving he said, "If you can interest her to the extent that a ring is required, Norman, we will see that you get just the right one. However, don't wait for a depression. That may be a long time off."

But it was only a few weeks later that the great stock market crash came on an October day in 1929. Factories began closing, breadlines were forming, people were taking cuts in salaries and wages. The economic collapse, later known as the Great Depression of the thirties, was beginning. At a Rotary Club luncheon that fall, I was sitting with Bob Pond and others. We fell to discussing the situation, and I recall Bob observing, "We will never again have prosperity in this country," a sweeping negative generalization dictated by the pessimism aroused by this major debacle. But as later events proved, never is a very long time and prosperity came again, though not until after some very hard times.

Even before this national calamity I was experiencing a depression of my own in the church. Again I had come to the leadership of a church that was down in many respects. The intake of new members had materially slowed before I arrived. Then, deaths in the congregation and a slackening of interest had caused a decline in church attendance of perhaps 50 percent. No wonder the balcony could be used as the storage place for a ladder. There was also an acute financial problem. Church income had been declining for several years before I became the pastor.

I have always felt that the church in Syracuse was willing to take so young a minister in part at least because he would have modest salary needs. There was no discussion of salary with me, and the bishop said frankly, "The official board is lowering the salary because the church is in debt. But come anyway. You can build up this church and the salary matter will adjust itself."

"Bishop, I did not enter the ministry on the basis of salary consideration."

"I know," he said. "However, you should be aware that this church is in financial trouble."

It was an old story. I had already been pastor of two churches in financial trouble; and later was to go to one in New York that was in even greater trouble. Evidently I had become a sort of troubleshooter. Through these experiences I learned that the bottom can really be a good place to start. The only direction from there is up. And if you lift your job up, in whatever work you do, you go up with it—and deservedly so. On the other hand, if you take charge when all is going well and everything is at peak performance, you are expected not only to keep things at the high point, but to take them to an even higher level. And to accomplish this may requrie an extra sort of genius. So, to succeed in life, it may be better to take a job where there is trouble and your help is needed. This is my personal philosophy, developed through experience and followed in every instance.

Life at Syracuse was exciting indeed, and some unusual experiences contributed. One night when I had just returned from a meeting to my hotel room, the telephone rang. A rather muffled voice asked, "Are you Reverend Peale?" When I answered that I was, the voice continued. "A woman is dying. She wants a pastor to read to her from the Bible and offer a prayer for her soul. She has heard you speak and asks you to come. We will send a car for you and return you to the hotel. Will you do this for her?"

Questions as to her name and address received vague answers. "All you need to do is read the Bible to her and pray for her. Nothing else matters."

I was a bit doubtful but, always being ready to serve human need, I agreed to meet the woman's representatives at the front entrance of the hotel in fifteen minutes. A big black car drew up. A man stepped out and asked, "Reverend Peale?" I nodded and was ushered into the backseat. The man followed me. I found myself in the middle between two men. Another was seated beside the driver. Trying to make conversation to find out a bit more about the dying woman elicited no response beyond grunts. Then I noticed that the car had shades pulled down on the side windows. I could not turn to see out the back window, and the hulking shoulders of the men in front effectively blocked my view.

Here I was with four starkly silent men dressed in dark suits and in a car in which the windows were shaded. Visions of a murder (mine) by gangsters (for they certainly looked the part) came to mind. Thus we rode in complete silence, the driver making many turns so that quickly I lost my bearings, with no idea of what direction we were taking. We drove for some thirty minutes. Finally the car stopped. The man who had ushered me in, likewise ushered me out, without a word, but nodded for one of the other men to follow him. We entered a house which from the outside was blacked out, no light at all that I could see. The man took me into a room where a woman lay in bed. He stood by the door.

The woman seemed to be in her thirties. Her face was pale, her hands on the coverlet were thin. "May I have your name, ma'am?" I asked.

"My name would mean nothing to you, Pastor. I am just a poor miserable sinner. It is good of you to come. Please read to me from the Book. I loved its wonderful words as a child. Mother would read the Scriptures to us kids every night when she put us to bed." All of this was spoken in a feeble voice which now and then trailed off so that it was somewhat difficult to follow. "Ask the Lord to forgive me for my sins and to take me to heaven," she said in a pathetic way.

"What would you like me to read?" I asked. "Have you any favorite passages?" She named a few, which I read, and she was obviously comforted. Throughout this reading the taciturn man still stood beside the door.

Then I took the woman's thin, cold hand and held it while I prayed for her. I asked the always merciful Lord for forgiveness for all her sins, praying for one who had strayed but who now, as the shades of death closed in, wanted the divine assurance and love.

When I said, "Amen," her fingers held on to mine. "Thank you, Pastor. I feel peace in my heart. I am ready now when Jesus calls me." Her hand fell back on the coverlet, and she smiled a faint smile.

"God loves you," I said. The man by the door led me to the car. The same two men got in the back again, seating me in the middle. We drove in silence, and at the hotel the man who alone acted as spokesman, though a very taciturn one, simply said, "Thanks," closed the door of the car, and was driven off, disappearing around the corner. Too late I thought of reading the license number.

I watched the paper for a few days with particular reference to death notices, but found nothing. To this day I have no knowledge of who the woman was or anything about the four strange men. But when I said my prayers that night, I again prayed for the poor dying woman. And to the prayer I added one of thanksgiving that I was still alive and safe.

My first task at Syracuse, after getting student activities going, was to eliminate the debt on current expenses, which had reached a total of over fifty-five thousand dollars, not much now, but a huge figure for those times. I called a meeting of the official board, which included some of the prominent businessmen of the city as well as leading members of the faculty of Syracuse University. When they had assembled, I made a little speech.

"Ladies and gentlemen," I said, "there is a debt on the running expenses of this church of some fifty-five thousand dollars and we are continuing to go further into debt with every passing day. There are two things we can do in such a situation: one is to curtail expenses, cut back on activities, reduce staff; on the other hand, we can raise the debt, get more income, go forward with important activities, and get the money to do the work God wants us to do.

"Personally I am for raising the debt and going forward. It can be done and we are just the people to do it. Please do not tell me that the times are bad. I am reading that fact in the papers every day. But so what! Christianity always does better when times are bad. It is true that man's adversity is God's opportunity. You have had this debt a long time. Too long, I would say. Anyway, I didn't come to University Church to run an institution on three cylinders. So, shall we start by raising that debt? I know that God will help us and bless our efforts."

These remarks started a discussion that lasted well into the night. Finally a decision was taken that "under the circumstances [a catchphrase for negative thinking] the total debt of fifty-five thousand dollars is too much to undertake so we will try something reasonable; viz. twenty thousand dollars."

While I was disappointed by this uninspired result of my talk at the board meeting, nothing daunted, I went out to raise twenty thousand dollars and maybe more. There was an older man, whose name was Harlowe B. Andrews. He was a prominent wholesale grocer in upstate New York. He would order perishable merchandise from Arizona, Florida, and California by fast express trains and sell it on Salina Street in Syracuse, to the confusion of his competitors. Andrews could very well be called the forerunner of present supermarkets and high-grade specialty shops.

A banker in Syracuse once told me that Brother Andrews, as he was generally called because of his Christian witness, was the best businessman in central New York. "All he needed to do," said the banker, "was to hold out his fingers and money sprang to him." I hung around with Brother Andrews in the hope of acquiring that same skill but, alas, without success. He was one of the greatest positive thinkers I ever knew, always a believer in potentialities, and a creator of positive results.

Brother Andrews was a generous giver to the church, so the

next day after the board meeting I drove out into the country to see him. Although he lived on Genesee Street in the city, he often stayed for days in the old farmhouse that was the home of his youth. "Brother Andrews," I said, "we had a meeting of the official board last night."

"I heard you did."

"I thought I would come out to see you."

"I figured you would."

"Well," I continued brightly, "we don't believe we can handle all that debt of fifty-five thousand dollars, so we have decided to go after twenty thousand dollars of it. And I wondered what you will give?"

"Well," he responded promptly, "the answer is, not a nickel; in fact, not a cent." I sat, disconcerted. "But," he continued, "tell you what I *will* do, I will pray with you."

While I am an avid believer in prayer, I must say that at the moment this offer was a bit of a letdown. But the prayer he offered to the Lord, like all of Brother Andrews's prayers, had power in it. Perhaps it appeared to be a bit less than formal, but it had genuine love and faith.

"Get onto your knees," he ordered. "Now, Lord," he said, "I pray for this young minister. What he doesn't know about people would fill a book. I know he has been to college and has several degrees, but he doesn't realize that faith and courage are required for leadership and that people will respond to bugle calls. So if he is going to go along supinely with those same old negative attitudes and go timidly out to raise only twenty thousand dollars, I will not give anything. But, dear Lord, if he will be courageous and decide to raise the whole fifty-five thousand dollars, I will give five thousand dollars. Amen."

"That's wonderful, Brother Andrews," I said excitedly. "You will give five thousand dollars, but where are we going to get the rest?"

"That's easy! Where you just got the first five."

"And where was that?" I asked a bit perplexed.

"You prayed for it, and you now have it and only need fifty thousand dollars more. So here is what you do. Go downtown and ask Dr. Roy Moore for a matching gift of five thousand dollars. He can do it. He doesn't know that he can, but he can. So picture him as doing just that, and thank God for working on his heart, for he is a good man."

Following his positive direction, I drove to the doctor's office. Then that old shyness of mine began to assert itself once again. Hoping there would be no place to park so that I would not have to confront the doctor, I immediately found a spot. "Hello, Norman," the doctor said. "I hear that you are out raising twenty thousand dollars."

"Well, that is what the board has ordered, but I've just gotten a good gift provided we raise the whole fifty-five thousand dollars. But I need a matching gift."

"How much do you want from me?"

I was about to say one thousand dollars. But I quickly upped it in my mind to three thousand dollars. Then I saw a vision of old Brother Andrews's face with faith written all over it. "Doctor, I'm going to give you the privilege of making a matching gift with Brother Andrews of five thousand dollars."

The doctor obviously was startled. I could actually watch his mind working. "It's a lot of money," he muttered, "but . . . but . . . tell you what, I *will* give five thousand dollars."

I could hardly contain my amazed excitement. Leaping into my car, I broke all speed limits to Mr. Andrews's house. Slamming on the brakes in a cloud of dust, I dashed into the house without knocking and cried, "He did it! He did it!"

"Of course he did," calmly said Brother Andrews. "Knowing how weak your faith was I sent a prayer of affirmation along with you right into the doctor's office."

"I know," I shouted. "I saw it hit him."

"Well now, young fellow, you have ten thousand dollars."

"But . . ." I hesitated.

"Oh, I know," interrupted Brother Andrews, "you are already wondering where you are going to get the remaining forty-five thousand dollars. And the answer is the same: where you got the first ten; namely, by praying for it, by believing in your mission, by knowing that God makes a way where there is no way, and by our getting out there and asking for it."

So it went. With the always present help of the Lord and the support of some dedicated Christians, the wonder-working power was put back into a great church.

The practice of real faith joined to the preaching and teaching of a strongly evangelical Gospel began to bring back disenchanted members and to draw in new ones in large numbers. The pews filled up; financial support became less of a problem. But more importantly, a new spirit developed, an exciting spirit, which brought about life-changing experiences in the lives of so many that the church became a vital center of spiritual growth.

Students at the university began flocking to the church every Sunday until from the pulpit, the preacher looked into a sea of faces, many of them youthful and excited, glowing with an inner spirit. This enthusiastic response continued unbroken until Hendricks Chapel was erected on campus. We then discontinued the emphasis on getting students to come to church, believing that their spiritual lives should not be separate from the totality of educational experience. Many of them, however, continued their attendance at University Church, especially the considerable number who had found new meaning and reality in their lives.

The spectacular Christian student work that developed at University Church during the years before the chapel was built became the talk of the campus. I began the practice of reserving sections of the sanctuary for particular student organizations. One Sunday the members of my fraternity, Phi Gamma Delta, were present in a body, not only the undergraduates but also many alumni members who lived nearby. Ruth's sorority, Alpha Phi, the Alpha chapter, would reserve a big section across the aisle. The next Sunday it would be another fraternity and sorority. So it went, Sunday after Sunday.

It became the "in" thing for students to attend University Church. This gave us not only the opportunity to bring Jesus Christ into their lives by the spoken word, but through small discussion groups as well. Getting to know them personally meant that many came to us with their problems; and the personal problems of youth are numerous and of crisis intensity. In my travels around the nation on speaking engagements I still meet Syracuse graduates who tell me that they found themselves spiritually in those services and through friendly contacts at our University Church.

In all this work I was ably assisted by Reverend Webster D. Melcher, a classmate from Boston University, who became an associate minister with me, and at another time by the Reverend Dean Richardson. Both these men subsequently gave distinguished service in the ministry.

The greatest thing that happened to me in Syracuse, indeed the greatest thing that has happened to me period, was my marriage to Ruth Stafford, the girl I had seen in the church doorway, the one I had instantly known was for me. Some months after I had, with assumed nonchalance, felt Bob Pond out on how much engagement and wedding rings might set me back, I went back to his place of business. "Bob, the time has come for that ring."

"Been pretty slow in getting to it," he observed. "Anyway, congratulations. You are lucky to find such a girl. Give her a kiss for me." So saying, he took a ring from the case.

That evening I called for Ruth as usual at the home of our friend Mrs. Calthrop where she lived while teaching at Central High School. Just before we went out to dinner (and now I am quoting this story the way she tells it), I took a little unwrapped box from my pocket and offhandedly gave it to her, saying, "Here is what I guess you have been waiting for." She opened the box, tried the ring on her finger, and rushed into my arms. Bursting with our great news, we kept it to ourselves until it was announced in the Syracuse papers a few weeks before the wedding day.

The wedding took place in University Church on June 20, 1930, at four o'clock. Guests packed the church to more than its capacity and hundreds stood on the church lawn waiting for the bride and groom to emerge following the ceremony. The officiating ministers were three in number, and a fourth, Rev. Frank B. Stafford, gave Ruth away as father of the bride. The three pastors who shared the ceremony were the father of the groom, Rev. Dr. Charles Clifford Peale, pastor of the First Methodist Church, Columbus, Ohio; Bishop Adna Wright Leonard; and Chancellor Charles W. Flint of Syracuse University. Dr. Howard Lyman, director of our sixty-voice choir, which I enthusiastically advertised as "the greatest choir in the Empire State," provided music with sensitivity and beauty. Mrs. Frank B. Stafford, Ruth's lovely mother, Mrs. C. C. Peale, gracious mother of the groom, and her young son Leonard DeLaney Peale, my brother, as well as Ruth's brothers, Charles and William Stafford, were in the place of honor. My brother Dr. Robert Clifford Peale acted in the capacity of best man, and Eleanor Stafford, wife of Charles M. Stafford, Ruth's brother, was the beautiful matron of honor. In the ceremony the groom, having returned to Bob Pond for the wedding band, slipped the ring, without dropping it, onto the bride's finger. Thus were our sacred vows exchanged.

As we passed down the aisle together, Ruth on my arm, I whispered, "Just think what a collection we could get out of a crowd like this!" I also directed my bride's attention to the tears being shed by the young women present at their having failed to capture this groom. To all of these irrelevant remarks Ruth responded, "Be quiet; the groom is a very secondary person at a wedding." With that, we stepped across the threshold of the church through the wide-open doors and were greeted with love and an obvious sharing in our happiness by the throng outside.

Following the wedding reception given by Chancellor and Mrs. Flint in the chancellor's mansion at Syracuse University, Ruth and I took off in the gathering twilight of that memorable June day to start on our long life together. For the first night of our honeymoon we had reserved a room in the old Cooper Inn at Cooperstown, New York, because the next day I had a speaking engagement at nearby Cazenovia Seminary. I was to deliver a commencement talk where my younger brother, Leonard, was a member of the graduating class. So, following the wedding dinner in Syracuse, we drove away in the gathering twilight down Route 20, one of the most beautiful roads in the Empire State.

The next morning we read in the *Syracuse Post-Standard* that "the most eligible bachelor in Syracuse" had been married the day before. I pointed this out to Ruth, but she seemed unimpressed.

We were late in getting away after the commencement exercises and the luncheon at Cazenovia Seminary. Upstate roads were hardly superhighways in those days, and the afternoon was well along when we resumed our honeymoon. Ruth philosophically observed that this was par for the course. Anyway, it was dark when we finally reached our destination.

Friends in Syracuse, Dr. and Mrs. Markham, owned a charming house in the North Woods area near Fifth Lake in the Adirondacks that they kindly put at our disposal. Night had fallen when we drove through the dense woods surrounding Fifth Lake trying to find the Markham cottage. We had picked up a newspaper that headlined the escape from the Auburn State prison of a desperate criminal who had been jailed for murder. It was thought that he was in the North Woods. Everyone living in that area was warned to take extra precautions because the murderer was armed and would not hesitate to kill again.

We finally located the house deep in the dark woods. The only light was the faint gleam of the moon. I stumbled onto the back porch and finally got the house unlocked. Then I built a roaring fire for, though it was late June, the night was chilly.

After my bride, who was and still is a topnotch cook, had prepared a meal, we sat in front of the fire, holding hands. But the silence was awesome and the thought of that lurking murderer possibly being in those very woods did not add to my peace of mind. At every noise or creak in the old house I envisioned his stealthy approach. Suddenly, a noise on the porch sounded like a footstep. A chill passed through me. Here I was alone with my bride. Were we to be murdered on our honeymoon? Something had to be done and it was up to me to do it. Ruth was unperturbed, obviously not nervous at all.

"Don't be worried," I said heroically. "Leave it to me. Whoever this intruder is I will handle him." Seizing an ax, which I had found in the woodshed by the kitchen, I advanced toward the door from which the sound of the step had come. With bravado I took hold of the knob and flung open the door. There, blinking up at me, was a little chipmunk. After one look at my formidable appearance, it scampered off among the trees. "Scaredy-cat," said Ruth.

"You have to be on the alert," I mumbled.

Came time to go to bed in the big bedroom upstairs. I looked through all the other bedrooms and closets while Ruth calmly unpacked and turned down the bed. Finally I came in sheepishly holding the ax behind me. "Whatever are you going to do with that ax?" she asked.

"If that convict gets in here he will have me to deal with," I said, putting the ax by the side of the bed where I could quickly reach for it.

"I'm sure that would frighten him," said my calm and unafraid wife. When morning light came, with the sun shining down among the trees and sparkling on the lake, I self-consciously returned the ax to the woodshed. The convict was apprehended the next day hundreds of miles from our North Woods honeymoon cottage.

A few days later we returned to Syracuse, and for the next two years the husband-and-wife team of Ruth and Norman Peale began to function in the many ways that have made an exciting life story for over half a century.

CHAPTER NINE

Sidewalks of New York

WINTER IN SYRACUSE was winter in the fullest sense of the word: cold, snow, ice. Indeed, back in the 1930s it was said that Syracuse weather consisted of eleven months of winter and one month of poor sleighing. While I always liked the stimulation and steely blue beauty of winter in Onondaga County, a steady diet of cold blustery days, with the snow lying thick on the frozen ground, could produce an occasional desire for respite.

In early March 1932, when an invitation came to preach at Marble Collegiate Church on Fifth Avenue in New York City, I rather welcomed it as a chance to have a day or two away from upstate weather. When I told Ruth about it, the matter was decided. She was not about to pass up a weekend in New York City. My friend Bishop Adna Wright Leonard happened to be in Syracuse and obligingly said he would preach for me at University Church. So off we went to New York blithely unaware that, as we subsequently learned, God had it in mind for us to minister not for a weekend, but for over more than half a century on the sidewalks of New York.

Marble Collegiate Church had been without a spiritual leader for two and a half years since its famous pastor, Dr. Daniel A. Poling, resigned to head a religious publishing project. I had met Dr. Poling when, as a young, black-haired giant of a man, he came to speak once for my father in Greenville, Ohio. I was thrilled by his eloquence, but little dreamed that one day I would succeed him in a New York pulpit, have his abiding friendship for a lifetime, and finally officiate at his funeral, eulogizing him as one of the greatest preachers in American history.

Dr. Poling had an outstanding ministry at Marble Collegiate Church and attracted a sizable congregation during his eight-year tenure. It was a great loss when he presented his resignation. He successfully blocked a movement to abandon the church, for he was convinced it had great potential for future development. But following his departure a steady decline took place, and the long interim without a pastor had left Marble Collegiate Church as a mere skeleton.

Many candidates had preached in Marble Collegiate. The search committee for a new pastor had looked far and wide. For some reason the committee had not been able to reach a decision. Of course, I knew nothing of this background when I went that Sunday morning, March 13, 1932, to the classic old church at Fifth Avenue and Twenty-ninth Street. The preacher scheduled for that day had suddenly taken ill—thus, the invitation to me as a guest preacher.

Ruth had arranged to meet several of her Syracuse classmates and sorority sisters, and they sat with her in church. A gracious lady, impressed by a pew filled with attractive young women, approached them after the service and asked if they were visitors in New York. When Ruth responded that she was from Syracuse, the church member said, "Our visiting minister this morning is also from Syracuse. You must allow me to present you to him." The lady seemed a bit startled when Ruth, so youthful-looking, announced that she was the wife of the visiting minister.

Again that evening I preached to a congregation of approximately the same size as the morning congregation, neither one filling more than perhaps one tenth of the available seats. There was a marked spirit of dedication, however, among the members of the small congregation. This, with the atmosphere of friendly hospitality and the beauty of the sanctuary, gave the church a definite charm and attractiveness.

The next Sunday, when I faced the great congregation back home in Syracuse, my visit to New York of the preceding Sunday had passed out of mind. Then I chanced to notice a face in the congregation that looked familiar, and yet I could not place the man. A few minutes later another face caught my attention. Then I realized where I had met both men. It was at Marble Collegiate Church. And I saw the same men at the evening service. One of them came forward afterward and told me that five members of their committee had come to Syracuse to hear me preach and to talk with me. Could I meet with them that evening?

At our meeting they told me about Marble Collegiate: that it was the leading church in the parent religious body bearing the unusual and impressive name the Minister, Elder, and Deacon of the Collegiate Reformed Protestant Dutch Church of the City of New York. The first religious service of the church had been held on Sunday, April 9, 1628, in a gristmill at what is now the Battery. The population of New Amsterdam at that time was probably little more than three hundred persons.

The committee members told me proudly that, as far as their knowledge went, no Sunday had passed since that early founding date that a Sunday worship service had not been held under the auspices of the church.

I found the history of Marble Collegiate fascinating indeed. It seems it was the policy of the Dutch West India Company when it established a trading post in faraway places always to bring a "Dominie" (pastor), whose duty it was to conduct services, minister to the sick, and in general watch over the souls of the company's employees. The first dominie's name was Jonas Michaelius. The governors of the colony, including perhaps the most famous of them, Peter Stuyvesant, were communicant members of the church. Indeed, Peter Minuit, who bought the island of Manhattan from the Indians for the equivalent of twenty-four dollars, was one of the first deacons of the fledgling congregation. Persons of Dutch ancestry, bearing some of the most illustrious names in American history, had been on the rolls of the church. It got its name from having been built of marble quarried at Hastings-on-Hudson. It was the leading congregation in the Collegiate Reformed Dutch Church of the City of New York. Four separate buildings, each with a minister and congregation but under one governing body, gave meaning to "collegiate" or colleague ministers. More than 125 years ago, the Collegiate Church had joined with the denomination known as the Reformed Church in America.

Although Marble Collegiate Church was currently at a very low ebb, the committee members voiced their belief that, properly directed and with a strong, evangelically minded preacher, it could make a comeback and have an impact on our time. And anyone preaching from that pulpit, located as it was on Fifth Avenue, could have a national and even an international influence on the advancement of Christianity.

I liked these men and found myself in harmony with their positive spirit and thinking. They said that the sermons I had given in New York and the two they had heard that day in Syracuse had convinced them that my preaching was what they were looking for. They admitted that the congregation of Marble Collegiate Church was small and scattered, but if I felt called of the Lord, they were convinced that an outstanding ministry could be developed with that church as a center.

Thanking them for their expression of confidence and their implied suggestion that I might be called to their church in New York, I informed them that I had already accepted an invitation to preach for a month at the First Methodist Church of Los Angeles. And furthermore, I shared with them my understanding that an invitation might be forthcoming to become minister of that church. If they were sufficiently interested to hold their implied invitation open for a month, I would then be in a better position to consider the opportunity they were affording me.

They agreed to this suggestion and said they would like to come again to Syracuse, upon my return from Los Angeles, and at that time present me with an official call to become minister of Marble Collegiate Church. We parted with this thought in mind, and I went to Los Angeles.

For a month I preached regularly to very large congregations in the First Methodist Church at Eighth and Hope streets. The church had three thousand individual seats, which were filled to overflowing at every service. The spirit of the congregation was dedicated and enthusiastic. At the end of the month I was given an official invitation to succeed their minister, Dr. Elmer Ellsworth Helms, who very much wanted me to follow him, for he felt I might bring the same emphasis that his ministry had given to that church and to the city of Los Angeles for a good many years.

I responded to this invitation by informing them a call would probably be forthcoming from Marble Collegiate Church in New York, and that I would require a little time to arrive at a decision between these two opportunities, separated by some three thousand miles.

Returning to Syracuse, Ruth and I suffered, as do people who walk in the valley of indecision. In which of these two fields could we best serve our Lord? Comparing the two churches seemed altogether one-sided. Under the marvelous ministry of Dr. Helms, First Methodist in Los Angeles had become one of the largest and most vital churches in America. The congregation, then numbering upward of seven thousand, was the largest in the denomination and one of the largest of all Protestant congregations in the country. Financially it was extremely well off and able to carry out any program, no matter how ambitious.

Services, both on Sundays and weekdays, were crowded. It was, in short, one of the most inspiring churches that I had ever seen. To be its pastor would be an honor and an opportunity comparable to that of no other church.

On the other hand, Marble Collegiate was so low in every respect that a motion offered in the church's consistory, or official board, to close it out and dispose of the property had been defeated recently by only a few votes. The listed membership was approximately five hundred. But many of these were only old names on old records, and probably the total valid, active membership was not more than 250 persons. The current expense budget, beyond endowment income, was approximately fifteen thousand dollars per year, ten thousand dollars of which was given by one man, Mr. E. Francis Hyde, a wealthy stockbroker. Attendance was approximately 215 at the morning service and 225 at the evening service, a pitiful turnout in an auditorium with balconies on three sides. It was actually a pathetically small and ineffective church, and its future was in grave doubt.

Why did I even hesitate in making a decision between a great, ongoing church and a formerly prestigious but now seemingly dying one? If I went to Marble Collegiate and brought it up to where it ought to be in terms of membership, strength, and spirit, it would be in every sense a creative activity; whereas the leadership of the great and successful church in Los Angeles could and probably would be a holding operation. By experience and by nature I was, or at least I had been, a church troubleshooter. The problem again was whether I wanted to take a church that was down, indeed so far down that some wanted to abolish it, and with God's help bring it up to where God wanted it to be, or one that was up, in fact way up, and keep it at its present high level or, if possible, raise it even higher.

It required one month to arrive at a decision. I think I really wanted to go to Los Angeles. It was a church in my inherited denomination, Methodist, and the living would be pleasant. I was offered everything I could possibly want from the standpoint of opportunity to reach people in great numbers, as well as established position and financial security.

The New York church, though it was more than three hundred years old, retained only an inadequate vestige of its illustrious past. It was located on Fifth Avenue, but in a down-at-the-heels section of the famous street in a decaying part of the city. The West Coast church included in its membership some of the most distinguished leaders in business, politics, and society. The Marble Church had no such distinction, with only a handful of people remaining from the distinguished old families.

Day after day I struggled with the dilemma. Did I want a church that was already great; or one where, maybe, I could make something out of practically nothing? The situation, perhaps, was not quite as either/or as the above would seem to indicate, but the distinction was crystal clear. The Los Angeles church was successful and the one in New York was deteriorating.

Finally after a month of struggle, I came home for lunch one day and told Ruth that time was running out and we had to decide between the two calls. We put the matter completely in God's hands and prayed for His guidance. It was not something to be decided on the basis of possible earthly success, but only from the standpoint of where we could serve most effectively. Where could we best invest our lives for Christ, which, after all, was our basic commitment?

We prayed on our knees, for the most part, earnestly beseeching our Lord to indicate in a clear and unmistakable manner what His will was for us. We asked Him to take all material considerations, all thoughts of physical comfort and success from our minds and help us decide solely on the basis of what our Lord Jesus would have us do. This prayer session must have continued for at least three or four hours. We lost track of time. I do recall that at the end, the time was late afternoon.

The poet James Russell Lowell in "The Cathedral" says:

> I, that still pray at morning and at eve . . .
> Thrice in my life perhaps have truly prayed,
> Thrice, stirred below my conscious self, have felt
> That perfect disenthrallment which is God. . . .

We, too, attained that spiritual state as we let go of all desire for earthly preferment, comfort, and ease, and were completely willing to let God direct our lives. We would go where He wanted us to go. In all sincerity we wanted only His holy will to be done.

Suddenly, in a definitive flash of insight as clear as a light, His answer came. There was no doubt about it. I knew what the Lord God Almighty wanted us to do with our lives. Rising from my knees, I asked Ruth, "Have you received an answer?"

"Yes," she said with certainty, "I have."

"And what is the answer?" I asked.

"I won't tell you for it is your decision. I will go where you go, of course."

"The answer," I said, all doubt having been taken away, "is to go to New York."

I called Mr. William S. Denison, chairman of the board, in New York and told him we had reached a decision to accept the call to Marble Collegiate Church.

Now comes what I regard as a miracle of divine grace. In that moment I had a feeling of great peace, and with it the knowledge that I had decided right. And from that minute, never again did I have a vestige of doubt about the rightness of that decision. More than fifty years later, as I write these words, the same sure feeling that God had directed me and that I had acted right still prevails, all of which proves that God does for a fact guide prayerful and believing human beings. And if one is willing completely to subordinate his own desires and follow the will of God, the right answer to any problem assuredly will come.

Shortly thereafter, I went to New York City to appear before the Classis of New York of the Reformed Church in America to be transferred officially from the Methodist denomination. (The Classis of New York is the local ecclesiastical authority of the denomination and is composed of ministers and elders in the metropolitan area.) While, of course, I have never been bound by denominational ties, yet I did feel a twinge as I left the church of my fathers. However, this feeling was dissipated as I listened to the prayer that followed my signing of the ancient book in which ministers of the Reformed Church in America had signed their names for centuries. I knew then I was in a caring fellowship of Christian brothers in Christ.

Through the years, I have been honored to be part of an ancient denomination that has its roots in the Protestant Reformation and the church in Holland. The certificate of my ordination in the Methodist Church, signed with warm recommendation by Bishop Francis J. McConnell, presiding Bishop of New York, was read and unanimously accepted. Thus, I was officially received into the Reformed Church in America. After the meeting I climbed to the open upper deck of an old-style Fifth Avenue bus, looked back at Marble Church as we moved up the avenue, and knew it to be my spiritual home.

The service of installation as minister of the Marble Collegiate Church was held on Sunday evening, October 2, 1932, in the presence of a congregation that overflowed the main sanctuary. Presiding was the President of the Classis of New York of the Reformed Church in America, Rev. Dr. Oliver P. Barnhill. The charge to the people was given by the President of the General Synod of the Reformed Church in America, Rev. Dr. Edward Dawson. The sermon was preached by one of the most famous preachers of the era, Dr. Charles E. Jefferson, honorary minister of the Broadway Tabernacle.

The charge to the minister was given by my father, Rev. Dr. Charles Clifford Peale. He was then pastor of the First Methodist Church of Columbus, Ohio. I can see him yet standing in the pulpit, looking down at me sitting in the front pew on the main aisle, for technically I was still a candidate.

In his straightforward, loving manner he said, "Norman, I've known you from the minute you were born. You came into this world yelling and you have been yelling ever since." Then with a tear in his eye and a bit of a choke in his voice, he added, "In all your life you have never disappointed me; and you will not disappoint me now."

When the congregation had entirely dispersed, I found my mother outside the front entrance on Fifth Avenue, alone. She was weeping.

Startled, I asked, "What is the matter, Mother?"

"I have just put my hand on one of the huge marble blocks of which this church is constructed," she said. "And it seems so strong." She choked up again and put her hand on my shoulder. "Always keep it strong."

CHAPTER TEN

Facing a Hard Job

I WAS IN MY OFFICE early next morning. The "tumult and shouting" of the night before had gone by, and I had let myself in for a tough job. The church was a shell, the organization composed of a very few people, though they were dedicated and efficient. My staff consisted of two people, Rev. Albert A. Leininger and Miss Mercé E. Boyer. That Monday morning we had a meeting and they reported what I had already been told, that there were about five hundred people on the church rolls and seldom more than two hundred attending morning service, and a few more came on Sunday night. A Wednesday evening prayer meeting was attended by fifty or sixty, and there were several other small organizations in the church.

The physical facilities of the church building were extremely limited. Behind the sanctuary was a large room called "the parlor," though actually it served as a passageway between the Twenty-ninth Street door and the offices. There were no meeting rooms for groups except for a large room above the parlor called "the lecture room," where the prayer meetings were held. For dinners, perhaps seventy persons could be accommodated in the parlor and served inconveniently from a minuscule kitchen.

Essentially the church building had been unchanged and unimproved since it was built in 1854. Indeed, beneath the sanctuary, which is of rare and striking beauty, was a dirt-floored basement, with about a five-foot headroom, in which were several furnaces with a brick walk connecting them. For carrying out an adequate program of a modern church the facilities and equipment were inadequate, to say the least. Indeed, the church was considered rather generally as a "preaching center," and little emphasis was placed upon building a membership with all the rounded programming that was usually expected.

But the board of elders and deacons and the staff were all eager to start an innovative program of activities. Their enthusiastic support of my ministry was sincere and loyal from the start. And when one has such a team of dedicated people, believing together, working together, and praying together, great achievements are bound to follow; and they did over the years.

From the pulpit on Sundays I looked at the empty balconies and the wide, empty areas on the main floor, and had to make another decision. How could those balconies and empty spaces be filled? A sensational type of preaching might do it and quickly; and in those days of the 1930s there were such preachers. In fact, I actually saw, with my own eyes, a sermon topic advertised on a Brooklyn church: "IF I WERE THE DEVIL WHAT IN HELL WOULD I DO?" But as a firm believer in the Holy Bible, I claimed the scriptural promise "If I be lifted up . . . [I] will draw all men unto me." (John 12:32) My purpose must be not to fill seats but to fill souls with the Gospel of the Lord Jesus Christ. This became my policy, and I preached to human need, always dealing with the definite problems of men and women in readily understandable thought and language forms. And I kept at it Sunday after Sunday.

Following our first year of dealing with the dismal condition of the Marble Collegiate Church, in the summer of 1933 Ruth and I took our vacation in England. We settled down in the town of Keswick in the Lake District, a region of hills and lakes renowned for charm and beauty and filled with historic places connected with the great figures of English literature.

But I was restless and depressed regarding the church back in New York. It seemed a hopeless situation; and why had I ever taken on such a job anyway? In a gloomy manner I poured my woes into the ears of my happy and positive young wife. The Station Hotel in which we were staying was surrounded by a beautiful formal English garden. Charming old hedges and venerable trees and glorious beds of flowers made it a place of serenity. We strolled its graveled walks and sat on its benches, particularly on one at the far end of the garden.

It was while we sat on this bench that one of the determinative experiences of my life occurred, one that dramatically changed me and my total existence. It was vital to everything that happened afterward in my personal history. As I sat there giving vent to all my discouragement and negative thoughts, Ruth proceeded to do a masterful job of therapy upon me. Normally Ruth is a kindly and good-tempered lady, but then she became firm and authoritative, psychologically and spiritually.

"You," she said, "are not only my husband. You are also my pastor, and in the latter department I'm frank to say I am becoming increasingly disappointed in you. I hear you from the pulpit talking about faith and trust in God's wondrous power. But now I hear in you no faith or trust at all. You just whine your defeat. And to put it bluntly, what you need is a deep spiritual experience. You need to be converted."

"I have been converted," I expostulated.

"Well, it didn't take," she snapped, "so you had better get really converted."

We sat in deep silence, broken finally by her statement that she was not going to leave that bench, nor was I, until I had found the Lord in such depth that I became a remade person. "How do I do that?" I asked meekly.

"You, a pastor, asking how you do it," she commented. "Tell the Lord you are totally lost, without strength, that you have no power within yourself, and that you are humbly throwing yourself on His divine mercy and that you are asking Him to change you now."

She took my hand in a strong grip. "Ask Him now aloud, and I am praying for you, too." So in a stumbling sort of way, I confessed all my weaknesses, entreating the Lord to come to me, defeated as I was. I kept repeating this, surrendering, self-giving, and I prayed with all intensity. And the prayer was answered instantly. I began to feel warm all over from the crown of my head to my feet. Joy such as I had never known welled up within me, intermingled with tears. I laughed and cried. Leaping to my feet, I paced up and down excitedly.

"It's wonderful!" I cried, "wonderful, glorious. He has answered me. He is in my heart, my mind. Nothing can defeat me now, not that church or anything. I want to get back to work. We are going to have a wonderful time from here on in." So I talked after my newfound tremendous experience of God. "Tell you what," I said. "Let's get going back to New York right now to tackle that job with power. We don't need any more vacation."

Ruth said with mock despair, "Oh my, I've gone too far with this." But she, as excited as I, went to pack at once, and a thrilled young couple were soon on their way back to dismal old Fifth Avenue and Twenty-Ninth Street. But it was no longer dismal, for we saw the problem in a different spirit and through new eyes. Sure, there were lots of difficulties, but never again was I really down, and that old deteriorating church became filled with new life and faith and joy and power and people. And from the bottom it started a strong upward movement toward the top, where it has been ever since. In such manner does the good Lord work when given the chance to take over in life, especially when the subject has such a strong, believing, wise, and loving wife.

Years later I was a guest on Ralph Edwards's famous TV show *This Is Your Life*. You may recall that the guest, unknown to him or her, was always brought onto the show in Hollywood by subterfuge; therefore, I was totally unprepared for questions. But before a big studio audience and millions of viewers, when Ralph asked me to state the greatest thing that had ever happened to me, there was no question as to my answer. Instantly I told of my experience of the astonishing grace of God on a bench in a garden in England.

I conceived the idea that if people were not coming to church, I would go to the people. So I accepted every invitation to speak that came along: at service clubs, community gatherings, commencement exercises, sales gatherings, fund-raising events. I didn't preach a sermon but always emphasized the fact that each person could become greater than he was, through the Higher Power. And very gradually the church began to fill with eager people and has stayed full, with overflow congregations for more than forty years. But it took a long time to accomplish this, and the lesson is, never give up no matter how tough the job may be.

That current expense budget was one of the first things I tackled, especially since Mr. Hyde (who gave ten thousand dollars out of the total fifteen thousand dollars) suddenly passed away. I told the congregation that we wanted to replace that loss, not with one annual gift by one person but with an aggregate of many small gifts by many people. To my deep appreciation, when we counted up the new pledges we had more than twice the previous total. We promised a powerful by-product of spiritual growth to those who learned the biblical admonition of tithing. That kind of giving has increased steadily over the years until millions have been raised in Marble Church for the Lord's work.

My ministry in New York was and is based on three factors: (1) I took charge of a down church, indeed a way-down church, and believed there was only one way for it to go and that was up. It could hardly go any farther down and survive at all. (2) I preached the Gospel of salvation and life changing through faith in Christ, with emphasis on Christianity as a practical way of life. (3) My presentation was invariably in simple, uncomplicated thought and language forms and in the vernacular of the people I grew up with in Ohio.

Sometimes I have been asked whether I have not had some of the troubles ministers have with people. I would not have you believe that it has all been sweetness and light. I encountered a bit of trouble and even opposition from two men, both of whom happened to be elders of the church and, therefore, occupied rather authoritative positions. Why one of the two men came to feel as he did is a matter of mystery even now as I write of it years later. In my early days at the church he was quite friendly and supportive. Ruth and I were often in his home for dinner, and he and his wife were gracious hosts. I was young and I think he had a paternalistic attitude toward me, which took the form of an attempt, probably unconscious, to control my actions, even to dictate my preaching style. While I realized my imperfections in preaching, I doubt he had ever spoken in public. His credentials for reconstructing my presentations seemed questionable. His attitude, though I tried to deal with it respectfully, caused some friction.

Moreover, he desired positions of preferment in the consistory, the governing body of the church. I tried to secure these for him, but could not persuade others, and perhaps he blamed me for his failure to receive what he considered due him. Finally and unhappily, there resulted a cleavage, one of the only two which developed in my more than fifty years of ministry at the church.

The other personality problem was with the senior elder, the presiding officer of the church board, a businessman named William S. Denison. He considered that his position in the church, in effect, made him the chief executive officer and my "boss." "I don't want you running off here and there to give speeches," he said, "at least not without clearing your absence with me." Again he would say, "We hired you to be on the job here every day from eight A.M. to five P.M., and the usual evening activities as well." When mildly I reminded him that a minister of the gospel was not "hired" but "called," he persisted in the attitude that I was his employee and that was that.

I recall once when Denison was my guest for luncheon at the Union League Club, he encountered a friend and introduced me as "our new man at the church." And another time when I introduced him to some distinguished New York clergymen, also at the club, he stated, "I'm Dr. Peale's boss." All this arrogation of authority and somewhat crude throwing of his weight around did not bother me unduly. I took him as he was, a rather insensitive man who had no authority elsewhere and, having attained it in the church, did not know how to handle it as a gracious Christian. One time at the conclusion of the weekly prayer service, he took out his watch and said sternly and disapprovingly, "You went two minutes overtime."

Though I must confess that Bill Denison rather irritated me at times, I let him know, as politely as possible, that I was the minister in charge and that, while I wanted to work with him in friendly comradeship, I was actually nobody's man but God's. Despite his crudities, as I saw them, I used to play golf with him. I really liked him personally and revere his memory. One night as Bill rode uptown in the subway, the Lord took him home to heaven. He was a good, upright man and deserved heaven, I thought. But I must admit that my path was smoother after both these men, dedicated and honorable as they were, departed—one to another church, the other to his reward. Invariably strong-minded and intelligent men have served on the church board, but no one, including the minister, has ever again tried to dominate, but all have worked together in cooperation without thought of control or position.

Late in the afternoon of Sunday, December 7, 1941, the radio brought the shocking news that the Japanese Empire had launched a devastating air attack upon Pearl Harbor. Naturally feelings ran high in the wake of this incredible action, and everyone was filled with resentment and hostility. I was scheduled to conduct the regular Sunday evening church service at eight o'clock that evening. The church was packed to capacity, people standing. The atmosphere was acutely tense. I opened with a short prayer for the President in that hour of crisis, for our beloved country and that humanity would be guided to rational response in this time of emotionalized reaction to events.

Then looking out at that great assembly and knowing its feelings, for they were mine also, I called for the singing of "The Star-Spangled Banner." I have heard our national anthem sung by throngs of Americans at great moments of history, but never have I experienced the depth of feeling as at this moment. It was moving and totally unforgettable as voices surged in a vast volume of sound against the very rafters of the historic old church: "O say, can you see, by the dawn's early light?"

Having been able to express their love of country, the congregation sat, but the feeling remained. I stood silently looking at the people. They were looking toward the pulpit, their pulpit, the ancient one from which the Gospel had been preached even before the founding of the Republic. It came to me to repeat the words of James A. Garfield, who had uttered them from a balcony of the old Willard Hotel in Washington to the multitudes crowded in the streets the night Abraham Lincoln was shot: "God reigns, and the Government at Washington still lives!" As that statement had quieted the throngs in the stricken capital on that dreadful night in Civil War times, so it brought quietness to the huge crowd in Marble Collegiate Church on the similarly dreadful night of Pearl Harbor.

The next night, Monday, a dinner for the men of the church was scheduled at which the speaker was to be the Reverend Sojiro Shimizu, pastor of the Japanese Reformed Church in New York City. Reverend Shimizu was a scholarly, quiet, and compassionate Christian gentleman. He telephoned me early Monday morning to say that he was sure that under the circumstances it would be embarrassing to me for him to fulfill his engagement to speak in our church, and he wanted us to know that he would not appear.

I replied that the political differences between Japan and the United States had no bearing upon our relations as Christians, that we were brothers in Christ, and that I loved him. By all means he should come and speak as planned. When he was introduced to speak, the audience rose and applauded him. He stood with tears running down his cheeks. It was to me, and I believe to all present, a demonstration of Christian brotherhood in action.

Another event that had also been scheduled was the ordination of a Japanese man to the Christian ministry. He was Toru Matsumoto, a brilliant person and a totally committed Christian. Some of those involved in the ordination ceremony timorously suggested postponing it until "a more propitious time." But others insisted that the affairs of the Kingdom of God should go on without interruption by war or any other secular event. Accordingly the ordination service was held in Marble Collegiate Church as had been planned, while platoons of police encircled the church. I was very proud that we insisted upon ordaining to Christ's holy ministry a Japanese national at the very time we loyal Americans and also loyal Christians were in a state of war with his country. Later after the war, Reverend Matsumoto returned to Japan where for a number of years until his death he became a popular radio speaker and a strong influence for Christianity among his people.

Suddenly during January and February 1942, the dress of the congregation changed dramatically. Looking out from the pulpit on a Sunday, I saw hundreds in uniform and the wearers came from everywhere. Again the nation was at war, and the country's youth was being mustered into military service. New York being the port of embarkation for great numbers of young Americans headed for the front in Europe, thousands passed through the city. Many of these men and women, away from home perhaps for the first time and lonely, crowded into the church. They knew that while it was not the old familiar church back home in the villages, towns, and cities of America, still the friendly welcome that they sought was found in full measure at Marble Collegiate.

Members of the church provided social affairs during the week and an old-fashioned church dinner on Sundays. People invited them to their homes and, indeed, showered these young men and women with affection. To this day, as I travel throughout the country on speaking engagements, men now turning gray will grasp my hand and ask feelingly, "How's everything at dear old Marble Church? I'll never forget what it meant to me when in wartime I came there lonely and maybe a bit scared of what lay ahead."

So it went month after month until that unforgettable summer day on August 9, 1945 at Pawling, New York, when the bell in the steeple of the beautiful white Christ Church on Quaker Hill rang out jubilantly in the still afternoon air. President Harry S. Truman had just announced that the war was over. General Douglas MacArthur had received the Japanese surrender on the deck of the battleship USS *Missouri* in Yokohama Harbor.

Summoned by the church bell (similar bells were ringing out the glad tidings all over America), people, dressed for a summer's day in the country, came in crowds from every direction until the Quaker Hill Church was packed to capacity. "We must have some speeches to express the deep feelings of our people at this great historic moment," said Rev. Dr. Ralph Conover Lankler, the beloved minister of the church. Thomas E. Dewey, Governor of the State of New York, was in his pew with his family, and near him sat Lowell and Frances Thomas.

"Ask them. They are our leaders," I said.

But Ralph came back from speaking to them. "They want you to speak," he reported. "They say this is a moment in which God should be thanked." We finally compromised, with the governor and Lowell saying a few words. Then I followed with a short talk stressing the old American concept of freedom under God for which once again hundreds of our finest youth had given their lives to preserve. This service, spontaneously offered to the God of our fathers, will forever remain in the hallowed memory of all who heeded the message of the bells that day at the end of the Second World War.

CHAPTER ELEVEN

The Going Gets Tough

RADIO, WRITING BOOKS, the speaker's platform were among the creative methods I used to bring life to an almost moribund New York City church in the 1930s. Shortly after I had come to New York from Syracuse in 1932, my old friend Frank C. Goodman, who had been so good to me when I was at the Kings Highway Church in Brooklyn, took me to lunch one day at the Prince George Hotel on Twenty-eighth Street.

Frank had kept an eye on my ministry in Syracuse, and said, "I still have a high regard for your potential," to quote exactly his complimentary statement. He was pleased that I had returned to the metropolitan area and continued, "You sure have a tough one in that old church at Twenty-ninth Street. But if you love people in these hard Depression times, if you tell all who will listen that the Lord loves them and will help them if they put their trust in Him, I believe you will get results—in time." Those last words, "in time," proved to be true and I had to learn patience.

Frank had become the executive secretary for radio of what was then called the Federal Council of Churches, later to become the National Council of the Churches of Christ in America, and asked if I would like to do a national network program for three months in the summer. I would be taking over in June, July, and August; the time period would be fifteen minutes on Saturdays at 6:15.

P.M.; and I would be substituting for Dr. Walter Van Kirk's immensely popular program, *Religion in the News*. In those days radio programs were not prerecorded, and if I accepted this opportunity, it would require making long trips from Southampton, Long Island, or Canisteo, New York, where we spent our summer vacations. However, even though summer radio programs were considered to have a much reduced listening audience, still I felt this was another opportunity to reach people with the Christian message. And it might possibly result in adding a few new members to Marble Collegiate Church. After many years of broadcasting, I do not believe that either radio or television brings very many people to local church membership. But that such exposure of the Gospel message affects the thinking and lives of countless persons I have no doubt at all.

Frank Goodman suggested that my program be called *The Art of Living*. It went on the air in the summer of 1933 and continued for some forty years. The message contained many of the ideas and principles which years later gave substance to my book *The Power of Positive Thinking*. I owe a debt of gratitude to Frank Goodman for helping me develop the type of thinking that came to be my basic message.

The Art of Living was a fifteen-minute program, given in the studio and geared not to a large audience, but to one or two people as though we were quietly talking together. The message was about things in life that really matter to all of us. It was broadcast from the old New York station WEAF of the Blue Network, which later merged with WJZ of the Red Network to form NBC, the National Broadcasting Company.

Then in 1962 we started a half-hour program on radio station WOR, a powerful local station that reaches 150 miles or more around New York. This, however, is a broadcast of my Sunday morning sermon at the church, and, since it is a public address to a large crowd and has a declamatory format, it becomes perhaps less intimate and personal. Any humorous episodes, however, produce an audience reaction that conveys the spirit and atmosphere of the church to the distant listening radio audience. But I never received the volume of audience mail from this type of religious broadcasting that came from the quieter, more personal studio approach.

Lowell Thomas, who undisputedly was the oldest voice in radio, often said, "Norman, when I die it will leave you as the oldest, or at least one of the longest-time, living 'voices on the air.'" At this writing I have been on radio continuously for more than fifty years.

I remember many dramatic stories of men and women who experienced extraordinary changes in their lives simply by hearing the message of Jesus Christ on radio. There was the woman deep in the dark shadows of despair and desperation who had, at last, come to the point of suicide. It was an August evening on the Jersey shore in a miserable little room in a rundown rooming house. She was down to her last dollar and to her last hope. No one cared. She was alone, forsaken, rejected.

She had a loaded gun, and it had been reserved for the final hopeless minute. She sat staring out into a violent storm, one of those late summer hurricanes that sometimes roar up the Jersey coast. Now was the time for the end. She would go out of life in a tumult in which no human ears would hear the fatal shot.

Unhearing, uncaring, she had left the radio on. Just as she mustered courage to lift the gun to her temple, a voice with love in it said, "There is no hopeless situation, only hopeless people. There is a way out of any circumstance no matter how dark it may seem. Write me and I will help you. God loves you. He will help you. *There is hope.*"

Perhaps this sounds a little too dramatic as I write these words, but the radio talk stopped her self-destruction, took the gun out of her hand. She did write. We did help her reorganize her life. She always said it was God Himself who saved her. And I'm sure that it was, for He loves His poor unhappy children.

There was another story, and this time the scene was North Carolina. Jack had spent the night drinking and gambling, and on this early Sunday morning he drove along a highway completely disgusted, discouraged, defeated. Then our radio talk began. He reached for the button to turn it off. But just then the voice said something that reached his consciousness. Hesitantly he withdrew his hand and listened. It was a positive kind of message that insisted that life can be a victorious, even happy experience, that

God has the answer to all of our problems, even the problem of ourselves. Jack drew to the side of the road, stopped his car. He thought and then he prayed. He made some decisions that were to change his life.

Some months later I had a speaking engagement in Greensboro, North Carolina, and a man came to see me at the motel where I was staying. It was Jack and he told me the story I have just related. Eighteen years later, I was seated in the dressing room of a big city auditorium in Kansas City, waiting to speak to an audience of some fifteen thousand people attending a positive thinking motivational rally. A rap came at the door and a fine-looking man, well dressed and a face written all over with joy, stood in the doorway. "I would like to speak with you for a moment," he said. "I am the minister who is to open today's meeting with prayer. May I take this opportunity to thank you for what you did for me years ago."

"I'm sorry," I replied, "but I do not think I have ever had the pleasure of meeting you."

"Oh, but you have," and he related the story above.

I interrupted him. "Was it in Greensboro?" I asked. He nodded. "You are Jack. And God Himself shines through you!" I cried out in astonishment.

A few moments later, he lifted fifteen thousand people up to God in a deeply moving prayer. Today Jack is the minister of an influential church in a big American city, beloved by multitudes whom he helps find life at its best. Radio reached out over the miles and found this unusual man.

One of my most interesting and perhaps creative experiences in radio has been the program called *The American Character*. It was conceived by John Scott, famous newscaster of station WOR in New York, and Howard Greene, a prominent advertising executive. Funded by International Telephone and Telegraph, it is a ninety-second program aired currently five days a week on over four hundred stations throughout the nation. The program consists of true stories of people everywhere who perform deeds of heroism and human service. Its intent is to counter the flood of bad news by reporting each day the good news of good people doing good deeds. A typical story written by Bill Buckley of the *American Character* staff is one that I recently recorded.

"Brakes gone, racing down mountain road at ninety miles an hour." This was the message sent out over his CB radio by driver Ron Kob as he fought desperately to keep his two-and-one-half-ton truck loaded with propane from careening off the road and down the mountainside near San Bernardino, California.

Highway Patrolman Chuck Downing picked up the message. The runaway truck with its explosive cargo was coming down off the mountain into a congested business area at breakneck speed. A major disaster was in the making. Sgt. Downing wheeled his police cruiser onto the road ahead of the truck, maintaining the same speed as they roared down the steep incline.

Ron Kob, realizing Downing's plan, maneuvered his truck carefully until both truck and cruiser were in direct line. A few bumps then the front of the truck settled against the rear of the cruiser. Downing applied his brakes gingerly, knowing one false move could mean disaster. Both vehicles slowed gradually and finally came to a complete halt a few feet short of the busy intersection.

Quick thinking and daring and courage of a cool, collected Sgt. Chuck Downing averted a major catastrophe on a California highway—death cheated by the strength of the American Character.

Our Foundation for Christian Living releases a national radio series called *Positive Thinking with Norman Vincent Peale*, which is aired on some of the largest radio stations in the country, being on seven 50,000-watt, twenty-four-hour stations in time periods never before allotted to religious broadcasting. Through such outlets we are reaching young people, non-churchgoers, businessmen, and a vast audience to which we seek to give spiritual answers to the problems of everyday living. This program has received a positive reaction from a sizable listening audience.

Through radio talks I came to know many remarkable people, not the least being a man with an exciting career. His name was Paul Soupiset and he operated a store in Houston, Texas. But, according to what he told me later, his was a negative, defeated life-style.

"But one day, on my knees I was reborn after listening to you on radio. And life became altogether new and exciting," he wrote.

Later he was transferred to a store in San Antonio. By this time he was so inspired he wanted to help everyone. He discovered a long-disused little church in La Villita, a section in the heart of San Antonio. Upon request he was permitted to use it for the purpose of giving a new-life message to anyone who would listen. And did they listen? The little church came to be thronged with people—black, white, Mexican, Catholic, Protestant, and those of no faith. Rich and poor alike, warmed by the compassionate heart of Paul Soupiset, attended his meetings, looking for a better life and many finding it.

Then Paul wrote asking me to come and dedicate some carillons to be installed in the steeple. He wanted to dedicate these bells to me, he explained. Well, never before had I had any bells dedicated to me, and I was so impressed by him and by all the good he was doing that I accepted his invitation.

At the service of dedication the church was crowded, people standing around against the walls and out into the street. The man who made the dedication statement, an ex-alcoholic and obviously not accustomed to public speaking, arose and solemnly said, "Friends and fellow citizens, we hereby dedicate these bells to the glory of God and in memory of Norman Vincent Peale."

The crowd roared with laughter, and I had to remind the embarrassed gentleman that I wasn't dead yet.

After my talk, Paul invited anyone who wanted an exciting new life to step forward. There was an old Mexican man, a little black boy, and an aristocratic-looking, well-dressed white-haired woman among the many who came forward indicating that they wanted to find the Lord. I must confess that I watched through misty eyes as Paul put his hand on the head of each one as he gave a blessing.

A few years later I returned to San Antonio to participate in a huge public meeting in an open square to honor, for all his good deeds, Paul Soupiset, a formerly confused, defeated man.

I have never had any desire to use television as a medium for preaching. I do not like to see myself on the screen, much preferring the relative anonymity provided by radio, in which only the voice is used in the communication process. Never having been sufficiently interested to explore whatever psychological reason might explain this attitude, I do think that perhaps it might be traced back to the inferiority complex of my youth.

But the primary reason I have never sought to preach on television is the enormous cost involved. I have always reacted against appeals on television for financial support for a religious program. That these appeals turn off thousands of viewers I have no doubt, judging from many people who have told me that such is their reaction. This I have felt so keenly that on one occasion I committed our magazine, *Guideposts,* to finance the making of twenty-six thirty-minute TV programs in which there were no references whatsoever to money. At the time—about 1973, when costs were much lower than in later years—*Guideposts* laid out approximately one million dollars, which it could ill afford. But we did have the satisfaction of providing what we hoped was a valid religious program to the viewing public without making any requests for financial support.

I realize the problems faced by ministers who do communicate the Gospel via television, and these comments are in no sense critical of their work, for they are my personal friends and I admire the dedication and talent which they give to this form of communication. I am only saying that personally I preferred other ways in which to fulfill the charge of preaching the Gospel to every living creature. My choice of tools with which to reach everyone on behalf of Jesus Christ is radio, the platform, and the printed word; primarily the latter.

A woman from a southern city once wrote me that she and her family had faced one of those crises that come to most of us at some time. She paced the floor in her anxiety, and prayed fervently for guidance. She tried to buttress her faltering courage. The family had only recently moved into a house that was a scale down from their previous unpretentious home. In her restlessness she decided to go to the basement to sort out some boxes which had not been touched since moving. In going through papers, old magazines, and books, as she was about to toss out a ragged, soiled book without a cover she was attracted by one sentence that seemed to leap out at her.

She took the book upstairs and continued to read eagerly for it seemed directly to meet her need. The only identification was the by-line at the top of a page, and it was months later that she learned the name of the author. It was *The Power of Positive Thinking*, written thirty years before but still reaching into people's lives.

Sermons, speeches, radio talks are so often, shall we say, gone with the winds of time. A man I encountered a while ago on an airplane provides a case in point.

"I heard you preach a powerful sermon once about thirty years ago," he said.

"Do you recall anything about it?" I asked hopefully.

"Not really," he replied in some confusion, "but it was at the Methodist conference where you were the bishop."

"Well, thanks anyway. It must have been a great sermon." Obviously he was not remembering me, as I am not a bishop or a Methodist!

On the other hand, I have encountered people with prodigious memories, like the woman who said, "I heard you give an illustration five years ago in a sermon," and actually named the title of the sermon. However, I still believe that the printed word, especially in the form of a book, may be the most far-reaching and longest-lasting medium for the propagation of the Gospel message.

The most difficult period of my life, one that lasted several years midway in my ministry in New York, was occasioned by the publication of *The Power of Positive Thinking*. It was my second book with Prentice-Hall, Inc., according to my contract.

In writing it, a rather curious incident seemed somewhat indicative of the effect the volume was to have on large numbers of people. Ruth, the children, and I went to Pasadena together with my secretary, Alice Murphy. We had a cottage on the grounds of the Huntington Hotel, where our longtime friend Steve Royce was owner and general manager.

I began work on the book by dictating the first chapter to Alice. We were in the living room of the cottage. I noticed a maid dusting the windows and furniture. The thought crossed my mind that she was taking an undue amount of time at her job. But she stayed close by during the dictation of the chapter.

Later my secretary informed me that after I had finished and left the room, the maid asked, "What was that man doing?" Informed that I was writing a book, she said, "Well, Miss, he was talking to me. I need what he was saying. Would you please send me a copy of that book when it is finished? I know it will help me a lot." Naturally I was encouraged, for that was my purpose in writing it.

When I showed the completed first draft of the manuscript to an editor assigned to me by the publisher, he declared that it wouldn't sell ten thousand copies and suggested that I cut up the manuscript and salvage some by putting it together under the title *How to Live Successfully Seven Days a Week*. Dutifully I tried to follow his suggestion, having respect for his insight and publishing knowledge. But it just would not jell, so I put it in a drawer and left it there for a year.

Then I went back to the manuscript, working on the original idea of faith and right thinking. A year later it was completed, but it still did not seem to be what I wanted. Ruefully I decided to chuck it a second and final time. And I did just that, literally, and deposited it in the wastebasket over Ruth's objections and made her promise she would not remove it from the wastebasket. She agreed, but in her own way. A wife may indeed disobey her husband and vice versa. They are rightfully independent of each other. She carried the manuscript to Myron L. Boardman, president of the trade division of Prentice-Hall. The next thing I knew, the publisher had accepted it.

The title of the manuscript was originally *The Power of Faith.* Myron Boardman came to my office one day and said he wanted to talk about a title. I told him that having tried maybe a hundred titles, the one finally settled on clearly indicated what the book had to say. In his own quiet and persuasive way, Myron said that my title was a good one, especially for committed churchgoing people. But he wondered whether it would limit the book's market, and wouldn't I like to move farther afield and help people who were not necessarily connected with churches?

"Of course, that is what I want the book to do, but I also want to be totally true to my message as a Christian minister."

"Well then," he countered, "what if we can come up with a title that has a wider appeal but is equivalent in meaning to *The Power of Faith?*"

His thought was reasonable. Then he surprised me by saying that in the manuscript there was a recurrent phrase and was I aware of it? He thought the phrase was so attractive, so deep in meaning that it might very well become a title that would live on for years and make its way into the thinking, even the language of our country.

"What is this phrase?" Ruth and I wanted to know. With a smile and confidently, as I remember the incident now, he took a large sheet of paper and wrote the words "The Power of Positive Thinking."

"Don't you agree that this phrase says what your title says but more attractively, indeed more compellingly?"

I was not sure, but Ruth was. "That's it," she declared excitedly. "It's a masterpiece of a title." And so it was that a title was born that has appeared on some fifteen million books that have gone around the world and even now, more than thirty years later, still come off the press.

But when the first edition of the book was ready for publication and the jacket had been imprinted with this title, I received a telephone call from my friend Fulton Oursler, senior editor of the *Reader's Digest*. He asked me, "Is it true that you are going to entitle your book *The Power of Positive Thinking?*"

"Yes, Fulton, that is it," I replied.

"Norman," he said, "I beg you, I implore you to take the word 'power' out of the title. In my experience the word 'power' just won't go."

I told him that the printing had already been done and that we had to go with it.

"Well," he said, "perhaps it is God's will and I pray that He will bless the book. It is one of the most helpful manuscripts I have seen in a long time."

The Power of Positive Thinking was published on October 13, 1952, and it was selling reasonably well when I found myself being honored by *This Is Your Life*. The book was mentioned by Ralph Edwards so enthusiastically on this national TV show that sales immediately skyrocketed, and overnight *The Power of Positive Thinking* had wide exposure.

Soon another extremely popular television show gave the book added publicity. This was Edward R. Murrow's famous TV program called *Person to Person* in which he went into the home of a subject for an interview with him or her and members of the family. Ed Murrow was a friend and neighbor on Quaker Hill at Pawling, and I admired him as one of the outstanding newsmen of the era.

These two exposures, plus the timeliness of the book, caused it to hit the best-seller lists and to zoom to the top position, which it held steadily for a lengthy period. The book was on the best-seller list of *The New York Times* constantly for a period of 186 weeks, which was then a record.

When the book attained this amazing popularity, the trouble began. A few highly vocal ministers condemned it as a "success, get ahead, become vice-president of the company" sort of book. They declared it was not in any sense a Christian book, that it was oversimplistic, that it was, in short, no good at all.

Then the attacks by this minuscule group of sophisticated left-wing clergymen became personal in the extreme and in some cases highly vindictive. I was castigated as an archconservative, a tool of capitalistic interests, who was turning Christianity into a way to get rich. Indeed, one wailed about what I was doing to "our" religion. Their reaction to the book was not merely an objective analysis of a work with which they did not agree. It mounted into a vituperative, uncontrolled hate vendetta, which was most astonishing. They even preached against some terrible thing which they labeled "Pealism." In time I discovered that some of these critics had not even read the book but were simply repeating phrases and ideas from critic to critic.

One minister, who surprised me by his violent attacks, was the then Methodist Bishop of New York. A scholarly and gifted man, usually dispassionate and objective, he became quite intemperate in his attacks on the book and upon me. He wrote a scathing article in *Redbook* magazine that was short on accuracy and long on violent diatribes. But I have always noted that to every disadvantage there is a corresponding advantage. And that principle proved true in this instance, for so curious did the publisher of *Redbook* become at this violent hate campaign by what he called religious intellectuals that he felt there might be another side to the story. So he sent one of his best interviewers and writers, Arthur Gordon, to see what sort of an awful person I might be.

Arthur Gordon came to our home for the interview, and subsequently became one of the dearest friends of a lifetime.

The more Arthur Gordon investigated, the more astonished he became. He had read the book carefully and, as a dedicated and intelligent Christian, he found it impossible to verify any reason for the violent attacks. One possible explanation might be that the book was written in simple language by an everyday man for the everyday person. It could be that "Norman has hit a sensitive jealousy nerve," he speculated.

He wrote a quiet, objective article on "The Rage of the Intellectuals," which was well received by the vast majority of readers. Arthur did much to put into perspective this attack on me by a small but violently hostile group of ministers. And I must add that his sturdy friendship became and still is a blessing to me. Arthur later wrote a biography, a generous treatment of my life, which is entitled *Norman Vincent Peale: Minister to Millions.* Still later, Arthur accepted my invitation to become editor of *Guideposts.* Under his skilled leadership, the magazine grew spectacularly. He is also the author of *A Touch of Wonder,* one of the most moving and truly inspiring books I have ever read. A recent sequel to it is *Through Many Windows.*

How did Ruth and I react to this clamor and to the violence of the attack, not only against the book, but also against me personally? In Ruth's case, it was simply to act like the in-depth Christian she is. She sat on boards and committees of the National Council of Churches, where the Methodist bishop also served. Her method was simply to pray that she would remain quiet, calm, and unemotional; indeed, that she would be sincerely friendly. After the *Redbook* article attack she knew she must pray that when she next met the bishop, her attitude would be one of love and not of hate.

Ruth well knew that others were watching her reactions, and of course she understood that some of them shared the bishop's antagonism. Through it all, though deeply wounded, she conducted herself with dignity, forbearance, and love like the great Christian soul she has always been. I was immensely proud of her, and of course she was a tower of strength for me.

I must admit that Ruth has greater control as a Christian than I. But I, too, have always believed that the Christian way to confront hatred is with love, to turn the other cheek, certainly not to fight back or even answer in kind. I sat down and reread *The Power of Positive Thinking,* word for word. I found nothing in it but plain, traditional fundamental Christianity, the kind taught me from childhood. True, it was written in a simple, direct, perhaps newspaper style. In this I had also been trained. It was written for the purpose of showing how our Savior Jesus Christ could help people live better lives. It told how Christ had helped me and how He would help any needy person.

The best thing to do about criticism is to control anger, study yourself, and ask, "Is it valid?" If you decide that it is, then correct yourself. If it isn't valid, then the best possible procedure is to rise above the criticism and not stoop to recrimination.

It so happened that I had a job of reviewing books, and a new book by the same hostile bishop came to my desk. It was a very fine piece; accordingly I wrote a favorable review. A long time afterward, he expressed amazement that I would write a complimentary review of his book considering his attitude toward me.

In reply I told him that my review of his book bore no relationship to him as a person. This seemed to appeal to his native fairness and goodwill. Ultimately he developed a kindlier feeling for me. In my opinion, the bishop was one of the strongest Christian leaders of our time, and he had of course the right to disagree and to voice such disagreement. I was only surprised at the heat and violence of his criticism, which did not seem to be like him.

There were others, perhaps even more hostile in their personal attacks, but there is no point in calling the roll of people who seemed to act the part of personal enemies. I prefer to share a very kind remark which my colleague, Dr. Arthur Caliandro, reported to an audience gathered to mark the beginning of the fiftieth year of my pastorate at Marble Collegiate Church. He encountered Mrs. Cynthia Weddell, a former president of the National Council of Churches, who asked him, "How is Norman?" Arthur replied, "He is fine. And I guess he has outlived his critics." Cynthia responded with a remark so characteristic of this lovely lady. "Oh no," she said, "he has outloved them."

But I would be less than candid not to admit that the attack upon me personally, even upon my integrity, by church leaders whom I respected affected me deeply. It made me question whether I really belonged in a ministry where my motives could be so questioned. Through all the controversy, however, I was strengthened and most grateful for the loyal understanding and strong support of my own church members and of my denomination, the Reformed Church in America. They evidenced belief in me, and that fact profoundly helped sustain my spirit and courage throughout the entire harsh experience.

However, at that time I began to feel that seemingly there was no place in Protestantism for any type of communication or methodology that was different. It appeared that one had to conform to a rigid, shall we say, "party line" set by some die-hard liberals who thereupon acted as reactionaries. I considered withdrawing from the church into an independent ministry where one could think and act innovatively rather than be forced into a uniformity rigidly imposed by some self-labeled liberal thinkers who assumed a position of wanting to control thought in the church at large. But as stated earlier, the loyal support of my own church members made such a step unwarranted. And, of course, I did not really want to leave a local church which had traditionally afforded a free and untrampled pulpit.

Ten years after Mother's death, Father had married a lovely lady, Mrs. Mary McDougall. She was a cherished member of our family until her death in 1967. During the time of all this controversy, they were living in the village of Harrison Valley, Pennsylvania. Word came that my father was very ill, and Mary thought I should come to see him. Even though I was about as low in spirit as I have ever been, I boarded an overnight train on the old Erie Railroad. I did not intend to burden my father with my personal problems. On the train I wrote out my resignation from the ministry and put it in my jacket pocket. I did not intend to show it to my father.

However, always sharp in his insights, Father read my troubled thoughts. Besides, even in that quiet and remote countryside, some word of the attack on me had come to his attention. He went straight to the point. "Norman, you have always been true and loyal to Jesus Christ. You believe in and preach Bible truths. You have always been in the mainstream of Christianity, never following any temporary faddism. You have united the pastoral office with the best in the scientific and healing arts. You have blazed new pathways of positive thinking to counter the old destructive negatives. You are my son, and your old father who has known good men and not so good men for eighty years and more, both in and out of the church, says you are a good and loyal minister of Jesus Christ." He was silent and thoughtful for a long minute. "Besides, and remember this, the Peales never quit. It would break my heart if one of my sons was a quitter, afraid to stand up and face any situation."

My father was a gentle-spirited man, and in all my life I had never heard him use any expression that included a swearword. Imagine my shock when he said, "And Norman, there's just one thing more."

"What is it, Dad?" I asked.

"Tell 'em to go to hell," he declared, to my astonishment.

Stepping into another room, I tore up my resignation and threw it into the wastebasket.

Needless to say, I came away fortified in spirit. That was the last time I ever saw my father alive. A few weeks later I stood with Mary by his casket. "He loved you to the end," she said. "He believed in you always. He knew the type of men who could so mistreat an honest brother in the ministry. The last thing he said was, 'Tell Norman never to quit. Tell him the Lord Jesus will see him through.'" As she spoke, over the years came the sound of Dad's voice that day so long ago when he took me to enter college as a freshman: "Always stick to Jesus." This simple admonition of a great father, a strong man, lifted up my heart, and I hope that from heaven he looks down upon me as I have tried to keep the faith. Anyway, so ended the furor over *The Power of Positive Thinking*.

I am grateful for the sound wisdom of the plain people of this world, the everyday Christians who, because they lived closely with Jesus Christ, became practical philosophers, and I have been so blessed by this sort of person. I can think of one, a lady whom I never met personally but knew her son, Governor A. Harry Moore, the only four-term governor of New Jersey, who later served a term in the United States Senate. He was a dedicated Christian and taught a large Bible class for men every Sunday morning in Jersey City. Often he and Mrs. Moore would come to services at our church. I got to know him very well indeed.

Governor Moore came up out of poverty to the distinguished positions he held. He attributed his success in life to two basic truths taught him by his widowed mother. One day he came home to find his mother preparing their frugal evening meal in their modest home. He slumped into a chair and idly watched her stirring a kettle of soup with a big spoon.

"Why are you so down, son?" she asked.

"Oh, I can never amount to anything. We are poor, no money, no friends, no pull, no opportunity."

His mother stopped stirring the soup, pointed the spoon at him, drops meanwhile falling unheeded to the floor, and said, "Don't talk like that. It's not Christian and besides, it's no way for an American boy to talk. All you need is God and gumption."

CHAPTER TWELVE

·

The Pace Steps Up

A FAST-PACED, EXCITING LIFE can produce a tension and stress that destroy, or it can result in a strong life thrust that moves ever faster but still remains under control. When a life is lived in an attitude of complete faith in Christ, there is peace at the center and inevitably power flows from inner quietness. The streams that turn the machinery of the world rise in quiet places. As Edwin Markham put it, "At the heart of the cyclone tearing the sky is a place of central calm."

By nature I am prone to stress and tension. But Jesus Christ has given me inner peace and with it the quietness of mind that produces continuous energy along with the capacity to regulate it. Ever since I met Jesus and gave my life into His hands I have had the gift of vitality, energy, health, and enthusiasm. It is a secret I had the rare good fortune to find. And ever since finding it I have been speaking and writing in an effort to convince others that they, too, can find the same incredible secret.

In New York the pace of life stepped up. I took on more responsibilities, became involved in an increasing number of activities, embarked upon additional book-writing projects, and moved out onto the national speaking circuit.

There was a member of my church, Harold Peat, who was

famous at the time as "Private" Peat, so-called because he was a rather prominent veteran and character of World War I.

He was a gifted man: imaginative, fluent of speech, highly articulate with a consummate ability to describe the life of a soldier in the First World War. Harold had brought home from the front some captured German guns, gas masks, helmets, and other military equipment. These items he used as props in speeches before large audiences throughout the country.

About this time I accepted an invitation to speak at a dinner attended by what were described as "rising young New York executives on their way to the top." The dinner, with some three hundred men, was held at the University Club. I was seated between two pleasant fellows whose company was enjoyable. One remarked, "This is the closest I've been to a minister in a long time." The other assented to this statement. "You said it. It's the nearest I've gotten to a pastor since I was married."

"Well, you two guys are getting up in the world," I responded jocularly.

Then I turned to the one on the left. "What church do you belong to?" He named a Westchester Episcopalian church but added, "I'm not a regular attendant. In fact, they only see me on Easter. You see, I take my religion in my wife's name. She goes pretty often, takes the kids to Sunday School."

I turned to the bright young executive on my right. "And what is your record of churchgoing?" I asked.

"Well, you see, it's like this. My parents were good solid Presbyterians, and they made us go to church every Sunday. So when I got out on my own, I dropped off. And like Jack here, Easter or maybe Christmas too, I warm up the old pew."

Thus inspired, I asked the two, "How many of the three hundred or so men in this dining room tonight would you think might be churchgoing, practicing Christians, not occasional show-ups like you fellows?" They kicked the question around and finally came up with the guess that maybe twenty or twenty-five percent might be the answer.

This experience turned out to be one of the determinative moments of my life. Here were highly educated, competent men, most of them from good old Christian families, to whom the church had become merely a loose attachment that was perhaps good enough for women, children, and old folk, but had only minimal importance for them. The mighty church of God, full of power through the ages, turning civilizations upside down, forming the political foundation of their own country, giving freedom for the economic system that was showering blessings upon them, did not grip these men enough even to warrant their regular attendance. My dinner companions happened to be Protestants, but they said their Catholic and Jewish friends reacted to religion about as they did.

As I walked home that night, down Fifth Avenue from Fifty-sixth Street to Eleventh Street where I lived at the time, I experienced a powerful surge in my mind. It was like a call. Indeed it was a call, an awakening to an exciting new purpose for my life. I suddenly knew my task was to speak and write and present Jesus Christ and Christianity to the men of our times as the most exciting, practical, tremendous way of life available. If there were men not coming to church in large numbers, I would go to them, everywhere. So help me God, I would dedicate my life to bringing men into a vital Christian life-style in the church if it took me fifty years. Before reaching my apartment, in my mind I had embarked on a one-man crusade to make the businessmen of America realize the dynamic, spiritual, exhilarating fulfillment awaiting them by following Jesus Christ, the most exciting Man Who ever lived and Who still lives.

Early the next morning I went to see Harold Peat. He had established a successful lecture agency, providing speakers for business conventions. I told him of the meeting the night before, of my conversation with the two young up-and-coming business executives, of my newly made commitment. "I want to speak to such men in a nonchurch setting. I am going to write books designed to make them reach for the Christian life." And I did a little banging of the table as I spoke.

"Hold it, son." He lifted a restraining hand. "I go along with your thinking and purpose, but it has to be done with finesse. I can try you out at a couple of small meetings, but you can't go there and preach a sermon. You can give your message, but in a nonsermonic, humorous, practical manner. If you succeed, I will work you up to bigger conventions and more important secular

gatherings. Just give them your philosophy of life and of successful living, remembering that your audience is composed of people of all faiths or perhaps of no faith. Just love them. Be sure to
tell them the great persons they can be. I really think you will
make it."

The emphasis on men is due to the fact that in those days there
were few women in executive positions in business. And beyond
that, I had been annoyed since youth by the arrogant assumption
by some men that the church was not for them. The emphasis that
being a Christian and especially a minister was sissy stuff had
made it difficult for me to enter the ministry. But now, I am glad
to say, the whole "religion-is-sissy" concept that had riled me in
small Ohio towns in earlier years has pretty well disappeared. At
least, I never seem to hear it anymore, for which I thank the Lord.

For Harold Peat to put me on the program of a secular convention, even a small one, was not all that easy. Ministers brought
into such a setting were looked at askance. They were all right for
the invocation or benediction at a banquet or convention opening, but it was generally regarded as the kiss of death for a program to feature a preacher as the main speaker. It just wasn't
done.

For a long time I had to face this lack of enthusiasm for having
a preacher on a program. The first talk Mr. Peat sent me to make
was at a county convention in a small town in upstate New York.
The man who met me at the train greeted me with the remark,
"I've been a member of this business association for thirty years
and this is the first time we ever had a preacher as our speaker.
Guess our budget wouldn't get us a regular one this year."

When he took me back to the station later, he said, "You
weren't bad; no sir, not bad at all. In fact, you were pretty good
for a preacher." Then sort of reflectively, he added, "You didn't
sound like a preacher at all. But you could really make a sermon
out of the stuff you gave us today." He didn't know that the
speech was the same "stuff" I had used in a sermon, just reshaped
a bit. Anyway, as the train sped toward home, I had the feeling
that maybe I could succeed on the secular platform if I kept on
working at it, tried to find out the pressures and problems of
businessmen, learned to communicate with people outside the
church.

After a while I began to receive invitations to speak on the program of state conventions, thereby moving up from the county level. And at one of these state conventions, an incident occurred which I was able to use ever after to great advantage. I was the speaker at the annual dinner of a certain eastern state bankers association. I arrived at the hotel where the dinner was scheduled about an hour late, unavoidably. Going at once to my room, I changed into a dinner jacket. Thus attired, I descended in the elevator to find that all the bankers had gone into the dining hall save one stray man whom I encountered in the elevator.

This banker was unsteady on his feet. He fixed a thin, watery eye on me and looked me over speculatively. Dressed as I was, he did not take me for a preacher. In an intimate sort of way he said, "Hello there, buddy." This was not the form of address to which I was accustomed, but I answered in kind, and for a moment a conversation ensued which might be described as jocular. Finally, growing more expansive, he asked, "Where you going tonight, buddy?"

"I'm going to the meeting of the bankers association. Where are you going?"

"Oh," he replied in disgust, "I suppose I'll have to go in there also. But I don't want to, for it won't be any good."

"Why won't it be any good?"

"Oh, they've got some preacher from New York to speak in there tonight."

"You don't mean it," I exclaimed. "Why would they have a preacher to speak to a bankers association?"

"You've got me, buddy, unless they're running out of money."

"Well, I guess I'll go into the meeting anyway. There's nothing else to do around here."

He said he guessed he would too but reiterated, "It won't be any good."

"Brother, you don't know the half of it. I know it won't be any good."

Having agreed that it wouldn't be any good, and having gotten that matter settled to our mutual satisfaction, he went his way and I went mine.

I went up to the head table, took my seat, and forgot all about my friend of the elevator until when I rose to speak, the first eye I caught at the rear of the hall belonged to this man. He was what you might call embarrassed. He threw his hands up in a gesture of dismay and sank down out of sight. But presently he came up for air and listened to me. When the meeting was over, I was at the head table shaking hands with persons who came forward to greet me, when I saw the man coming from the left. It was evident that he hated to come up to speak to me. But I liked him, for he proved to be a good sport. When he finally reached me, he put out his hand and said, "Put 'er there, buddy. We were both right, weren't we!"

Why preachers have acquired a reputation for being men and women of another sort, and for the most part dull and uninteresting, I don't understand. For actually they are among the greatest people I've ever known. And I am delighted to report that gradually this erroneous concept is passing away. At least, I no longer seem to encounter it as in former years.

I feel accepted and understood for what I am. This was brought home to me after speaking to a trade association convention of some three thousand people in the grand ballroom of the old Sherman House in Chicago. A big genial man, smoking a big cigar, came up to me and said, "Reverend, that was a damn good sermon."

"Well, thanks," I replied, "but that wasn't a sermon. It was a talk."

"Oh, you may fool some of these fellows but you don't fool me. I know a sermon when I hear one whether it's labeled or not." Then he punched me affectionately in the chest. "You're on the right track. Keep it up. What you are handing out is what we all need." As he moved away with a big smile, I realized I was accomplishing my goal of reaching men, even the apparently hard-boiled ones.

Further verification came from the fact that men were crowding into our church on Fifth Avenue. And ministers around the country were telling me that I had been, in part, responsible for men coming back to church in their communities. I was also smart enough to know that when men go to a church, the women will be there, too. I began to note the increasing number of business-women at the conventions where I was a speaker. To win them

163

to full commitment to Christ became an important part of my goal. Women executives are most responsive to a positive concept of religion as a motivating force in life, and it is gratifying to see them in large numbers in my church and, indeed, in churches everywhere.

Sometime I would like to write about all the outstanding Christian businesswomen I have known, women like Josephine Bay, for example. She had been secretary to Charles Ulrick Bay, who had vast oil interests, shipping concerns, a New York stock brokerage house, to name just a few of his enterprises. And for several years he served as U.S. Ambassador to Norway during the Truman administration. Josephine became Mrs. Bay and after his death, his successor in business.

Rick Bay was a very remarkable man. He was a genius in making hard business decisions. One day he asked Josephine to come in the library after dinner. "You have the capacity to become a great businesswoman," he said. "I have a tough decision to make which I want to describe to you in detail and tell you my decision. I want you to argue hard and forcefully against any point in which you think I may be in error."

Josephine applied her brilliant intellect, as requested. And she reported that the "battle that ensued was terrific, for Rick was smart and very tenacious." Finally the matter was settled, Josephine having made, as Rick told me later, an important contribution "to the nubbin" of the problem. After his death Josephine gave lectures to business organizations and conventions on the topic "Teach Your Wife to Be a Widow."

Josephine Bay knew well how to be one herself, for at the death of her husband she and I rode back from the cemetery together, and she asked, "Norman, what shall I do about all of Rick's business interests? His men associates all want me to follow their advice. To whom shall I listen? You know these men."

Suddenly the answer came to me. "Josephine," I said, "you are just as smart, just as knowledgeable as those men. Indeed, I think you are more able than any of them. You take charge. Run the businesses yourself. You can do it."

She looked at me wonderingly. Then in her own beautiful, simple way, she asked, "Will you pray that God will help me?"

She went on to head a great shipping line, an oil company, and a New York brokerage house. Later I read an article in a national magazine headed, "Josephine Bay, the greatest businesswoman in Wall Street." One Sunday I was raising money for an addition to the church and enumerated various gifts that might be given, the most expensive being a hall costing $75,000. Josephine phoned me after church. "I'll take that hall," she said.

"But that costs seventy-five thousand dollars."

All she said was, "I heard you the first time." It is now called Bay Hall in the church.

At another time Ruth took on the project of raising $250,000 for a chapel in the Interchurch Center on Riverside Drive in New York City. This $20,000,000 building houses the national headquarters of many of the Protestant denominations. She went to see Josephine Bay to ask her advice about approaching ten people for $25,000 each in order to build this chapel. Josephine asked to see the list of those Ruth intended to approach. Her name was not among them. Ruth sincerely was only asking for advice.

"Ruth," she said, "you have so much to do and shouldn't be taking time going around seeing a lot of people. I will give the total of two hundred fifty thousand dollars." Later she added an organ, bringing the full amount to more than $300,000. The chapel was dedicated in memory of her husband, Rick. The plaque reads: "TO THE GLORY OF GOD AND THE SERVICE OF MANKIND THIS CHAPEL IS DEDICATED IN LOVING MEMORY TO CHARLES ULRICK BAY, AMERICAN AMBASSADOR TO NORWAY, 1946–1953, AND AS A TRIBUTE TO DR. & MRS. NORMAN VINCENT PEALE BY THE CHARLES ULRICK AND JOSEPHINE BAY FOUNDATION."

Josephine wanted a house in the country, especially for her three children. So I helped find her The Hill Farm, a beautiful white-pillared old Colonial house on a hilltop with a magnificent view in three directions, one of which was west to the Catskills. She was so happy fixing it up. I called on her one day when she was planting a hedge of pine trees in front of the house, and that hedge has now grown tall and wide. Then suddenly God took her home.

A few years later our daughter, Elizabeth, and her husband, John Allen, wanted to live on Quaker Hill in Pawling. John was an executive at the *Reader's Digest,* only thirty miles away. They purchased our home, Sugar Tree Farm, on which our children had grown up, and we bought The Hill Farm from the Bay estate. When the deal was complete, Michael Paul, Mrs. Bay's second husband, said, "Josephine would be so happy that you are to live in her house." Indeed, the spirit of this brilliant, gentle, Christlike woman seems to hover over the place, ever to bless it. There we have lived for many years when we are not in our present apartment on Fifth Avenue where we have lived since 1950.

When we are not in New York City or Pawling, we are on the road, going everywhere on speaking engagements. In one typical ten-day period I spoke in Portland, Oregon; Las Vegas, Nevada; Findlay, Ohio; Minneapolis, Minnesota; Ocean Grove, New Jersey; Austin, Texas; Memphis, Tennessee; and San Francisco, California.

I would not be surprised if the records show that I have made close to as many speeches as anyone on the circuit, to all manner of organizations, and over a good many years, traveling at least 200,000 air miles a year. Some weeks I may give as many as four speeches, sometimes only one, and now and then none. And the speaking engagements have taken me to every state in the union, and every province in Canada. Three times I have spoken in Australia, including two professionally sponsored tours in the major cities of that country. Other speaking engagements have been in England, Ireland, Japan, Hong Kong, Taiwan, the Caribbean islands, Switzerland, Holland, Malaysia, Brazil, Mexico, the Philippines, South Africa, and last but not least, the greatest ship ever to sail the seven seas, the Queen Elizabeth II, on which I have given sermons and lectures.

My speaking dates have included every kind of business and industry convention from the National Sporting Goods Association to the American Banker Association, and from the National Association of Realtors to the National Selected Morticians, and indeed hundreds of other fine organizations at home and abroad. Once I recall speaking in Wisconsin to a farm-supply convention in a huge tent. Farm machinery was displayed around the inside walls of the tent, and crates of chickens were also in evidence. In view of the setting, I started my talk by expressing the hope that in my speech I would not "lay an egg." At that point, a chorus of cackling came from the crated hens. Needless to say, this just about broke up the meeting.

In Chicago on another occasion, when I was being introduced to the national undertakers convention, the chairman read the subject of my talk, the title of a book I had recently written, *Stay Alive All Your Life.* This also seemed to cause considerable merriment in the audience.

I was the speaker at the annual dinner of a state association of funeral directors and embalmers. They had sent instructions that it was a black-tie affair. Accordingly, I arrived in the anteroom off the main ballroom where the head-table guests were gathering, the leading undertakers of the state. All were attired in black tuxedos and black ties, and each had a white carnation pinned to his lapel. It only remained to have a white carnation affixed to my lapel.

This job was assigned to a lady undertaker, a charming though somewhat diminutive woman. It was with some difficulty that she got the flower into my lapel from a standing position. Nor was she all that dexterous, for she stuck her thumb with a pin and also rammed a pin into my shoulder. Finally in complete exasperation, she said, "I could do a much better job at this if you were lying down."

Many are the persons whose lives are changed in meetings, even secular meetings, especially those that are motivationally oriented. I have spoken to many such gatherings, particularly at sales rallies, where the attendance often runs into the thousands. I especially like this type of meeting, for the men and women attend for the definite purpose of learning how to improve themselves. Their motive may be of course to do a better job, to get further along in business, to improve performance. But from the speakers they soon learn that to be better at anything, one has to be a better person attitudinally, mentally, and spiritually. Actually in many such meetings, I feel that it is but a step from a sales meeting to a spiritual meeting. The religious note sings out through all the proceedings, perhaps not articulated specifically but felt realistically.

I recall one such meeting in a large midwestern city. It was a bitter-cold winter night, and a high wind was driving snow across the avenue as I went to the hall in a taxi. We were stopped at an intersection by a red traffic light. On the far corner was a gasoline station above which a huge banner flapped in the wind. On the banner in large letters was printed the slogan "A Clean Engine Always Delivers Power." It was an advertisement of some kind of motor oil. The statement struck me forcibly.

The hall was packed with several thousand young men and women, mostly sales personnel. Hardly anyone there was as old as forty years. Paul Harvey was speaking in his inimitable and fascinating manner.

The slogan on the banner, "A Clean Engine Always Delivers Power," was on my mind when my time came to speak. I looked into the faces of that great assembly of young people, sensing the power represented there. I told them about the slogan and commented that there were in that auditorium several thousand "mental engines," each known as the head. I made the point that if those engines were unclean, the power needed for a great life could not get through.

I defined an unclean mental engine as a mind that is full of negative thoughts, self-doubt thoughts, hate thoughts, envious and resentful thoughts, lustful and dishonest thoughts. "Now," I said, "I know that I am not speaking in church, not preaching a sermon, but there is only one sure way by which a mind can be washed clean of such corrosive thinking which blocks off the power flow. And that procedure is for each in his own way to ask the Lord to cleanse the mind, empty out that old debilitating mass of stuff, wipe it clean, and then to fill that mind with positive thoughts of faith in God, hope, love, and enthusiasm."

I went on with my speech on how positive thinking can change one's personality and improve life. I had no sooner finished and gone backstage when a big, fine-looking strapping fellow came charging back. He rushed up to me, threw his arms around me, nearly crushing me. "Boy," he shouted, "do I like you!"

"Well," I responded, "I like you too, but why be so vociferous about it?"

"Because," said he, "my life has been changed in the last thirty minutes, and I don't mean maybe. I have been a flop, a failure, a washout. I am the lowest man on the totem pole on our sales force. Can't understand why I haven't been fired. And that isn't all. I'm a failure as a husband, as a father, a failure period.

"There I was slumped down in my seat and you started talking about that dirty engine and no power coming through. I knew you were talking about me. For my mental engine, my mind, couldn't have been dirtier, filled as it was with negativism, jealousy, resentment, excuses, dishonesty, low in morals. You name it. Anything bad, and it has been there in my mind. When you said to turn it over to the Lord, brother, you had me for sure. I talked to the Lord Jesus and I meant it, deep down, every word of it. I asked Him to change me and He did. I could feel it in my mind, in my heart, all over. I am a new man." And as I looked at his face and into his eyes, I knew that he spoke the truth. The great old words came to mind: "If any man be in Christ, he is a new creature: old things are passed away; . . . all things are become new." (II Corinthians 5:17) As I returned to my hotel after that meeting, I thanked the Lord that the one-man crusade I had embarked upon back there at the University Club meeting in New York was still getting results, still bringing men and women into the spiritual life.

I recall the thirtyish businesswoman at a huge sales rally in the Kansas City auditorium. The speakers' platform was built up high, a flight of some ten steps leading to it. Fifteen thousand people filled the great hall for a P.M.A. (Positive Mental Attitude) rally sponsored by W. Clement Stone of Chicago. When I walked down those steps after my talk, a young woman was waiting and weeping, though there was a light on her face. "I met Him just now," she said. "Yes, I met Him and He has changed me. I feel like a big heavy burden has been lifted. I'm so happy." I led her aside where we could talk, and she told me she had been reared in a "paganistic, totally irreligious family and that she knew nothing about spiritual things." Apparently that did not deter her from a profound and valid spiritual experience of life changing.

In great meetings of this type, a spirit is generated that transforms it into a fellowship, a unity of feeling, so that in degree at least it approaches that of a religious meeting. It calls to mind a definition of a church service by an honored associate of mine who served for years at my New York church. Mary Brining said,

"A church service is the creation of an atmosphere in which a spiritual miracle can take place."

Mine has been, and still is, perhaps now even more than ever, a fast-paced life. But I love it and thrive on it. I believe in work, lots of it. An interesting, work-filled life is an exciting life. It is ever fresh, ever new. Problems galore, challenges every day, new goals, new experiences, this is the stuff of which living is made.

But it has not been all work. We have had a lot of fun and many thrilling times. Let me tell you about just one of them. The late Theodore E. Seiler of the famous Zermatt hotel family, in existence for well over one hundred years, was a close friend. We often stayed with him either at his chalet or in the Mont Cervin, one of his hotels in Zermatt. One day I asked, "Ted, have you ever climbed the Matterhorn?"

"Oh, yes," he replied, "and it is a glorious experience." Glumly, I told him I would have liked such a thrilling and "exalting" experience, for that is the word Ted used in describing his own reaction. "It was an unforgettable spiritual experience," he said.

"Tell you what," he said. "I will see that you go to the top of Matterhorn—by helicopter. Wait for just the right day."

I am going to let Ruth describe what happened on that never-to-be-forgotten day. I like her dramatic account of our flight in a small helicopter to the top of the lonely, aloof, and gigantic Matterhorn.

The doors swung shut. The pilot adjusted his earphones and spoke a few words in German to the controller inside the hangar. His right hand held the stick. With his left, he twisted the throttle between the two forward seats. The helicopter vibrated, stirred, began to lift. Suddenly, with a heart-stopping lurch, it seemed to me that we simply jumped off the concrete platform into thin air. There was no forward taxiing, as in a conventional aircraft. We leaned into the wind—and leaped!

Up the little valley we rushed, not more than two hundred feet off the ground. The pilot and the passenger in the front seat could see almost straight down; I was glad we couldn't. On the instrument panel I could see the air-speed indicator; the needle was hovering between forty and fifty knots. The altimeter indicated that we were about six thousand feet above sea level, and climbing.

Up the valley we flew, between towering rock walls on either side, past lacy waterfalls, over green meadows filled with mountain wild flowers. The helicopter banked steeply and started back, still climbing.

Below us, now, we could see Zermatt spread out like a toy village, its chalets and hotels dominated by the spire of the church. We were following the contours of the ground to the east of the town. Once or twice it seemed to me that our rate of climb was too slow to enable us to clear the ridge just ahead, but we always slid over with something to spare.

Moments later we were over the Gorner-glacier itself, a huge river of ice, blinding white, strangely scored and indented. Where it ended, a torrent of water, gray with glacial sediment, poured from under the wall of ice. To our right, a lordly peak, the Stockhorn, pierced the sky. The altimeter now read eleven thousand feet, and some dim unwelcome memory reminded me that as a rule pilots are not supposed to fly over ten thousand feet without oxygen. We had no oxygen.

Up the glacier we raced at sixty knots. Tortured and barren as the ridged ice was, I was glad to have it there, only a couple of hundred feet below. If our engine stopped, I told myself cheerfully, we could just sit down on that nice solid ice and wait to be rescued—perhaps by a friendly St. Bernard. But then, looking ahead, I saw that the glacier ended. And not just the glacier, but the mountain, the world, creation ended. Rushing toward us was a fine white line, sharp as a knife blade. Then nothing. Just a kind of livid emptiness.

Over the line we went, straight out into this awful chasm. I felt my feet pressing against the floor, as if by doing so they could somehow hold us back. Beneath us the precipice fell sheer, straight down, for more than a mile. We hung suspended over a stupendous void, ringed by the great peaks, floored by purple shadow.

I grabbed Norman's hand. "Ruth, are you nervous?" he asked, surprised, for it takes a lot to trouble me.

"Oh, no," I answered feebly, "just excited!"

My rational mind knew that we could fly just as well over a mile of nothingness as over a glacier, but my stomach didn't seem to know it. My stomach, in fact, seemed to have stayed back over the glacier. I saw that our writer friend had reached for the side of our plastic bubble as if to brace himself, and I knew he too was wondering what four infinitesimally small and unimportant human beings were doing in such a sublimely terrifying place.

Only the pilot seemed unconcerned. We swung behind the twin peaks of the Monte Rosa, still higher than our heads although our altimeter now indicated twelve thousand feet. Below us a few ants seemed to be toiling painfully across the vast snowfields. Climbers. "That can be dangerous," said the pilot, pointing at them, "unless you know what you're doing. There are snow bridges that can break. See those holes that look like caves? If you fall in one of those, you're finished. No one can get you out."

The Matterhorn is impressive at a distance. Close up, it is overpowering. And we were close, so close that it seemed to me we could see the cracks in the towering walls. But when the pilot pointed out some climbers, they looked unbelievably tiny, just dots of color clinging to the naked rock. Past a small hut we went, perched like an eagle's nest on the edge of a stupendous precipice. "Climbers spend the night there," the pilot said. "They start climbing at dawn."

We were still climbing ourselves, in a tight spiral that circled the Matterhorn three times. It seemed to me that our engine was laboring in the thin air. I was beginning to feel some shortness of breath, and I could see that Norman was too. Now the altimeter read fourteen thousand feet; we were almost on a level with the summit. I could see clearly the iron cross that marked the spot where Whymper and his companions had stood so long ago. Higher still, so that we could look down on the summit itself. There on that dizzying height, three tiny figures stood, waving at us, and I felt a sudden surge of admiration for the restless, unquenchable spirit of adventure that had made them challenge and conquer those frowning heights. Perhaps our generation was not so soft and effete after all.

Then we were dropping down through the luminous air, the great mountain receding behind us. "Swallow hard," the pilot said, "it will ease the pressure on your ears." Zermatt came into view, tranquil in the sunlight. The landing pad looked like a linen handkerchief. We made one last turn, came up into the wind, settled down exactly in the center of the painted circle. The flight was over.

Our friend Ted Seiler had arranged for the hotel van to meet us. The two splendid horses trotted back to the village, bells jingling gaily. We sat in the old coach—it had been old when he was a boy, Ted Seiler said—not saying much. The spell of the heights was still on us, and the transition from twentieth-century helicopter to nineteenth-century horse-drawn van was so abrupt and so strange that it seemed unreal.

All through the rest of that day, and many times since, I have found myself reliving the exaltation of that moment when we swept over the edge of the glacier into that vast emptiness, and the thought has come to me that perhaps dying is like that: an outward rush into the unknown where there is nothing recognizable, nothing to cling to, and yet you are sustained and supported over the great void just as you were over the comfortable and familiar terrain.

Fanciful? Perhaps. But I remember that when we said our prayers that night, thanking God for the privilege of seeing all we had seen, and also for our safe return, it didn't seem so fanciful. Not at all.

CHAPTER THIRTEEN

The Message Goes Nationwide

IT IS REALLY A THRILL when you make significant progress toward attaining your chief goal in life. And ours, Ruth's and mine, is to communicate the practical Gospel of Jesus Christ to as many people as we can possibly reach in our lifetime. Currently we are reaching approximately twenty million every month by means of just two of our projects, *Guideposts* magazine and the Foundation for Christian Living. And this reckoning does not include the large numbers of people with whom contact is made by books, radio, television, preaching, and public speeches. Our goal is a simple one. And we have a terrifically interesting time in working toward it in successive stages.

To begin something small and help it grow is surely one vital element in an exciting life. Most of us are impressed when we read about business ideas that started small and grew into giant enterprises. It is the stuff of which the romance of achievement is made.

Back in 1940, eight years after I came to New York, when the great influx of out-of-town visitors began at the church, many began asking for printed copies of the sermons given on Sundays.

There finally were so many requests that it was decided to respond to this demand. The messages have always been delivered extemporaneously, without manuscript or notes, actually without even a podium. So it was necessary to capture the speech or sermon, first stenographically, later by recording. Several hundred copies of a sermon were run off by mimeograph and were quickly gone. Often visitors requested that their names be put on a mailing list to receive copies regularly.

Mercé E. Boyer, director of church activities, at once saw the possibilities for service and growth inherent in the development of a sermon-by-mail enterprise. She enlisted William "Bill" Groll, a dedicated Christian layman, along with another efficient member, Russell G. Shepherd, and a publication committee was formed. Sermon Publications began as an activity of Christian Endeavor, the young people's society in the church. The stuffing and addressing of envelopes was done in the church basement by volunteers.

The mailing list grew so rapidly that it was necessary to expand to other rooms of the church. Meanwhile the activities of the congregation were increasing and the Sermon Publications enterprise had to move to an office building on Fourth Avenue. When Ruth and I purchased a farm on Quaker Hill in Pawling, New York, in 1943, we moved this enterprise to a large room over the garage on our farm property, and Ruth took charge. The list of recipients numbered approximately 1,200 at the time. It was not long before this space proved inadequate, and the activity moved into a rambling old residence on Quaker Hill. Soon the mailing list grew to twenty thousand persons in all sections of the United States and Canada, and in foreign countries. This necessitated enlarged space and more efficient direct-mail facilities. Accordingly, acting on faith that the Lord would help in providing adequate financial support, a lot was purchased on Route 22 in the village of Pawling and a small building was erected.

As stated above, before the Sermon Publications work was moved to Pawling, it became evident that it was destined to be an independent venture. An elder of the church, McClelland F Stunkard, at a meeting of the deacons and elders, offered a motion that the church transfer ownership and control of Sermon Publications to Dr. and Mrs. Peale, and the proposal carried unanimously. We in turn asked our attorney, Gerald Dickler, for many years our close friend and advisor in all our activities, to take the necessary steps to incorporate the project into a non-profit Christian publishing organization, and it was officially made a church corporation under the laws of the state of New York.

As such, it has its own board of directors with John M. Allen of Pawling, a vice-president of *Reader's Digest,* as president. The name was changed to the Foundation for Christian Living and its chief publication is in pocket-size format and called *Plus The Magazine of Positive Thinking.*

The current mailing list is close to one million persons in every state of the nation, every province of Canada, and 120 foreign countries. The original building has been expanded five times, now comprising over sixty thousand square feet of working and storage space. The plant is fully computerized, and contains the best and latest equipment for mailing nearly forty million items yearly and for handling the large volume of mail received from readers. The Foundation for Christian Living has become the largest direct-mail enterprise in the world for spreading the Gospel in this form. During its phenomenal growth it has never varied from the initial purpose of winning men and women to Christian commitment and giving its readers practical messages on living the Christian way of life. Its 130 employees are themselves dedicated to the purpose of the organization for which they work daily.

All of this growth and achievement has been financed on the spiritual principle of voluntary giving. No charge is made for material published by the Foundation for Christian Living beyond an occasional statement of what it costs to manufacture and mail it, and this serves only as a guide to giving. This Christian publishing enterprise has been supported, as is any church, by the free-will gifts of those whom it serves and who want to share in its evangelical work. It has never been in the red, always in the black. Nor have I personally ever received compensation for the writing I do for the Foundation, or for the time spent in helping direct its activities.

As a strong believer in Christian volunteerism, I am convinced that the more we do freely for the Lord, the more joy will we have and the greater blessing will we receive. A particularly rewarding experience I have in connection with the Foundation for Christian Living is participation in its prayer work. Requests for prayer come to the headquarters in Pawling by the hundreds, and everyone's problem is made a personal object of prayer. A slip of paper containing the name of the individual and the nature of the problem is placed on the altar in the chapel, and workers go there daily at 9:50 A.M. to pray for those seeking spiritual help. On Good Friday, a special day of prayer, people come from near and far to join with the employees in offering prayer, since as many as sixty thousand prayer requests are received for that day alone.

Every week I receive as many as four or five hundred special prayer requests and I set aside time to pray for each person by name and problem. Over a period of years I have noted that problems seem to come in the following order: (1) health; (2) job; (3) money; (4) youth; (5) marriage. However, the requests range over every known human difficulty. Constant attention to this phase of the work of the Foundation for Christian Living results in an in-depth and compassionate awareness of the hurts of people.

Often long-distance telephone calls come to the office of the Foundation. The call may come from any of the fifty states or from Canada or even from overseas. Having read our publications, the callers seem to feel that someone in our organization can help them. At least they know that we are their friends, even though we have never met in person. One man, calling from the far northwest, wept over the telephone about his little girl, who was in a coma. He said, "I didn't know where to turn. And then I thought of you, Dr. Peale, for I read you regularly."

I told him, "Put her in God's loving hands. See her as whole and well. Visualize her coming out of that coma. See Jesus putting His hands upon her and completely restoring her to health."

Then I prayed with him over three thousand miles on the basis of the scriptural principle of "two or three": "Where two or three are gathered together in my name, there am I in the midst of them." I pointed out that by the telephone he and I were "together," and that the loving and healing Jesus was with us. The troubled father choked up as he thanked me. Twenty-four hours later he called back joyfully to give me the good news that the little girl had opened her eyes and said, "Daddy." And the doctor assured him that she was going to get well. "Thank you for your wonderful, caring Foundation for Christian Living," he said with feeling.

There was also the man who had been let go by his company, along with others, when management had to cut back because of economic conditions. "Whatever will I do at my age?" he asked me nervously. His wife was on an extension telephone, and together the three of us prayed on that same "two or three" principle. I urged them to seek first a spiritual and mental state of calm, for especially in crisis one must think clearly and objectively. Creative thinking is not possible when the mind is agitated and anxious.

We prayed for guidance, for an idea. I assured them of my continuing prayers and urged them to pray constantly. The solution did not come immediately; but it did come, and it led this couple into a self-employed business from which, working together, they could make an adequate income. Though no suggestion was even hinted, they sent a tithe of their first year's income to the Foundation for Christian Living and now are convinced that "by tithing we have even more prosperity." Of course they do, for does not Scripture say, "Bring ye all the tithes into the storehouse, that there may be meat in mine house, and prove me now herewith, saith the Lord of hosts, if I will not open you the windows of heaven, and pour you out a blessing, that there shall not be room enough to receive it." (Malachi 3:10)

Ruth is the actual founder and directing hand of the Foundation for Christian Living. By her faith, administrative ability, and executive skills as well as her dedication and love of people, she has built this great Christian service agency into the most outstanding institution of its kind in the history of Christianity in America. This has been an exciting experience for us both. Ruth has developed an extraordinary team of executives and a competent group of dedicated co-workers. The Foundation for Christian Living is an important enterprise in our lives and has helped me reach millions of people over many years. We hope we have contributed to the extension of Christianity in our time. So the message went nationwide, indeed worldwide.

* * *

In the autumn of 1944, Raymond Thornburg, my neighbor and longtime friend from college days, came over to our place on Quaker Hill with the suggestion that Ruth and I join him and his wife, Pherbia, and drive over into Connecticut for dinner at an old country inn. We would visit a couple of antique shops on the way. He said he had an idea he wanted to try out on me.

It was one of those glorious days in autumn with clear blue skies, a haze on the far horizon, the odor of burning leaves in the air, and every tree aflame in beauty. So we accepted the suggestion, and enroute, "Pinky," as he had been called since boyhood because of his complexion and reddish hair, outlined his idea. It was that businessmen needed something besides financial reports and production papers to read, something inspirational and spiritual. He thought it might be a good idea to develop a spiritual letter service to reach the desks of businessmen on a Monday morning to help them start the week in positive spirit. Ruth and I liked the notion, and we discussed it during the afternoon and evening.

Sometime later we attended a dinner party where the guests included Lowell Thomas, J. C. Penney, Captain Eddie Rickenbacker, Branch Rickey, and others. During a sprightly conversation the suggestion was made that this country needed a new and different type of publication, one that would not run down our system of free enterprise but build it up instead, one that would show, by true stories, how faith helps people in everyday life. It would be designed to motivate American youth to be what they could be, that the sky was the limit under the American way of life. It would stress the fact that if a person thinks positively, is of good character, works hard, and practices his or her faith, that individual could develop creatively. The assembled group became very excited. They "elected" me editor and told me to go out and start this publication (which became *Guideposts*).

"Well, friends," I said, "I do appreciate being made editor of this nonexistent magazine, but even though I am a preacher I was not born yesterday and am smart enough to know that to float any such enterprise some capital is necessary. Since I know all of you to be very well fixed, I will pass among you to receive your contribution for the starting of this publication." I am sometimes pained by the reactions of human nature, as in this instance the alacrity with which all present suddenly discovered that the hour was late and they had to get along home. And they left me, the editor of a nonexistent magazine, having no editorial know-how, no subscribers, no equipment, no office, no employees and no capital, which was what might appropriately be called an unpropitious situation.

I was about to abandon the suggestion, but the idea had taken hold of me. It was obvious that funds were needed, but where could I raise the necessary money? Who did I know who was very wealthy and had a generous disposition? These two qualities are not always found in the same person, but presently I thought of a friend, Frank Gannett, founder of the Gannett chain of newspapers. Frank lived in Rochester, New York. So I went to see him, outlining enthusiastically the idea of the proposed publication: to support freedom under God and to motivate youth to be the great persons they can be under the American system of free enterprise. I told him that it would be a spiritual publication to build once again into our nation a deep faith in God. Frank Gannett made a contribution, which enabled me to purchase part of a mailing list called "The Good Givers List."

I prepared an appeal letter outlining, as persuasively as possible, what we intended doing. We received approximately seven thousand dollars from this mailing, and with this small amount of money, *Guideposts* magazine was started as a nonprofit inspirational publication. We tried Pinky Thornburg's idea of a spiritual letter and printed the first issues as small four-page folders or flyers, measuring 4½ by 6 inches, which could be carried easily in the pocket. However, this form did not seem practical; so in August 1948, we began stapling the folders together to form a small magazine of twenty-four pages. With the July 1949 issue, the size was enlarged to 7¼ by 4⅞ inches. Then the overall size and number of pages was increased to the present dimensions of 7½ by 5⅛ inches and forty-eight pages printed in full-color gravure process.

It was in connection with the development of *Guideposts* that I learned two of the most important lessons of my own life: positive thinking and imaging. Both of these practical principles have been developed in my books. Starting a new magazine today may require the investment of several millions of dollars. Ours was begun on the proverbial shoestring. In fact, it came within a hairsbreadth of folding on several occasions. Once I recall spending the night as a guest of Mr. J. Howard Pew, then head of the Sun Oil Company. I told him how close to bankruptcy we were. He did not seem responsive, but a few days later my wife came running across the lawn waving a piece of paper. It was a check for five thousand dollars from Mr. Pew. It saved the day in that crisis, for our organization was short about that amount to pay the current printer's bill.

Tessie Durlach, a wise and loyal friend and a great lady, gave generous contributions to *Guideposts*. She also contributed creative ideas that became vital to the future of the magazine as well as helpful to thousands of people in audiences all over the country where I have talked about them. On one occasion, when the cash flow was extremely low, Tessie suggested writing to the subscribers outlining the need for more operating cash and asking if any would be willing to make a loan to *Guideposts* in any amount at 6 percent interest, the going rate at the time. The note would be for one year, at which time the principal would be repaid plus the accrued interest. Over $100,000 was raised by this method. At the end of the year each lender received the interest payment and was afforded the opportunity to extend the loan for a second year on the same terms. Tessie also suggested that the lender be given the opportunity of donating the principal amount to *Guideposts* as a tax-deductible gift. About fifty thousand dollars was given this way. Many reloaned the money for a second year. Others asked to have the principal returned. Financial problems became less difficult for a time. "Always take a positive attitude toward a problem," said Tessie. "There is always a way; or you can make a way where there is no way. Believe and think positively and trust God to help you. And He will, too."

In 1950, perhaps the most critical period in the early history of *Guideposts,* Tessie came forward with another brilliant suggestion based on a sound creative principle that can be used successfully by anyone, in any situation. At that time *Guideposts* had grown to some forty thousand subscribers, but costs were mounting faster than income. Debts had accumulated alarmingly and unless some miracle happened, we could very well go out of business. But a miracle did happen and the company went on to spectacular success.

In this crisis I called a meeting of the board of directors, but no constructive ideas were forthcoming to deal with the grave situation. I had a tall spindle crammed with bills, most with old dates and not a few with some rather mean remarks. I recall one from a dealer who had sold us a typewriter on time—lots of time —who rather petulantly wanted to know why we hadn't paid for the typewriter. I never even answered him, for any fool should have known the reason: We didn't have any money. I put those bills before the directors, saying, "Look at those bills." A deep silence fell upon the room. Finally one director said in a small voice, "What do you know? Look at those bills." Truly an uninspired observation!

Tessie had been invited to this meeting, in part, because of her past generosity plus with the hope that lightning might strike twice in the same place. But Tessie said instead, "I might as well put you out of your misery. I'm not going to give another nickel." Which, of course, did not put us out of our misery but, on the contrary, threw us more deeply into it. "But," she quickly added, "I will give you something of far greater value than money, a creative and dynamic idea with which you can secure all the resources needed to make *Guideposts* a success.

"Now," she continued, "let us examine the situation. You lack everything. You lack money, you lack subscribers, you lack equipment, you lack ideas. And why do you lack? Simply because you have constantly and consistently been thinking in terms of lack and have thereby created a condition of lack."

Her statement struck me with a powerful impact. It gave me an insight into truth like a flash of lightning illuminates, in sharp detail, a landscape on a dark night. In that moment, for the first time in my life I knew the important fact that as we think, so do we create.

"What shall we do then to correct this situation?" I asked.

"Do?" she echoed. "Stand up affirmatively and command these destructive lack thoughts to get out, to vacate your mind."

"Now, Tessie," I objected, "any student of the human mind knows that if one tries to mount a frontal attack on an unhealthy thought pattern the result is not to exorcise or cast out defeatist thoughts, but it tends, on the contrary, to drive such thoughts more deeply into consciousness. Besides," I concluded, "we do not control our thoughts. Our thoughts control us."

I shall never forget the look of disgust that Tessie leveled at me. "Don't you know what the great Plato said?" she asked.

Frankly, I hadn't the slightest idea what the great Plato said, but, not wanting to reveal my ignorance, asked brightly, "To which of the many familiar sayings of Plato do you refer?"

She said, "I refer to the one you never heard in your whole life!" I shall never forget hearing Tessie say what she said was a statement by Plato. As I recall it, she quoted the philosopher as saying, "Take charge of your thoughts. You can do what you will with them."

"So flush those lack thoughts out of your minds and do it now, forcibly, and with determination." And we did just that. We cleansed our thinking of the lack concept.

"Now," said Tessie picturesquely, "those lack thoughts have been ejected from your minds; but they are waiting around expectantly to return where for so long they have been hospitably entertained. The only way you can keep them from returning is by a process of displacement in which you fill your minds with a more powerful and positive thought pattern, thus crowding out the lack thoughts which have hitherto dominated your thinking.

"How many subscribers do you need to keep this magazine going?" she asked. I did not know for sure, but picked a figure at random and said that a hundred thousand would do it. "All right. What I want you to do is to look out there and see, visualize, image a hundred thousand people reading *Guideposts* who have paid for their subscriptions."

As she said this I happened to look into her snapping brown eyes, and I was reminded of the exalted look of the believer. Tessie was not of my church. She was Jewish, a compelling combination of spirituality and sagacity. Mirrored in her eyes I "saw" the required hundred thousand subscribers. In excitement I leaped to my feet and shouted, "I see them. I see them."

Tessie jumped up also and threw her arms around me. "Isn't that wonderful?" she exclaimed. "Now that we see them, we have them."

"How's that?" I asked incredulously.

"Ah yes," she repeated firmly. "Now that we see them, we have them."

Being a spiritual person, Tessie offered a prayer. It is etched on my mind after all these years. She did not ask God for anything. But she thanked Him in advance for everything, including our hundred thousand subscribers. She quoted a passage of Scripture: "Whatsoever ye shall ask in prayer, believing, ye shall receive." (Matthew 21:22)

What happened? I looked over at those bills and they were still there. I guess I had expected the Lord to come down in some sweet chariot and carry them all away. But that isn't the Lord's method. When He wants to change a situation, He does not proceed in some magical fashion. His method is much more adroit and subtle. He changes people, and changed people change situations.

And that is precisely what happened in this instance. Our directors came alive and began to throw out ideas, one after the other. Of course some 90 percent of them were of no value. But 10 percent were very good ideas indeed. And as a result, those bills melted away.

In the early days of *Guideposts*, DeWitt Wallace of the *Reader's Digest* was fascinated with the notion of an interfaith publication telling true personal stories of spiritual experiences. He even said he wished he had thought of it himself. He helped in many ways, chiefly by asking the senior editor of the *Digest*, Fulton Oursler, to guide the struggling publication. This was an incredible benefit to a fledgling magazine. But that wasn't all, for Mr. Wallace generously made available stories of high quality that the *Digest* editors had not used. And frequently Mr. Wallace would select a *Guideposts* story for publication in the *Digest*. He did this so often that the name *Guideposts* began to be known. Indeed, he once sent me a letter from a subscriber who asked, "What in the hell is *Guideposts*?" But when the magazine passed the three-million-dollar mark in paid subscribers, I went again to DeWitt for help in something. But this time he said, "You are now strong enough to handle that on your own. You are a big magazine now."

After a shaky beginning over a grocery store in Pawling, we moved the magazine into a house on Quaker Hill owned by Lowell Thomas, which burned to the ground one Sunday afternoon. In a photo taken after the fire, the steeple of Christ Church on Quaker Hill rose majestically above the ashes, a portent of victorious things to come. The organization then moved into a larger house not far away, but soon it was not large enough.

One day I heard that the land and buildings of the Drew Seminary for young women at Carmel, New York, were for sale. Fred Dill, a prominent businessman of Carmel, was a member of the board of the defunct school and, with his help, *Guideposts* acquired a splendid property of fifty acres overlooking Lake Gleneida. A modern building was erected to house the business and outreach departments. The editorial department is located at 747 Third Avenue in New York City.

Throughout the history of *Guideposts,* Ruth and I have been editors-in-chief and publishers. I have served as its president and Ruth as executive vice-president. There have been four editors of the magazine over the course of its history: Grace Oursler for three and a half years, Leonard E. LeSourd for twenty-five years, Arthur Gordon for nine years, and Van Varner, since 1982. Under the editorial leadership of these brilliant people, *Guideposts* has had the most spectacular development in the history of religious publishing in the United States.

Since Ruth and I have a very heavy schedule, we asked Wendell Forbes to be our deputy publisher to coordinate all activities of the magazine. Mr. Forbes had been circulation director of *Life* magazine and was with Time, Inc. for twenty-five years. Skilled in publishing, circulation, and marketing, Mr. Forbes's opinion is widely sought throughout the magazine publishing industry. Under his extraordinary leadership, *Guideposts,* at this writing, has a monthly paid circulation of more than 4,700,000 and a readership every month exceeding 15,000,000. In the seven years of Mr. Forbes's administration, the circulation increased from 2,124,248, or a growth of 76 percent. It is currently the twelfth largest magazine of any kind from the standpoint of circulation in the United States. It is the most widely read religious inspirational magazine in the world. Mr. Forbes acknowledges that this amazing increase could only have been achieved by having an editorial product of superior quality. The outreach department under the inspired leadership of Bedford F. "Chuck" Lawley helps advance the Gospel in many ways and is vital to the magazine's aim of building up the spiritual life of America.

On an unforgettable day—Friday, February 18, 1983—Ruth and I attended a luncheon celebrating the attainment by *Guideposts* of four million paid subscribers.

As we stood on the platform observing the four hundred-plus happy employees who packed the ballroom of the Danbury Hilton Hotel, we were very deeply moved. My mind went back over many years to the publication's humble, even minuscule, beginnings. I recalled how *Guideposts* started with one paid employee (and not very much pay at that). She had a shaky old card table for a desk, a paper-box filing cabinet, and a second-hand typewriter in a cubbyhole of a room. It was always touch-and-go about paying the printer's bill, and it seemed there was a perpetual state of crisis. As Ruth and I stood there recalling those years, we agreed it was all a very great miracle.

Our computer had given us the name of the four millionth subscriber, Mrs. Vauncile Bell of Branford, Florida, a gracious lady, a schoolteacher, and a church worker in a village of 650 population. She was flown to New York as our honor guest. Mrs. Bell presented to Ruth and me on behalf of all the employees of *Guideposts* a gift of four cylinders set in wood and having a bronze plaque on its base; the cylinders contained the names of four million subscribers.

I told the assembled crowd that six words determine the success of any enterprise: "Find a need and fill it." "*Guideposts,*" I stated, "is doing just that—filling a need. Hence the spectacular response it has received." Ruth emphasized that it was God's blessing upon *Guideposts* that made it one of the phenomenal religious influences of our time.

Van Varner, our present editor, has been with us in an editorial capacity for some years. Actually we think of him as *Guideposts* personified. In his view the magazine is something very special, not so much a publication, but rather a life-style, vibrant faith in action.

To spend an hour with the editorial group over which Van presides is to savor a fellowship that enriches you greatly. Some think of *Guideposts* as a spiritual fellowship, national in scope. Perhaps that may account for its unprecedented growth.

Ruth and I feel that *Guideposts* and the Foundation for Christian Living are the major contributions we have been privileged to make. And, of course, through books also we have had an incredible opportunity to communicate the Gospel to millions of persons.

CHAPTER FOURTEEN

Exciting Family

EXCITEMENT, ENTHUSIASM, ENERGY! Like golden threads these three dynamic qualities have run through Ruth's family, the Staffords, and mine, the Peales. The Crosbys and the DeLaneys too, our mothers' families, were always an interested and enthusiastic lot of folk.

Mother's father, Andrew DeLaney, was raised by two maiden aunts in the village of Ballynakill in Ireland. But apparently the village was too small and perhaps too dull for young Andy, motivated as he was by dreams of far-off romantic places. One time he went to the seashore, and, standing on some rocky eminence, visualized himself on a ship sailing over the earth's horizon to the golden shores of America where hundreds of Irishmen had preceded him.

How could his dream be fulfilled? His loving but stern aunts would never allow him to set forth into the cold, unknown world. Then, lying in bed one night, a thought came, perhaps from his subconscious where it had been long incubating. Why not go away, steal off quietly on his own, with his few shillings in his pocket? The thought frightened yet exhilarated him, and he continued to nurture the dream, fascinated by it.

As a thought is always ancestor to a deed, there came a night

188

when, with his few belongings wrapped in a parcel, Andy crept on stocking feet down the cottage stairs. On the hall table he left a note telling his aunts that he just had to go, that voices were calling him, but that he would always love them. Next morning when they found the note, one aunt said, "Little Andy always had something special in him. We couldn't hold him here. But oh, how we shall miss his bright and happy spirit."

Meanwhile, Andrew was trudging the dusty road to Dublin, where he slipped aboard a packet, hiding from the officers, and presently found himself on the Liverpool docks. There he haunted the waterfront until finally he was able to stow away on a ship that he had learned was bound for America. Stowing away successfully was more difficult on this better-policed vessel. But Andy, a bright and personable Irish lad, had a way with him, and the motherly women passengers took a fancy to him and helped hide him. They also smuggled food to him so that he fared well on the long voyage across the North Atlantic. So when the ship arrived, he slipped among the crowd down the gangplank to the riverfront and onto the sidewalks of New York.

He had packages of food in the bag flung over his shoulder, and not a little money in his pocket given him by kindly people on the ship. Many had promised prayers and some offered to help him in his life in America. Years later he tried to repay his fare to the shipping company. Appreciating his honesty, someone at the company wrote him, saying the financial accounting of his voyage had long since been closed and wishing him well.

Andy's adventures are too many to record here, but in due course he arrived in Lynchburg, Ohio, where he was able to find employment. Years later he married a beautiful blue-eyed girl named Margaret Potts, descendant of a distinguished Pennsylvania family, one of whose members had been—so the story goes —an officer under General George Washington in the Revolutionary War. She made a Methodist of Andy, who became one of the leading citizens of Highland County, a sturdy, upright man of great integrity.

From childhood I faintly remember Andrew DeLaney as tall and stately, with a great head of white hair and a white beard. At his funeral in the crowded house of my uncle and aunt, Herschel and May Henderson, I was lifted up for a last look upon his face as he lay in his casket. The minister payed tribute to him as "one of the noblest Christian men this county ever had."

My grandfather Andrew still lives on in another; for on August 31, 1972, my daughter, Elizabeth Allen, gave birth to a beautiful baby boy who was named Andrew Peale Allen for Andrew DeLaney and his own grandfather.

My mother, Anna DeLaney Peale, had her dreams, too, and one of them was to go someday to Ireland to see her father's birthplace. So Ruth and I took her and my father to visit the old country. Mother had always told me that the DeLaneys were descended from the kings of Ireland. When we disembarked from the ship at Cork, the first thing I noticed was a building with the name in large letters across the front: "DeLaney's Saloon." My mother was a sworn enemy of alcohol; so pointing to the saloon, I said, "Must be one of your relatives," to which she snapped, "There's a black sheep in most every family."

Mother rode in jaunting carts along narrow romantic roads, visited ancient castles, and kissed the Blarney Stone. We spent some time at the lakes of Killarney, passed through Limerick, Kilkenny, and Tipperary. The lush green of Ireland and all the old names familiar from childhood thrilled her. How she loved it.

Then we came to Ballynakill, the small village of her father's birth. I went to the town hall to ask if we might see the records of births of the early 1800s and was told that all such records were kept at the Catholic church. There we found the priest was kind and helpful. He got out the old record of baptisms, and, sure enough, there was the name of Andrew DeLaney. As my mother looked at the clear but faded writing, she wept. The priest then took us to the home address given, and showed us the typical Irish cottage where the little lad was born and lived who in far-off Ohio became her father and my grandfather.

The Stafford family had its roots in England and later in Canada. Dr. Frank Stafford, an outstanding physician in Detroit, was the self-appointed historian of the family. Once, years ago, when I told him we were going to England, he insisted that we take a train to the village of Whisendine from which the first Staffords had emigrated to Canada and Michigan long years before.

Ruth and I spent most of a day brushing grass away from

tombstones in order to photograph the inscriptions to Stafford men and women who had lived good lives in the beautiful village. We felt that they must have bade a sad farewell to family members when they felt the urge to take up their lives and carry their traditions to the new world. We had tea that day with an elderly lady of the family in her picturesque home surrounded by a beautiful English garden.

The Peale family likewise traces its beginnings to England. Urged on by an advertising promoter who wanted to use it for some purpose, I employed a well-known genealogist, Mrs. Dickinson, to go into my family background.

It appears that at various times across the centuries the family name has been spelled Peel, Piel, Peele as well as Peale. There is a distant connection with Sir Robert Peel, originator of the London police force, called "bobbies" from Sir Robert's first name. His statue stands in Westminster Abbey.

Thomas Peale, or Squire Peale as he was called, was one of the early settlers in Lynchburg, Ohio, and has the most imposing monument in the older cemetery there. His sons, my grandfather Samuel Peale and his brother Wilson "Wilse" Peale operated a dry-goods store called Peale Brothers. They do not seem to have been go-getters, for my father told me how they liked to play checkers. One day during business hours they were engrossed in a game in the back room when a customer came into the store door and stood there waiting to be served. "Shush," whispered Wilse, "keep quiet. Maybe she will go away."

Samuel Peale was a four-year veteran of the Civil War, serving in an Ohio regiment that saw action at Antietam, Chancellorsville, Gettysburg, and many other famous battles.

Ruth's parents were Canadian; her mother, Loretta Crosby, was born in Markham, Ontario, and her father, Frank Burton Stafford, in Elora, Ontario. They lived for some time in Iowa and later in Detroit. Ruth was born in Fonda, Iowa, and has two brothers, Charles and William Stafford. Charles is a retired chamber of commerce executive, and William, a former professor at Penn State University. Her father, who died at eighty-one, lives in my memory as one of the finest men I have ever known. He was a white-haired stately gentleman whose inner spirit of love and strength of character were chiseled on his countenance. He served churches in Iowa and concluded his ministry in Detroit. Ruth's mother lived to eighty-eight years of age. She was a saintly woman, but had considerable strength and firmness when required. Her loving spirit endeared her to me and to all the family. Ruth's parents passed on a distinguished heritage to their children and grandchildren.

On my father's side, we are descended from a long line of Fultons, the name Robert Fulton appearing in every generation of the family. My grandmother was Laura Fulton and her father was Dr. Robert Fulton, one of the most prominent physicians in southern Ohio in his lifetime, and a pillar of the Methodist church; indeed he was a lay preacher. My parents had twins who died in infancy, a little girl named Anna Grace and a boy named Charles Fulton Peale. Genealogy traces our ancestry to Robert Fulton, inventor of the steamboat, whose body rests in Trinity churchyard in New York City. It has been said by some wag that Robert Fulton made lots of noise with his steamboat upriver on the Hudson, while his descendant Norman Vincent Peale made lots of noise in his pulpit downriver.

Our immediate family circle, Ruth's and mine, began one rainy evening, November 17, 1933, at 11:20 P.M., when our eldest daughter, Margaret, first saw the light of day, or more accurately the electric light, in the delivery room of Doctors Hospital in New York City. Mother Nature can be a little rough on an expectant father by keeping him alternately sitting in a hospital waiting room or pacing a corridor, nervously waiting for news from the front. When Ruth was wheeled away to the delivery room, she said in her usual composed manner, "Just sit here, Norman, and think about next Sunday's sermon. Everything will be fine." As she passed through some ominous-looking doors, I wondered if I would ever see her again.

In the waiting room there were several men biting their nails. However, one by one they received the good news, and suddenly they became jovial. After seeing their babies and their wives, they walked off jauntily, saying with an exasperating air, "Don't worry, old boy. Nothing to it. All is well. Good luck. See you next time." Finally about 8:30 P.M. only one man and I remained. Nine o'clock came, then half past nine, then ten o'clock. His lips moved. "I've just said my Jewish prayer," he explained.

"I've already said my Protestant one," I responded.

We sat on, talking; now and then we paced the hall together. He and I became friends by half past ten; brothers by eleven. Then came the nurse with a big smile on her face. We both leaped up expectantly. She came toward us, then grabbed his hands. "Congratulations. You have a wonderful baby daughter."

My friend was ecstatic. "Can I see her?" And the nurse led him off. I slumped down alone, my friend gone. Then he returned, jauntily, like the others. "I'm going out and celebrate. Good luck." And the elevator doors closed behind him. Now totally alone, I paced the corridor. Then suddenly that same nurse returned, a big smile heralding the good news. "You have a beautiful baby girl. Congratulations."

"May I have a look at her?" I stammered, overjoyed but still unnerved.

"You just come along with me, Daddy," she said, and I straightened up in pride. And there she was, vociferously crying.

"Good lungs," I commented. "Like her father," I added.

Then I asked, "Does she have ten fingers, ten toes, two ears, everything she is supposed to have?"

Assured that she was fully endowed, I went to join Ruth in that beautiful happiness young parents have together when a baby comes.

I went out into the misty night, driving home, stopping at an all-night luncheonette on Lexington Avenue. I could hardly contain myself. Ruth was fine, the baby was wonderful, and I, what do you know?, was a father.

Almost three years passed with baby Margaret in complete charge of the house. Then one lunch hour on September 2, 1936, while Ruth was washing the dishes and I was painting a kitchen chair for our newly acquired larger apartment, Ruth suddenly showed all kinds of disturbing symptoms and said, "Get the doctor on the phone." I dashed to comply, fouling up the action by dialing the wrong number, but finally I reached him. Whereupon Ruth took the receiver from my shaking fingers and calmly explained something about a water bag breaking. At her unhurried pace, I took her once again to a maternity ward, this time at the French Hospital on West Twenty-ninth Street, not far from my church. There Ruth sat up in bed, chipper as you please, even though she occasionally went into a paroxysm of pain that sent me scurrying for a nurse. Each time the spasm passed, Ruth said, "You don't ever seem to learn anything. You know nothing about having a baby." Sheepishly I admitted I had never had one.

When the doctor came, and to further underscore my uselessness, he said, "You aren't doing any good here. Go over to the church and work on your sermon for Sunday. When anything happens we will send for you." Glumly I walked along Twenty-ninth Street, grumbling, "This is the second time I've been told just to go off and work on a sermon." At 4:00 P.M. they called me to come back to the hospital. I rushed up to Ruth's room. No Ruth; the bed was empty. "Where is she?" I asked excitedly to the nurse who came in to straighten the room.

"Your wife?" she asked. "Oh, she is in the delivery room having a baby."

"But what about me?" I asked, pretty upset.

"Oh, you. What can you do? Just sit here and relax." And she paused at the door. "And maybe say a prayer." With a smile she was gone. Well, I did pray, that's for sure; but as for relaxing, well, that was a different matter.

After what seemed an interminable wait (although it was only about forty-five minutes), a nurse came in. "Well, sir, congratulations. You've got a fine baby boy." She was followed by a sister, this being a Catholic hospital. "You have a beautiful wife," she said. "When she was in labor, a big tear ran from her eye and lay like a pearl on her cheek. What a lovely mother that baby boy has." It was one of the most beautiful remarks I ever heard.

The little fellow was named John Stafford Peale. When sometime later he was baptized in the church by my father, he made the second issue of the old *Life* magazine. He was shown being baptized by his grandfather while held by his father. The caption over the picture was "Three Generations."

Thus I survived two births, but I wasn't through yet. Six years later a lady, shaking hands with me after a Sunday morning service, said, "Congratulations!" When she noticed my blank expression, she realized at once she had committed a faux pas and clapped her hand to her mouth, shocked. "Oh, no," she exclaimed, "don't you know?"

While mystified, I forgot the incident until after lunch when we were in our apartment and I remarked, "You know, Mrs.—— said a strange thing to me this morning. She congratulated me for something. I don't know what." Then I looked at Ruth, for she had a strange expression on her face.

"I hadn't told you, because you are so busy and you get so nervous and distressed. We are going to have another baby."

Aghast, I sank into a chair. "Oh, no," I gasped. "I just can't go through that again."

She patted me on the cheek. "Don't worry. I'll stay close to you. We will go through this together."

As the time drew near, we went to Canisteo, New York, where my father lived; he was then superintendent of the Hornell district of the Methodist Church. Canisteo is in Steuben County on the Pennsylvania border, seventy miles south of Rochester. Mother had passed away three years earlier, and Ruth moved us all to Canisteo each summer for the last three years in order to run the house and take care of my father. My brother Dr. Robert Clifford Peale lived in nearby Olean, New York, and agreed to deliver the baby. When birth seemed imminent, we went to Olean and occupied the home of my brother Rev. Leonard DeLaney Peale and his wife, Josephine. They say it never rains but it pours, and in this instance the old saying was literally true, for a tremendous flash flood struck Olean, flooding the streets to a considerable depth. Ruth was prepared to go to the Olean hospital in a rowboat, but the water receded just enough so that the bridge was opened. She took it all calmly. By early morning she knew "this was the day." She arose without waking me, finished some ironing, got breakfast, then called me. In early afternoon she went to the beauty parlor and about four o'clock, after consultation with my brother Bob, she checked into the hospital.

That evening while we were at early dinner in Bob's home, a call came that the birth was imminent. Bob departed for the hospital to deliver the baby, taking me along but telling me to sit in the waiting room, again putting me down with the dismissal "You can't do any good, so just sit and keep quiet." For once, however, he didn't tell me to work on my Sunday sermon, for it was summer, July 22, 1942, and I was on vacation.

The baby came at around 7:30 P.M., a lovely baby girl whom we named Elizabeth Ruth. As in the two previous births, Ruth took it all in stride, a healthy, normal mother. Bob, the doctor and the uncle of the baby, was also an enthusiastic photographer, and when she was one day old, he took Elizabeth's picture. This photograph shows the baby holding up her right hand with the two first fingers in the V-for-Victory sign, popularized just then by Winston Churchill. Elizabeth came into the world a natural-born positive thinker and has been one ever since.

From the beginning ours has been a closely knit family. We love each other. We like to be together. We have fun. Our house was always filled with excitement. Everyone was busy and into things. All were involved, to employ an overly used word, in things of interest to every member of the family. Dinner was an exciting babble of conversation and discussion, even argument. Very little of the table talk ever had to do with personalities, or trivia, or the food we were eating. The latter was always good, for it was cooked by Alice Brown, a Jamaican lady with an English accent, one of the loveliest, kindest, sweetest people the Lord ever made. She was with us, dearly beloved by all, for more than twenty-five years. The conversation raced on, the good food was enjoyed, and we had the time of our lives.

Sometimes I would bring home a problem that someone had presented in a counseling session. No names were ever mentioned, of course, but I would outline the problem and ask advice from the family, who would go at it wholeheartedly but compassionately. Often I was amazed at the children's insights, and many times solutions and answers would emerge from those dinner discussions.

When the children were little, and even up to their teenage years, they used to get after me for an original story. I made them up as I went along, and never have I had such an audience. The children would hang on every word, and if I happened to repeat one and it was not done precisely as it had been the first time, they would loudly call my attention to the incorrect detail and demand that it be corrected. If I could not remember a detail, someone would always straighten me out.

One of my make-it-up-on-the-minute stories was a series called "Larry, Harry, Perry, and Their Magic Airplane": Three boys had an airplane that could be carried in a pocket. After a few mysterious and magic words were mumbled, it would grow immediately to whatever size was required. Then the three boys would take off quickly to any designated place in the world.

To vary the storytelling, I invented another series called, for some reason I cannot for the life of me explain, "Jake the Snake" and his brother, "Hake the Snake." I never liked those reptilian stories quite as much as the stories about "Larry, Harry, Perry, and Their Magic Airplane," but apparently the three children enjoyed both. Now my grandchildren clamor for the same stories. There must have been several hundred chapters of these "masterpieces" for children.

We always say a blessing at the table, and it was a custom for our children to be prepared when called upon to offer prayer. Now that they have their own homes, the same practice is followed. Our children not only attended Sunday School but church as well, sitting with their mother in a pew with a silver plate inscribed "Pastors" on it. At one stage they rebelled against this pew, which they claimed gave them more attention than they wanted. So their mother told them they could sit wherever they chose. John sat in the east balcony, Margaret in the south balcony, and Elizabeth was almost directly above me and to the left of the pulpit at the front end of the north balcony. All these locations were probably the most prominent in the church.

It became my habit after entering the pulpit, looking as dignified as I could manage, to sit down, then look up at Elizabeth in the balcony. She would give me a big smile, which I would return in full measure. This, I subsequently learned, caused the congregation considerable enjoyment. Once I noticed that I was losing the attention of the congregation, all of whom seemed to be looking toward the south balcony where Margaret was completely wrapped up in the effort to mimic my gestures—raising her arms, pointing, repeating every motion I was making. "It was," as John said later, "a riot." Finally the children all came back to the Pastors pew.

In the family pew Ruth sat on the aisle, the children strung out on her left. Then John went off to be a student at Deerfield Academy. The first Sunday he came back, Ruth was already seated in her accustomed place at the end of the pew when John walked masterfully down the aisle and signaled to his mother to move over. Thereafter, when home, he took the end seat. Perhaps feminists wouldn't think it was funny, but Ruth liked it.

John graduated from Deerfield, then from Washington and Lee University. He went on to study philosophy at Boston University and at the University of Chicago. He received his Ph.D. from the University of North Carolina at Chapel Hill. Between times he spent three years at Union Theological Seminary in New York City and graduated with a Bachelor of Divinity degree. It was at this time that *The Power of Positive Thinking* was "breaking all book sales records" and some liberal ministers were becoming quite aggressive in their attacks on me. As a student at the seminary, John frequently had to listen to professors or students take me apart, sneering at me as the apostle of something supposedly onerous they called "Pealism." John's controlled emotional mechanism held steady under what must surely have been a profound embarrassment. It did not seemingly cause any trauma, or affect our relationship, which has ever been one of love, trust, and mutual respect. I always admired John's inner strength and inner peace, for he could listen to hostile criticism of his father and at the same time maintain a pleasant relationship with professors and students as well as with me.

We have always endeavored to keep a travel fund with which to visit interesting, instructional, and inspiring places around the world. It has been our opinion that directed travel would help our children to become good citizens not only of their country but of the whole world as well. However, before we started a program of overseas travel, we wanted them to see the United States. Therefore, one of our first family trips was to the national parks out West: Yellowstone, Yosemite, Grand Canyon, and others. And, of course, in those days travel was by train.

There being five of us, we reserved accommodations in which a Pullman bedroom, sleeping two, and a compartment having three beds could be opened into one area. As night came on, the porter made up the five beds perfectly, without a wrinkle. But before going to bed, the children had to have what they called their evening exercise. This consisted of swinging on the top bars and leaping from bed to bed, and was accompanied by pillow fights and shouts of joy. When breathlessly they called it quits, the beds were a shambles. It was their job then to make up their own beds and ours, too. My feet would detect many a wrinkle, but I didn't mind, for we were adventuring together as a family and having lots of fun. Those nights on the train from coast to coast have become a long and happy memory.

Then there was that unforgettable trip on the Canadian Pacific Railroad when all day long the train took us through the Rocky Mountains, up long grades, around curves, and over trestles. There was an open roofless observation car at the rear of the train, it was like being right outdoors, among some of the most majestic mountain scenery in the world. Elizabeth had the habit of slipping off her loafers and wiggling her toes. One time, as the train whipped around a curve, one shoe slid off the train and went bouncing down a steep mountainside to land in a gully far below. Elizabeth was inconsolable, not because she had lost a shoe, but because the shoe would "be lonesome and frightened out there in those dark mountains all alone at night." When she went to bed in Vancouver that night, Elizabeth cried about the lost shoe, so I said a prayer asking our Heavenly Father to watch over it as well as every one of us. After that she went to sleep. But the shoe that was lost amidst the Canadian Rockies remains a tender tradition in our family.

Then came the question of marriage. That their children marry the right person with whom they may live always in happy companionship is a concern to parents. Mrs. Daniel A. Poling, whose twelve children all married very well, had a creative idea: If one of them became enamored of someone who didn't seem right, she persuaded that child to bring the friend home to stay for a week. Before the week was up he or she would sense deficiencies, if any, and incompatibility, if any, and the budding romance would wither on the vine. If, however, the person was all right, that would also manifest itself.

Our son, John, had new girls regularly, and each "the greatest." He couldn't live without being with this one or that one, he would tell us fervently. Once, we were going to Europe as a family, and John refused to go unless a girl from out West could go along. She was able to pay her way and was with us every day from morning until night. This constant proximity and presence in the family effectively revealed the flaws in that romance.

Then one night I went to Boston to give a speech and had dinner with John and his latest "greatest." This one really struck me. "Bring her home for a holiday," I said. He did, over Thanksgiving, a family day. I knew we would all love her. The more John spent time with her in the family, the more convinced he was that she was the girl—and for sure. "Don't let this one get away," I told him and he didn't. Lydia is the daughter of the late Reverend Dr. Edgar Woods and his wife, Lydia. John's Lydia was born when her parents were missionaries in China. Edgar and I officiated at John and Lydia's marriage in the beautiful Rivermont Presbyterian Church, Lynchburg, Virginia. John is Professor of Philosophy at Longwood College, Farmville, Virginia, and Lydia is an English teacher at Prince Edward County High School, where she also helps coordinate a program for gifted students. John and Lydia have three children, Laura, Clifford, and Lacy.

Margaret graduated from Friends Seminary, a private Quaker school in New York, and was Phi Beta Kappa at Ohio Wesleyan University. Once, when I stopped off on a speaking trip to see her, she asked me how she would know when she was in love. "Well," I said, "as you know, I'm no 'Dear Abby,' but I would say that when the relationship is compatible and exciting, and you just can't wait for the other person to appear, like I can't wait to hear your mother's footsteps returning when she has been out, then it's pretty surely the real thing. But it's always wise to pray about such a relationship to be sure it's right; for if it isn't right, it's wrong and nothing wrong ever turns out right."

Well, she found him, and right in Marble Collegiate Church, a personable, highly capable young man who had a top buyer's job at Macy's. He got involved with our young adults group, had a deeply spiritual life-changing experience, gave up his well-paying position, graduated from Princeton Theological Seminary, and became an ordained Presbyterian minister. Margaret married Paul F. Everett in our church, and so popular were these young people that there was standing room only at the wedding. Paul heads the Pittsburgh Experiment, a religious fellowship of businessmen and women which is established now in many cities. They have two children, Jennifer and Christopher.

One Sunday my wife happened to be away and I had made an

appointment to see an editor from the *Reader's Digest* in my office after church. So I pressed Elizabeth into service. "Honey," I said, "I have this young man coming to see me on business. He says he is coming to the church service. Ordinarily your mother would take care of him. How about pinch-hitting for her. Will you take care of him until I can see him after church?" Elizabeth is always efficient. She took such good care of him that they were married a year later, and they have three children, Rebecca, Katheryn, and Andrew. And to our rare good fortune they live only a half mile up the road from us on Quaker Hill. John Allen, who grew up in Scarsdale, New York, is at the *Reader's Digest,* where he is vice-president for corporate and public affairs, U.S.A. John and Elizabeth are leaders in church and community affairs.

On a wild and wintry night years ago, I was going to visit my parents in upstate New York on an old Erie Railroad train. As I was talking casually with a fellow passenger, he asked, "Where are you headed tonight?"

"I'm getting off at Hornell to spend the night with my mother and father who live in nearby Canisteo," I replied.

The man sat silent for what seemed a long time. Then he said, "I hope you are thankful that you can spend a night with your mother and father. You see, I can't do that. My parents are gone from this world. So, my friend, be glad that you can be at home with your mother and your father, particularly on an old-fashioned winter night like this."

The snow lay deep in the fields. But the road had been cleared, for they know how to handle heavy snow upstate. I arrived in Canisteo at my parents' home, a white house with white pillars on a hill. Every window was ablaze with light because one of their sons was coming home that night.

I sat with my parents in front of a big open fire. We drank cider and ate doughnuts and talked about everything until one o'clock in the morning. By then the storm had ceased and the moon was shining on the snow, which lay inches deep on the ground. Mother and Father came into my room. She kissed me good-night like she did when I was a child. Dad punched me in the chest and said that they were glad to have me there. Both had tears in their eyes as did I.

I cannot make such a visit anymore, for they have both gone on to the other side, but I am thankful I can still remember that night I spent with them long ago, experiencing the deep, wonderful, fundamental values of love. A happy, loving, and exciting family is surely the dearest of all human relationships.

CHAPTER FIFTEEN

Friends and Acquaintances

ONE SPRING MORNING in late April, I spoke to a convention of the drug industry at the Greenbrier Hotel in White Sulphur Springs, West Virginia. Afterward Ruth and I took a drive among the hills and at a crossroad, became intrigued by a little road meandering off whose weatherbeaten sign read: "Sunshine Valley."

"Shall we go down Sunshine Valley?" I asked.

"Yes, let's," said Ruth. And I am glad we did, for it was there that we encountered Tommy Martin.

We came to a small bridge, under which surged a mountain stream washing over rocks and murmuring on its way through a meadow. We parked the car and walked upstream through the woods. There we came upon a boy, dressed in old jeans rolled up above high boots. On his head was a very ancient sloppy hat with holes in it. His checkered shirt was open at the neck, and he was chewing gum mightily, puffing it out in huge bubbles.

He fixed a level brown-eyed gaze on us and said nonchalantly, "Hi. Where's your fishing pole?" I had to admit that I had none. "O.K.," he replied, "I'll fish for all of us."

"Are you using lures?" I asked.

"Nope. Just plain old worms." So saying, he pulled out of the water a beautiful trout, which he held up for us to admire. "Put it on a stick," he said, tossing it to me. I was a bit nonplussed but complied as best I knew how.

"What's your name?" I asked.

"Tommy Martin," he replied, then added, "My father shot a deer in these woods last fall." In this statement, I had a touching vignette of the comradeship of a son and his father.

"Shouldn't you be in school, Tommy?" I asked with adult stupidity. I got a vague, inconclusive answer and was sorry I had asked. But after all, it was Thursday.

So the three of us fished together, Ruth and I accepted as friends by this ingenuous country lad. It happened that at the time I was preparing a talk on "How to Stop Worrying." So I asked, "Tommy, do you ever worry?" As he chewed his gum and put another worm on his hook, he fixed his clear, honest eyes on me and in his mountain drawl, replied, "Shucks, no. Ain't nothin' to worry about."

Well, Tommy Martin would now be close on to forty years of age. I never saw him again. But often since that April day, I have thought of that clean, natural, appealing boy and have wondered if he is still the same. I've also wondered if he had any idea of what he did for those two city folk who met him one day, long ago, up Sunshine Valley.

My life has been enriched by the people I have met through the years. Some have been prominent persons, others not so well known. Some are living, others have departed this world. All have added immeasurably to my total experience and have been an important source of inspiration in life.

I have been speaking to business audiences for many years and as has been stated, have probably addressed as many national conventions as anyone: realtors' conventions, national insurance meetings, and, indeed, every sort of business. I am sometimes asked to speak at conventions when my knowledge of the activities involved is limited. However, I am in the "people business." All industries are operated by human beings, and I have dedicated my life to a study of people and to trying to help them as persons. So when speaking at a convention, I address the message to each man and woman present.

In recent years a kind of meeting has developed known as a motivational or success rally, which are usually attended by big crowds. One of the largest of such rallies was in Minneapolis, where more than seventeen thousand people packed a giant arena with an overflow crowd. I have had the pleasure of appearing with some of the outstanding motivational speakers in our country. Notable among them are Art Linkletter, Paul Harvey, Zig Ziglar, Earl Nightingale, Cavett Robert, Ira Hayes, and others —all of them are some of the greatest inspirational speakers of our time. Other exceptional speakers with whom I have shared platforms are Millard Bennett, who is always popular; Jennings Randolph, distinguished United States Senator from West Virginia; Kenneth McFarland, and many more.

Traveling throughout the country, I have of course encountered thousands of people. People are fascinating, wonderful, and they have made my life exciting.

Sometimes it is only a casual encounter as the one I experienced one day in an airport waiting area when a mother and child attracted my attention. The child, a little black boy, was one of the most beautiful youngsters I had ever seen. The mother was a handsome young woman, but the scowl on her face gave her a rather mean look, and I thought she was a bit cruel to her little boy. She slapped him hard on the face a time or two, although he wasn't doing anything that I wouldn't have done at his age (which of course isn't saying much). Finally, hesitantly, not knowing whether to do it or not, but charmed by the child, I said, "Ma'am, I beg your pardon, but may I say something to you?"

"Why, yes," she said, surprised.

"I have seen thousands of children but that little boy of yours is someone special. He is a prize. He is one of the most beautiful children I have ever seen. And I just cannot resist complimenting you, for he is really wonderful."

"Yeah, I guess he is," she replied. "He takes after his father, who is a very handsome man." And then she smiled and it illuminated her face.

"But," I said, "he has your smile. With his father's looks and your wonderful smile just think what he is going to be."

"Now, sir," she said, "I appreciate what you are saying, but you know you are not telling the truth, for you can see that I am a mean-looking woman."

"But your smile . . ." I countered.

She picked up the youngster and made ready to go to her plane, saying, "You are a kindhearted man. I get the message." And the mother and son were gone.

I performed the wedding ceremony of Governor John Y. Brown of Kentucky and his lovely wife, Phyllis, a former Miss America and a charming and talented young woman. One day when their baby boy, Lincoln, was only some weeks old I received a telephone call from John and Phyllis that the baby had some obstruction and surgery was required. They were just about to take Lincoln to the hospital, but wanted to put him into God's loving and healing hands with prayer. So over the telephone I prayed the prayer of the "two or three" with the Governor and First Lady of Kentucky. As the Scripture tells us, "Where two or three are gathered together in my name; there am I in the midst of them." We were three and we asked that He grant healing for the little boy.

The thought came to me that in such a crisis, wealth, power, honor, prestige meant nothing. Only the grace and love of God could be depended on in that anxious hour in the lives of a believing mother and father. When, some months later at their hilltop home in the Kentucky bluegrass country, I held their rugged and vigorous boy on my knee, I was truly moved by the way God grants His blessings to those who trust Him. Later they brought Lincoln back to my church for baptism.

Governor Brown told me of the final tribute paid to a rare and remarkable character, Colonel Harland Sanders, founder of Kentucky Fried Chicken, the nationwide franchise business. At Governor Brown's suggestion, the funeral service for the colonel was held in the statehouse at Frankfort. Clad in his white suit, the great old Christian and famous Kentuckian lay in his casket in the rotunda. A huge crowd filled all available space, including the encircling balconies all the way to the dome. The governor and Phyllis each gave a tribute. A pastor spoke the words of faith, read the Bible, and offered prayer. Christian hymns were sung. Then the service concluded with the entire throng singing "My Old

Kentucky Home." "John," I said to the governor, "the colonel would have loved that."

"I thought he would. And we all loved him," he replied.

In earlier years Colonel Sanders had operated a restaurant in a little town. He did a modest business until the highway was rerouted. This put the restaurant on a secondary road with reduced traffic; so presently the restaurant went out of business. To make matters worse, he was then sixty-five years old. How can one begin again at sixty-five? At such an age most people retire. It would seem life was running down, but actually the circumstances were readying this man for one of the most spectacular careers in American business.

He was sitting on his porch in a rocking chair when the mailman came up the walk and handed him an envelope. In it was a check for $157, the first payment of his social security. The United States government was now his sole support.

He rocked back and forth in the chair and finally said to himself, "I don't like this. Here I am being dependent on the government for a social security payment." So, rocking in his chair, he started to pray and to think—incidentally, an effective combination. He remembered the delicious fried chicken his mother always made. Colonel Sanders was the oldest of a large family, and since his father was deceased, his mother had to go to work in the mill. She would get breakfast for the kids and leave him, the oldest boy, to handle other meals. And in so doing, he learned his mother's formula for fried chicken. So he thought, "Wonder if I could do something with Mother's fried chicken recipe?"

He set out in his battered old car, calling on restaurants in an effort to franchise his fried chicken formula. But nowhere was he able to sell it until he persuaded a restaurant proprietor in Salt Lake City to accept his proposition. He went on to make a great success of it, and hundreds of other people profited from that success.

The colonel always wore a white suit and black string tie.

I was with him one day in Montreal when a girl came up to me and said in astonishment, "That man looks like Colonel Sanders."

"It is indeed the colonel," I said.

"You mean he is really alive?"

"Yes, very much alive."

"Well," she said, "I thought he was a statue that stood around in Kentucky Fried Chicken shops."

"No, he is not a statue but one of the most creative men in business," I assured her.

He often worshiped in my church, and I had the pleasure of conferring upon him the Horatio Alger Award for achievement.

Some years ago Lucille Ball married Gary Morton at Marble Collegiate. I was speaking to Gary and Lucy before the wedding and commenting on Lucy's vitality and excitability, and asked, "When Lucy takes off and heads for the ceiling, how are you going to handle the situation?"

To which Gary replied calmly, "Oh, I'll just wait until she comes back down again."

Lucy said, "Humph!"

Lucille Ball came from Jamestown, New York. One May day in Los Angeles I was talking with her and she stated wistfully, "It's lilac time back in New York. Smell them for me, won't you?" Spoken like a true New York Stater. This extraordinary, talented woman has a deep religious feeling that has sustained her in the many trials of life. Her humor is of course proverbial. One evening when Ruth and I were having dinner at her home, a maid came in and said, "Mrs. Morton, Father Flanagan is on the phone and wants to speak to you."

Quick as a flash Lucy quipped, "Tell him to call tomorrow. This is Protestant night." Lucy is always interested and interesting, very dynamic, eager, a true positive thinker. She is also unusually sensitive. One day in my office she started crying as I talked about her success from a poor girl in Jamestown to the heights of popularity.

"Why in the world are you crying?" I asked.

"I'm afraid my success won't last."

"Oh, yes, it will," I replied, "and one reason is that your humility will always motivate you to keep on being your best and"—I added—"that best of Lucy Ball's is superbest."

The famous Olympic track champion Jesse Owens, one of the immortals of American athletic history, once told me an unforgettable story. We were sitting together at the head table at a dinner in Columbus, Ohio, where he and I, Lowell Thomas, Cardinal Kroll, and several others were each to be given an award by Governor Rhodes called, believe it or not, the "All-Time Great Ohioan Award." This was during the celebration of the bicentennial year in 1976. I had read an article praising Jesse Owens as one of the few truly great athletes in American history. Modestly he disclaimed this tribute when I referred to it in our table chat. "But," I asked, "how did you become the supergreat Jesse Owens?" He seemed in the mood to talk, since as a once poverty-stricken kid, he was now receiving an award as an all-time great of his state.

Born poor, Jesse was also quite frail and skinny, not at all rugged. His mother, a devout Christian, was a positive person, and she told her son that he was to become "a somebody."

"But how, Mama? I'm just a little fellow and poor and black."

"Never talk that way, son. God made you and He loves you and if you believe and follow our dear Lord Jesus Christ, you will make your old mother's heart glad."

One day in school there was an assembly of students to listen to a talk by a great athlete named Charlie Paddock, hailed by sports writers as "the fastest man alive." Paddock was going around to schools with the avowed object of "motivating kids." Jesse, sitting down front, told me that Paddock came onstage, rammed his hands into his hip pockets, looked the crowd over, while a dead silence ensued. Then he asked, "Do you know who you are? Well, I'm here to tell you. You are children of God. You are Americans and you have it in you to become what you want to be if you know what that is, if you will form a goal, if you believe in that goal and in yourself, if you work and never give up. If you trust God all the way, you can be what you want to be; and that is the plain truth about every one of you."

These remarks burned into young Jesse's mind, and in that instant he knew precisely what he wanted to be. Indeed, he saw an image of himself as being just that. He could scarcely wait until Paddock finished speaking. He rushed up, grabbed Paddock's hand, and as he told me later, "An electric shock or some kind of impulse passed from him into me. I could feel it all the way from my head to my feet." Jesse then ran into the gymnasium to the coach, exclaiming, "Coach, I've got a dream. I'm going to be the next Charlie Paddock. I'm going to be the fastest man alive."

The coach, a wise and kindly man, put his arm around the shoulder of the slight, skinny kid. "That's right, Jesse; have a dream. You can never go higher than you can dream. But you can go as high as you can dream." Then the coach added, "But you will have to climb a ladder to your dreams and it can be steep and hard going. And on that ladder to your dream are four rungs: the first is determination; the second, dedication; the third, discipline; and the fourth rung is attitude."

The coach discoursed on the importance of each rung, but stressed the extra importance of attitude. "Your attitude toward your goal, toward yourself, toward life, and toward the Lord God Almighty will determine whether or not your dream will come true."

The little boy responded in full measure, and so came the day at the Berlin Olympic Games when he won four gold medals, running the 100-meter dash and 200-meter dash faster than any human being of record. His broad-jump record achieved that day was not equaled for twenty-four years. And when the American Hall of Athletic Fame was established, high on the list of American sports immortals was the name of Jesse Owens.

Later that evening in Columbus when Owens acknowledged the "All-Time Great Ohioan Award" before that big audience, he said impressively, "When I came home from Berlin, I put those medals in Mama's hands and together we thanked that Man, the Lord Jesus, for all He had done for us." A few years later when Jesse Owens died, flags were at half-staff to honor the memory of a great Christian and a great American. I have often related this story as an example of what a person can do in life to counteract the pernicious mental negative attitude which comprises what I call the three Ls—lack, loss, and limitation. A positive attitude may not take all of us to Jesse Owen's level of success, but it can lift us to heights we would not otherwise attain.

A lovely, sensitive, and intelligent Swiss girl named Ursula von Aesch (later Stingelin) lived with us for three years and added much to our family life. Then she went back to Switzerland. When we first met her in Switzerland, Ursula wanted to come to the

United States to learn English. We liked her right off, but I wanted to know whether she could cook.

I have always liked Swiss cooking, so I asked her in my very limited German, *"Der wiener schnitzel und der spaetzle und der rustig potatoes—machen Sie sehr gut?"*

"Oh," she replied with a big smile, *"ja, ja."*

I said, *"Ja, ja,* we're in."

So Ursula came to live with us and cooked the most delicious meals. She presided over our household so Ruth could be free for her many activities. She came to mean a great deal to us.

At Christmastime a lot of people send us gifts, sometimes they are from people we do not even know. They are not expensive presents, just loving thoughts, many handmade, and we are very grateful. We gave Ursula the responsibility for opening these presents and keeping a list of who sent each gift and all the details of what it was. She was impressed by so many packages, and she didn't know what to give us for Christmas. Apparently the flood of presents confused her. So, on Christmas Eve she went to a store nearby on Lexington Avenue and bought a beautiful little baby dress. She didn't have much money, but she wanted it to be a beautiful dress. Ursula asked the salesperson to wrap it in colorful paper. Then she went out into the street and started looking for a home of a very poor family with a little baby to whom she could give the present. She went up to one of those resplendent majordomos known as doormen and said, "Please, Herr doorman, where can I find a poor street?"

"What's that, Miss?"

"I want to find a poor street where poor people live."

"Well," he said, "maybe you should go down to the Lower East Side or way uptown." And he named some other locations. But she had never heard of any of those places, and she wouldn't have known how to get to them if she had.

So she walked on down the street. It was bitter cold, and she was fighting the wind and swirling snow. Suddenly, in the midst of the traffic noise, she heard the tinkling of a bell: a Salvation Army man. This was familiar. Back home they also had Salvation Army men on the streets. So she went up to him and said, "Herr Salvation Army man, where can I find a poor baby in a poor street?" She said that she had heard of poverty sections of New

York, but she was on Park Avenue now, and it didn't look all that bad. Then she asked, "Where is there such a place?"

"Why do you want to find a baby of a poor family?" he asked.

"I want to give a poor baby this little dress," Ursula replied.

"Well," the man said, impressed by her sweet sincerity, "I will be off duty in a few minutes. As soon as my relief man comes, I will take you. I know many poor families who have children with no nice dresses."

So they got into a taxi, and as they drove along Ursula told him all about why she wanted to do this, and he listened attentively and the taxi driver listened also. They finally came to a poverty-stricken section. She looked at one of the bleak houses, and the taxi driver said, "Take your time, Miss, I'll be waiting for you here. Don't you worry." She went with the Salvation Army man and gave a nice young mother the beautiful dress. The mother opened the package, burst into tears, and said to Ursula, "Why did you do this?"

"It's a gift not only to you, but it's also a gift to a family in Manhattan with whom I live." (On Christmas morning she told us this story and said, "That is my Christmas present to you.")

Ursula got into the taxi and was driven back to our apartment. When the taxi stopped at the door, she fumbled in her purse for some money. But the taxi driver said, "No charge, Miss. You've paid me like I've never been paid before. You're a sweet girl. Merry Christmas." And off he drove.

Lowell Thomas owed the charm of his personality in part, at least, to his unusual way of doing things, to his innovative unpredictability.

One day when I was in Los Angeles on a speaking engagement, my hotel room telephone rang. Lowell, who was also in that city, had learned I was there. He told me he was toastmaster for a big dinner that evening of the Screen Producers Guild, and most of the famous motion-picture personalities would be there. He said, "I don't know what you're doing, but you've got to show up around ten o'clock. I'll have a seat for you. Just ask about it at the door."

I demurred, but he wouldn't take no for an answer; and so late in the evening I was shown to a seat at a table in the middle of the audience alongside the famous columnist Louella Parsons. No one else knew me. Then from the podium Lowell said, "I've always thought it would be interesting to try an experiment at a banquet like this. My theory has always been that the most eloquent, most interesting speakers are not at the head table but somewhere down in the audience." Lowell always chuckled as he told this story. "You should have seen the faces of the dinner committee. Their jaws dropped."

Then he appeared to be looking over the big audience speculatively and pointed a finger at me. "You there by Louella Parsons, that fellow with a face like a moon, partly bald, who looks like he might be the head of the chamber of commerce. You come on up here and make a speech and prove my point." Thus singled out and embarrassed beyond words, I ambled up to the head table. "Give them two or three of your knockout stories," he whispered.

I couldn't let my old friend down, so I tried to do my best to please him. Later he told about it. "Norman did a thing that is very clever in winning an audience. He began by stuttering. And if a speaker does that, he immediately wins sympathy—oh poor fellow. After a little bit of stammering, Norman swung into his act and absolutely rocked the place. They just cheered and cheered." Actually he exaggerated, but out of the bigness of his heart Lowell always exaggerated about his friends. He had other emcee tricks which he pulled from time to time, but he always seemed particularly to enjoy this one.

I knew Lowell for fifty years as friend and neighbor on Quaker Hill. He was a truly great human being, one of the most remarkable men of our time. Once at a dinner party he asked me across the table, "Norman, where is your next speaking engagement?" Knowing him as I did, I realized he really wasn't all that interested in my engagements, but wanted me to ask him where he was speaking, which I proceeded to do. Whereupon he discoursed at length on his experiences on the lecture platform, enthralling the guests with story after story of his adventurous career in all areas of the world.

As the dinner party broke up, one man said to me, "I've heard him tell all those stories before."

"And so have I," was my response. "But you and I are privileged to hear them from one of the greatest Americans of our time." Came the day when I gave the eulogy at his funeral in New York, as he had left a request that I do, concluding with "And so, Lowell, we shall miss you here until we meet again over there. It is not good-bye, but in your own words, 'So long until tomorrow.' "

As I think about it, how fortunate I have been in my lifetime to know and count as friends so many interesting people. Some have been well-known and famous, while others have walked in the quieter ways of life. John Imre manages our Hill Farm on Quaker Hill in Pawling. He and his wife, Maria, escaped from Hungary when the Communists seized control in that country. The Imres walked all the way from Budapest to Vienna, sleeping in haystacks along the way, proceeding determinedly to freedom. A Catholic organization helped them get to America, and John has been with us for many years, more like a son than an employee. He has the courtly manner of the old Europe, kissing Ruth's hand when we return from a long absence. He will nurse a plant or a tree as long as it shows the slightest sign of life. He tries to hide his kindliness, but it shows through. He is a loyal American and shakes his head when he talks about some things going on in this country that remind him of the Communist takeover from which he and his wife fled years ago. He watches over us with affectionate concern. And Maria's Hungarian-style cooking is out of this world.

Knowing people, admiring and loving them, learning what makes them what they are have been a large part of my education and of my motivation as well. Tennyson in his poem "Ulysses" said, "I am a part of all that I have met." How right he was. For my part I like to add that all I have met are part of me, too. The mountains and the sea, the sky and the changing seasons, dawn and sunset are all thrilling and contribute to our lives; but it is people who mold us, beginning with our families and including friends and acquaintances. They can inspire, turn us on or off, depress or excite us. And I have found that if one looks for the best in every person, the best will reveal itself. Every human being has a story rich in drama, humor, pathos, greatness, and perhaps tragedy. Perhaps someday I will catalogue all the thrilling individuals I have met across the years. But how could such a book ever be completed, for I'm still meeting interesting people every day.

Indeed, I met one recently after making a speech. I never eat before speaking; so following the talk, I perched on a stool at a lunch counter behind which stood the proprietor with a clean white apron draped around his ample middle. A tall white chef's hat was perched rakishly on the southeast corner of his head. "What will you have, brother?" he asked with a big smile.

"Please give me a dish of Jell-O without whipped cream and a cup of black coffee."

Putting his hands flat on the counter, he asked, "Why?"

"Well, to be frank I don't really know why except I'm trying to take off a few pounds." Whereupon he picked up a beautiful pie.

"Just look at that pie," he said admiringly. "It's a work of art." Twirling it deftly around, "Did you ever see anything to equal it? And it's made of good old New York State apples, the finest in the world." And to give a final touch, he added, "They're sprinkled with cinnamon." So saying, he cut me a sizable wedge and laid a piece of what he called "luscious New York State cheese" over it. Then he expertly slid a big steaming cup of black coffee to a stop besides the pie. "Refresh your soul on that," he said.

I looked at him with admiration. "You," I declared, "are a philosopher, a connoisseur, and a poet." I forgot all about the Jell-O.

There is another man I think of sometimes as being one of the last of a great breed of Americans. Although actually there will never be the last, for there is something in the very air of America that will continue to turn out that kind of human being forever. The man I have in mind is the late Justin Dart of Dart Industries, Inc. I saw a story in a Washington paper in which he was referred to as a "crusty tycoon." The story was designed to be complimentary, but Justin only talked crusty occasionally, and usually he was quite right in doing so. He really had a heart as big as all outdoors. He was a rugged, admirable human being who had convictions and defended his beliefs against all comers. In my book he was usually right in his beliefs about God and country. He never wanted political office, not even an appointive one from his friend

Ronald Reagan. Once when a quick, devastating fire swept through the canyons and over the hilltops of the Los Angeles area, his house was destroyed. Hearing of it, I telephoned him. His reaction: "Oh, don't you worry about that. Jane and the children are safe. Only wood and furniture have gone up in flames. It was only a house. We can build another." Long afterward he told me that one of the few things saved from the fire was a copy of *The Power of Positive Thinking* because he had loaned it to a friend who had not yet returned it. But he did not need that book, for no man I've ever known had a more solid faith in God and a more positive attitude than Justin Dart.

When Justin was a student at Northwestern University, he was a guard on the football team. On an October day between halves of a game, the coach gave the team a vigorous talk, then dismissed the squad to go back on the field for the second half. As they started out, the coach called, "Wait a minute, Dart. I want to say something to you." The coach hesitated a moment, then put it to him straight. "If you realize your potential, you can be the greatest guard Northwestern ever had. Now go out there and be great, running tall." Justin says he squared his shoulders, lifted his head high, and dashed out to the field. And I might add he lived the rest of his life "running tall."

CHAPTER SIXTEEN

I Found That Prayer Works

IN A LIFETIME of positive thinking and positive living, one of my greatest discoveries is that prayer is not a fanciful procedure. It actually and definitely works. It is real. It is an amazing power available to everyone. Always it has been an important factor in my life, guiding and supporting me in decisions and crises across the years.

One of the greatest insights about prayer was given me by my wife, Ruth. She said, "Prayer is answered in three ways—yes, no, or wait awhile." I have had yes answers and no answers and delayed answers. But there has always been an answer, and in each case it has proved to be right, whether negative, "wait awhile," or positive.

Elsewhere in this book I explained how self-conscious I have been when about to give a speech. And my business is speaking. To do it effectively, I have found that I must have help, the sort of help that only God can give. Never have I made a talk or given a sermon without asking divine help; and what I pray for is clarity of mind to say the right thing in such a way that it will help people. I never ask that I may make an impression. I am not too smart, but I am smart enough to avoid that prayer. Such is not the purpose of giving a talk, and I'm aware in advance that no prayer of that sort merits an answer.

In 1940, I spent three months in Hollywood acting as advisor in the making of a motion picture called *One Foot in Heaven.* It was the story of a midwestern country preacher. Fredric March and Martha Scott had the leading roles of the pastor and his wife, and I came to admire them both.

In the cast was a famous character actor, a wise and philosophical man. He told me that early in his career, motivated by a rather extraordinary success, he became, as he put it, "pretty cocky." As a result of his egotism, people began to turn away from him, his roles became less important, and gradually he all but ceased to get work. He had practically abandoned God, he said, but in his extremity turned once again to the Lord. He became genuinely humble, and his comeback started when he was given a small part in a stage play.

Peering through the curtain at the gathering audience, he noticed a man in the front row who looked terribly despondent, even sad. He found himself praying for that man, asking that something in his few lines might help cheer the fellow up. Suddenly, he said, "I sent a love thought to him and to others I could see out front." From then onward, his life and career changed and ultimately the actor became a beloved figure of stage and screen. That conversation made an immense and lasting impression upon me.

From that day to this, I have never stood in the wings of an auditorium or in a pulpit in church without offering a prayer in which I "send out love thoughts" to the people in the audience or congregation. I pray simply that through my talk or sermon they may find help and courage and faith to meet the sorrows and difficulties which they face. This is one prayer that inevitably receives a "yes" answer, for when you are able to forget yourself and love others, you are on the Lord's great beam, working for Him and His children. At least I feel it to be so.

Many times I have had remarkable feedback from this process of prayer. Once it happened when I was the speaker at a chamber of commerce annual dinner in a Texas city. While I was seated at the head table, suddenly I caught sight of a face in the audience that seemed to have a hatred of me written on it. Although the man was some distance from the head table, he appeared to be glaring at me. I shook it off as imagination, but I kept being drawn back to him. It was no one I knew and I was at a loss to explain his attitude.

I made this man a special object of prayer, sending out extra-loving thoughts toward him and asking the Lord to be especially near to him. I sent love to counter hate. Going into my talk, I still looked in his direction at times and kept the love thoughts going. At the end of the speech I was shaking hands with people when suddenly here was this man. We were face to face. "I have a confession to make," he said. "When I learned the speaker at our chamber of commerce dinner was a preacher, I was angry for I hate preachers, not you necessarily but all preachers. It's a long story, and I won't take your time, but I've felt since boyhood that a preacher wronged my father. But as I sat out there in that audience, something changed in my mind. That unreasonable hate suddenly left me. I actually found myself liking you. What do you suppose happened to me?" I was awed as he spoke and said, "I believe something spiritual happened to you." To my surprise he put out his hand. "That's it. That's it," he said. After a firm handclasp he was gone. There is miracle-working power in prayer, especially when it is linked with love.

One of the most difficult experiences I ever encountered in speaking was at a convention luncheon of a large national association in a big hotel ballroom in Boston. Prior to the luncheon there was a reception at which cocktails were offered, but no liquor was served at tables. However, there were two tables in the center of the large audience where whiskey bottles were clearly evident. The men at these tables were becoming unruly, and people nearby were showing their annoyance.

I am sensitive to this sort of thing and said to the chairman seated beside me that it was going to be a problem to talk over this ribald demonstration of drunkenness. He said he would quiet them, but it was soon apparent that he had no control whatsoever over the situation. Not wanting to have a shouting match with drunks, I finally suggested to the emcee that we skip the talk and let me leave and return to New York. He was upset at this suggestion, reminding me that I had promised to speak and had been widely advertised; and further, this big crowd was present to hear me.

So I acquiesced, though reluctantly. I began the talk with a couple of sure-fire jokes which evoked general laughter and drowned out the loud talking of the inebriates. Finally I went into more thoughtful discussion, but this proceeded with difficulty due to the noisy men at the two tables. Then came one of those pauses and deep silences which sometimes occur during the giving of a speech. At this precise moment one of the drunken men shouted in a profane way: "Jesus Christ." Instantly there was an intense hush. Even the offending people were shocked into silence. I sent up a quick prayer that included a loving thought toward the man who had shouted the Holy Name.

During the quiet I said, "That's right. You have spoken the name of your best friend, the One who will never let you down." Then I went on with my speech. Apparently this incident sobered these people, for they were as quiet as mice the rest of the time.

After the talk I was shaking a lot of hands when I noticed a man standing off to one side. I was conscious that he was waiting to say something to me. Finally he stepped over and said, "I am the man who shouted the name of our Lord and I am so ashamed. I'm a member of the Holy Name Society. This has shocked me into taking a new look at myself. I just want you to know, Dr. Peale, that I've learned my lesson. I'll never do that again. I'm a pretty poor Christian."

"So am I. I guess many of us are pretty poor Christians. But if we stick to Jesus, we'll do better, won't we?"

He grasped my hand. "You forgive me, don't you?"

"Of course," I said. "And I like you, too. You're an honest man."

It seems that my quick prayer and loving thoughts actually reached him. Prayer for a fact is power especially when it is offered with loving concern for persons.

And prayer is power also in dealing with problems. After a luncheon meeting of the Rotary Club of New York, of which I am a member, one of the Rotarians said, "I have a problem, a toughie, and it's vital, too, for my future may depend upon the right solution. And I am not able to see my way through it. Will you pray for me?" I of course said that I would and I did.

"But Lou," I said, "tell you what; when you return to your office shut your door and tell the Lord all about it. Believe that He hears you and that He will give you the answer that is eluding you. Then thank Him for His help in advance. Go about your business confidently. The answer will come."

The next day Lou went to lunch at his usual restaurant on Madison Avenue and decided since it was a nice day he would walk back to his office. As he stood on a street corner waiting for the traffic light to change, suddenly like a light coming on in his mind there was the answer to the problem. It was clear and distinct. It was not what he expected but he was absolutely certain that it was right. And subsequent events attested to its validity.

J. L. Kraft, founder of the cheese company, once told me that he built up his business in its early days through prayer plus hard work. It was pretty much a one-man business, or as he whimsically put it, a "one-horse business," in those days. The horse was named Paddy, and it drew a wagon with the young Kraft perched on the driver's seat. In the wagon he made deliveries, picked up supplies, and wrestled with the problems of making ends meet.

Often as Paddy clumped along, Kraft would talk over his problems with the horse. And Paddy would twitch his ears and look back at the young man. Mr. Kraft said with a chuckle, "I'm not sure I was talking to the Lord or to Paddy or to both, but somehow answers would come and I was guided every step of the way." And he looked piercingly at me and said firmly, "When you really need your answer, if you are a believer in prayer, your answer will be there for you. For example, if I needed my answer the next Thursday at nine A.M., I would tell the Lord so. I didn't dictate to Him, I just told Him I needed guidance by then as I had to come up with a decision at that hour."

"Did you get answers that way and at the required time?" I asked.

"Sure did," he replied. "At nine A.M. Thursday, whatever thought came into my mind at that time I took as being the answer I had prayed for, and it is remarkable how many times it was just right." Mr. Kraft taught me much about the way the Lord works with an all-out believer.

Many verifiable experiences, remarkable in nature, have fortified my personal belief that prayer releases powerful forces. This power has been demonstrated in changes in the nature of human beings, in lifting people out of complete personal failure to become outstanding individuals, and in physical, mental, and spiritual healing. One case in particular may serve as an example.

Harry DeCamp is a successful businessman in West Long Branch, New Jersey. At age sixty-six, he was physically healthy. Not a churchgoer, he was a believer in God, in Jesus Christ, in prayer, and in the Bible. Mr. DeCamp might come under the classification of "a good old boy," outgoing, gregarious, and popular. He was also an enthusiastic bicycle rider and a very good golfer.

Suddenly, feeling ill for the first time in his life, he was sent for tests and a cancerous mass was discovered behind the gall bladder. Further examination at a famous New York City cancer hospital confirmed the diagnosis and he was sent home to die. He had no appetite and lost weight rapidly. Treatment confirmed a losing battle. Every day all day, the formerly active Mr. DeCamp sat staring unseeingly into the television screen. Then he received a get-well card which said, "With God all things are possible." (Matthew 16:26) "I have never done anything for God. Why should He do anything for me?" reasoned Harry. Still, he put the card where he could see it, and in his own direct and humble way finally began to pray to God.

A friend sent Harry a copy of *Guideposts* magazine that contained an article by a former star basketball player who had been so shot up in the war that he was declared a perpetual invalid. But this man began imaging himself as he had been when in full vigor, and he mentally visualized shooting baskets following the trajectory of the ball, with most shots breaking through the meshes. The practice of such imaging together with his believing prayer brought him healing in time. He became as he had imaged himself as being.

The article written by the basketball player gave Harry an idea. He began to image thousands of healthy white cells cascading down from his shoulders to meet the unhealthy cells in mortal combat. And finally he began to see a small figure of Christ leading the onslaught of the army of white cells. Perhaps a hundred times a day he would visualize this battle as he continued to talk to the Lord in prayer until he developed a profound friendship with Him.

Then one day he felt hungry for the first time in months, ravenously hungry. When he demanded a big meal, his wife, concerned lest his mind was affected, called the doctor. Examination revealed the astonishing fact that the disease no longer existed. The cancer hospital confirmed the fact, and now in the sixth year since the healing, he is a completely healthy, vigorous man.

In two articles in *Guideposts* magazine, Mr. DeCamp described his healing and credited the words "only believe" for bringing it to pass. I well realize that his case is outstanding and significant and may even be a landmark in the field of healing. If this can happen to one person, the same prayer-imaging formula when applied by others can produce similar results. Mr. DeCamp then wrote a book, *One Man's Healing from Cancer,* * which describes his healing in greater detail. Since the two *Guideposts* articles and the publication of his book, hundreds of sufferers have written or telephoned him. He has been able to help many and in each case he witnesses to the power of prayer. He says, "I am a man who lives in a state of amazement. For sixty-six years I had only a nodding relationship with God, how extraordinary, then, that when I was dying He would bother to reach down and heal me. And yet He did just that!"

All you have to do to believe the truth of this story is to see Harry DeCamp. Prayer and faith constitute the highest form of power.

*Fleming H. Revell Company, Old Tappan, New Jersey.

CHAPTER SEVENTEEN

Warm Friendships and Hot Water

MY MINISTRY has been greatly aided by the officials of our church, the elders and deacons. Over the years I have been associated with approximately one hundred men in this capacity. They have all been competent business and professional people and sincere Christians. I wish I could affectionately mention each person, but have to content myself with only one.

At the time of my coming to Marble Collegiate Church in 1932, Milton D. Ketchum was the youngest member of the board and is serving now as senior elder. A quiet, genial man of intelligence and faith, by nature conservative, perhaps even traditional, he has nevertheless supported me loyally and completely, even when some of my innovative procedures must have been a bit difficult to accept. Men like Milton Ketchum are able to think problems through objectively, dispassionately, and spiritually with total commitment to Christ and the church. He is one of the most capable churchmen I have ever known.

As commitments to speak before national business conventions and other public gatherings increased, taking me to all parts of the United States and Canada, and as responsibilities developed in the expansion of *Guideposts,* the need for an executive minister to supervise church administration in my absence became apparent. I decided upon a young man whom I had known since his college days, a classmate of our daughter Margaret at Ohio Wesleyan University. I had followed his career and knew his parents. His father was also an able minister. He is Arthur Caliandro, then pastor of a church in Brooklyn. I asked our officials to call him to Marble Collegiate Church, and he filled this position effectively. Then I decided to restrict my preaching program to the 11:15 service on Sunday morning, and asked Arthur to take the preaching assignment at the early service each Sunday. Noting his development as a preacher, I became increasingly aware of his ability and of his strong evangelical convictions. Finally I decided that after I relinquished this ministry, he would be a fitting successor, and I asked the consistory of the church to confirm him as such—which was done. As a truly great preacher, he will continue to deliver in his own way the type of strongly positive and life-changing message that has characterized the church through three pastorates—those of Dr. David James Burrell and Dr. Daniel A. Poling, and mine—totaling nearly one hundred years altogether.

After working with Arthur Caliandro for several years, I suggested to the church board that the congregation was entitled to a younger minister in total charge as preacher and pastor. This would give me time to concentrate on my many other responsibilities. When I indicated my decision to relinquish the ministry, board members strongly resisted and asked me to continue. I accepted their reaction as indicative of God's will and agreed to continue for a time.

In more than fifty years of ministry in one church, the lives of thousands have been touched. Space limits me from telling the thrilling stories of the many men and women who, through Christ, found new life in Marble Collegiate Church over the years that we have worked there. Perhaps it may suffice to tell of just one. I choose this great human story, for I believe that it typifies the power of the Gospel I have preached for so long.

Once, when I was speaking in Roanoke, Virginia, I met Charles and Hazel Kennard. The Kennards lived in Staunton, Virginia, where Charles was in the automotive parts business. After my speech that night, he related the following story.

He had become an alcoholic and was warned repeatedly by his employer that, even though he was their most valued employee, he was in danger of losing his job unless he could bring his excessive drinking under control.

Finally Charles made an appointment with the late Dr. Edward Silkworth, who practiced in New York City and was an expert on the cure of alcoholism. Arriving in New York, Charles immediately got completely drunk and was robbed by a bellboy of all his money. Next day, penniless, he walked into the hospital and was put into treatment by Dr. Silkworth. Later, upon completion of the standard procedure, the doctor called him into his office.

"Charles," he said, "we have completely boiled the alcohol from your system and we have tried to reeducate your mind. At this moment you are cured. But there is an area in your mind where lurks a reservation. That we cannot reach. How wonderful if we could use a scalpel to probe into your mind and operate to exorcise this reservation, which in due course will bring you back to us, still a helpless drunk."

"But, Doctor," said Charles, "you are acknowledged to be the greatest physician in this field. If you cannot cure me, who can? Is there no doctor who can cure me completely?"

Dr. Silkworth hesitated before replying, "Yes, there is one Doctor who can cure you, but He is very expensive."

"That's no problem, sir. I can raise whatever his fee may be," declared Charles.

"Yes, but this Doctor wants everything you have and are; indeed, He wants nothing less than you yourself. His name"—he paused rather dramatically—"is Jesus Christ and He keeps office in the New Testament! And what a Doctor He is, with the long, slender, probing, and sensitive hands of a gifted surgeon. He alone can reach that control center in your mind and remove that reservation. Without such surgery you will never find healing. But He can for sure heal you if you put yourself in His hands completely and without reservation."

This remarkable manner of a modern doctor referring a patient to the Great Physician affected Charles Kennard profoundly. He walked the streets in battle with himself. He had always been a believer and a churchgoing man, yet the idea of complete surrender to Christ was a mental problem for him. And being of a thoroughly honest character he had to be sure he could keep a lifetime commitment before he made it. My name came to his mind as the only minister he knew in New York, for he had read *The Power of Positive Thinking*.

As evening came on, rain mixed with snow was falling, accompanied by the kind of cold wind that bites into you. Still trudging, overcoat collar turned up, Charles located my church at the corner of Fifth Avenue and Twenty-ninth Street. He was hoping to find me even at this very late hour. He tried the front door of the darkened church, and it was locked. He tried all the other doors, but they too were shut tight. With the rain and snow pelting down upon him, he stood by the door numbered 1 West 29th Street. He took his business card from his wallet. On it he wrote, "Dear Dr. Jesus: This is your unworthy servant, Charles Kennard. Dr. Silkworth says only You can heal me. Here and now, for always, I give myself to You, body, mind, and soul. Please heal me, dear Jesus. Thank You." And he signed it "Charles Kennard."

Slipping the card into the mail slot of the locked door, he continued to stand there as if expecting an answer. And an answer did come, for all of a sudden he began to feel warm all over. Like a glow, beginning at the crown of his head, the warmth flooded his entire being down to the soles of his feet. He began to cry and laugh at the same time. A glorious ecstasy of relief encompassed him, and in that moment he knew that the Great Physician had laid His hand upon him and that he had been healed.

When he told me this story in Roanoke, it seemed that I knew it all, that in some strange way it had been transmitted to me. So I asked, "Have you ever told this story before?"

"This is the first time," he replied. The card which he had put through the mail slot that night, to my knowledge, was never found. But the Lord Jesus knew about it, for Charles Kennard was completely healed of his problem. He became a field representative of *Guideposts* magazine, and throughout his territory of the Southland, he became a blessing to all sorts of people in all types of trouble. He was beloved everywhere. One Sunday morning some years later, looking down from the pulpit as the congregation sang the old hymn "What a Friend We Have in Jesus," I saw Charles. He was singing, without a book and with his head flung back. A long shaft of sunlight through the stained-glass windows spotlighted his face. There was a glory on it. I watched, deeply moved. He knew the Friend about Whom he was singing. Today he is in heaven; but he will ever live with me in loving memory as typical of the redeeming ministry in the old church on the sidewalks of New York.

It is said that to every disadvantage there is a corresponding advantage. When we went to New York in 1932, the Great Depression was at its very bottom. The situation was depressive in the extreme. It was difficult to see any advantage in it. But out of it came an agency of human helpfulness that might never have been born had it not been for the extraordinary needs the Depression created.

People were receiving cut after cut in salary and wages. Thousands were being thrown out of jobs and onto the streets, where they looked futilely for work. Business closings were reported every day. Shops all up and down the avenues were closed, hundreds of banks had failed, the savings of thousands were lost. It was a strange, sad time. Some people shot themselves, others suffered breakdowns, and many came dejectedly through the church doors, looking for comfort and understanding. All needed healing of their thinking; and, above all, they needed hope.

As I tried to meet the flood of need by personal counseling, I became aware of my lack of knowledge of how to help troubled people. Aside from a beginning course in psychology in college and a scarcely more advanced one in the theological school, I had no knowledge in the field of counseling. I did have, however, two positive qualities—a caring attitude, and a willingness to let burdened and hopeless people talk out their fears. But I knew that I must do more . . . become more effective.

Finally in 1935, I was directed to Dr. Iago Galdston, then secretary of the New York County Medical Society. I went to him to ask whether he knew a psychiatrist who had a Christian view, from whom I could get guidance and perhaps assistance in this dire situation.

Some days later he telephoned me to meet him for lunch at the Harvard Club, and there he introduced me to a man who was to become my partner in service for many years. He was Dr. Smiley Blanton, a graduate of Vanderbilt University, formerly of the Royal College of Physicians and Surgeons in London, then a professor of speech and mental hygiene at the University of Wisconsin and assistant professor of clinical psychiatry at Cornell University and Vanderbilt School of Medicine. Dr. Blanton listened silently to my story and my need for help. When finally I ran down a bit, he asked, "Do you believe in prayer?"

Astounded by this seemingly irrelevant remark, I replied, "Of course."

"And so do I," said the doctor. "For years I have been praying that sometime I would meet a pastor with whom I, as a psychiatrist, could work, thus uniting in a partnership, psychological science and pastoral methodology. That partnership could be the greatest advance in pastoral counseling in a hundred years." I liked this man at once, who had every advanced degree in his branch of medicine, but characterized himself as a "hillbilly Methodist from Tennessee."

At first I would meet with Dr. Blanton once a week and go over cases with him. I was impressed by his ability to get at the heart of personal problems even in absentia and based solely on my inexpert description of them. His amazing counsel proved invaluable. Gradually over the weeks I began to see the pattern of his methodology. Finally he became so interested in the cases that he began to see the people themselves two afternoons a week. Conscious that we were working as a team—psychiatrist and pastor —Dr. Blanton would say to a patient, "Now, as a doctor, I tell you go to Dr. Peale, a pastor, and he will give you the cure which the Great Physician provides." To me he would say, "This is the problem and mechanism. Just give this man the good old Gospel."

Gradually, as our caseload increased, Dr. Blanton began to bring young student psychiatrists to work with him. At first this activity was an arm of the church, but later Gerald Dickler, our attorney and board member from the beginning, incorporated it as the American Foundation of Religion and Psychiatry. Years afterward the name was changed to the Institutes of Religion and Health.

In the beginning, only a treatment department existed, but as we became aware that ministers should be trained in religiopsychiatric counseling techniques, a training program was instituted. Under the auspices of the Blanton-Peale clinic, educational credit is provided at several prestigious institutions. From the Institutes of Religion and Health more than one hundred Pastoral Counseling Centers have developed in cities across the nation. I believe Dr. Smiley Blanton will deservedly be honored for a long time to come as a pioneer in the mental-health field for having brought the pastoral office into a working relationship with psychiatric medicine. This has resulted in vastly improved skills in dealing with human problems.

Recently, in a line of passengers proceeding through security at an airport, I saw ahead of me a familiar figure. It was Dr. Iago Galdston. He said, "One of the best things I ever did was to get Dr. Blanton and you together forty-five years ago."

"I will never cease to be grateful to you for making it possible to know and work with Dr. Blanton. He was one of the wisest, kindest men I ever knew," I replied, "and his name will live on in the field of religiopsychiatric healing."

The Institutes of Religion and Health has had two chairmen whose fidelity to the work of healing is profound, W. Clement Stone and Neal Gilliatt.

Positive thinkers are bound to be positive doers. They are achievers and winners, and I have noted that they also have nonirritating though strong personalities.

The considerateness which I once ascribed to Donald Trump, the New York builder, surprised a reporter who interviewed me about him. Apparently it is assumed that a supersuccessful businessman has to be a tough guy, hard and ruthless, loud-mouthed, and mean all the way. However, I had an opportunity to be in on some church negotiations in which Donald was firm but polite and considerate in pursuing the goals he had set. In his quiet, somewhat low-key, but persistent way, he attained for the church one of the greatest assurances of long-term financial stability in its history. Characteristically Fred Trump, his father, acclaimed this contribution to the ongoing welfare of the church by saying, "Donald knows how to do it." And Donald said, "All I know,

Father taught me," adding his usual admiring remark, "My father is a very great gentleman."

Currently the Trump name is connected with Trump Plaza, the Grand Hyatt Hotel, and the spectacular Trump Tower on Fifth Avenue, as well as Trump Plaza on Atlantic City's famed boardwalk, and other structures. Donald Trump's career has only just begun, but what a beginning. Surely he is one of America's top positive thinkers and positive doers.

During my years in New York I have known some outstanding religious leaders. I was close to some, notably, Dr. Daniel A. Poling, my predecessor at the church and onetime editor of *Christian Herald* magazine. I first met Dan when I was twelve years old when he came to preach for Father in Greenville, Ohio. I was fascinated by this black-haired young giant who was a powerful orator. Little did I dream that one day I would succeed him in the pastorate of a Fifth Avenue church. He had one of the most notable Christian ministries in America. To me, Dan Poling was matched by few men or clergymen. He had the rare ability to inspire and lead people, young and old, to Christian commitment.

Billy Graham is undoubtedly the best-known preacher of our time, and I have known him from the beginning of his ministry. Perhaps no other man has preached the Gospel to more people than this gifted North Carolina country boy who has talked about Christ to kings and Presidents as well as to multitudes of us common folk. Always he is faithful to the Bible and to the Lord. His influence for the cause of Christianity has been incalculable.

Once at a meeting in Madison Square Garden, when I sat with him on the platform and looked out over a sea of faces in the packed arena, I turned to Billy in admiration and asked, "Billy, how do you do it?" With that winsome smile of his, he replied, "By practicing the power of positive thinking." We both laughed, but each of us knew that the real answer was the power of Christ working in him.

Over many years I enjoyed a very pleasant association with Bishop Fulton J. Sheen. He was, I believe, one of the most accomplished preachers in our country's history, and he used television with extraordinary brilliance. He endeared himself to all Americans regardless of their religious affiliation. I once asked him to preach in my church, and it seemed the whole city of New York wanted to crowd in to hear him. He gave a straight evangelistic message with fervor and persuasiveness. I told him afterward that he talked like a Protestant. "I hope just simply like a Christian," he responded.

There was no put-on about Fulton Sheen. He was always himself, which was plenty. His natural greatness of character gave him unadorned dignity of presence. Once when I was speaking with him on some important occasion in Radio City Music Hall, I donned my simple black gown and watched him as he put on his rich and colorful habiliments. "My, I wish I could dress up like you," I remarked.

"But you are," he replied with a chuckle. "Your native talents are such that you need no adornments like the rest of us simple mortals."

"Even you will never get to heaven if you stretch the truth like that," I said.

I was very close to him in our activity of speaking here and there, so much so that he claimed that once he was quite unconsciously introduced as Norman Vincent Sheen. And I reminded him of the night at a convention meeting when we were jointly referred to as Dr. Sheen and Bishop Peale. I commented that this error ministered to my ego as it was the nearest I ever got to being a bishop.

Another great Catholic dignitary whom I knew quite well was the late, inimitable Cardinal Francis Spellman of New York. Not only was he a spiritual leader of distinction, but his business ability and acumen were legendary among the city's business executives. As president at that time of the Council of Churches of the City of New York, a Protestant organization and perpetually faced with deficits, I once put to him a tongue-in-cheek inquiry as to whether he might be open to an offer to work for us. His reply, also jocular, was that he might consider the proposition if we all were to embrace "the true faith." But since he knew we would continue "in error," he was relieved from any responsibility for "pulling us out of the hole."

Cardinal Spellman was a kindly man and his sense of humor

was proverbial. People were always telling me of his remarks and would chuckle and shake their heads as if to say admiringly, "What a man." Once visiting him in his home on Madison Avenue, I made as if to leave. Courteously he helped me on with my overcoat. "What do you know," I commented. "I sure have arrived when I have a cardinal of the Roman Catholic Church helping me on with my coat."

"Might as well have the best," he quipped.

At a meeting in Washington, I introduced Cardinal Spellman to a large crowd as the speaker of the evening, and because of my feeling for him, went all out in extolling his qualities and service. Later he told me it was such a great introduction he would like a copy. Regretfully I informed him that I had spoken ad lib, and unfortunately it had not been recorded. Well, then, would I try to reproduce it for him? I did so and sent it to him, but he telephoned that it didn't quite come up to the spoken version, and wouldn't I really try to remember what I said? The second time I concentrated as in the ad-lib introduction, and it seemed to satisfy him. He was very genuine and likable.

On one occasion Cardinal Spellman invited me, in my capacity as president of the Council of Churches of the City of New York, to participate in an ecumenical gathering in St. Patrick's Cathedral. We met in the robing room of the cathedral. I walked just before the cardinal, who was in the rear of the procession. Two stalwart young priests marched on either side of me. "Your Eminence," I said, "tell me, do these two husky priests represent a bodyguard?"

"Not exactly," he responded. "You see, on the way to the high altar, we must kneel twice on the hard stone floor of the cathedral, and I doubt that your Protestant knees can take it. They will hoist you up." I must report with some embarrassment that they were indeed compelled to perform an assist. The humility of this great prince of the church was once again demonstrated in this ceremonial. He had to conduct a newly prescribed ritual, and I thought he presided to perfection. But apparently he did not think so, for in the recessional he asked, "Do you think I did it all right?"

As a minister I have known many pastors and preachers and evaluate them highly as dedicated, sincere, and competent helpers of mankind. Most have small churches in which to serve, whereas a relative few head larger churches; and a very few are famous television and radio ministers, such as Oral Roberts, Jerry Falwell, Rex Humbard, Robert Schuller, and others—all sincere and Godly men, each with his own particular flair and individualistic manner.

One interesting recollection I have of Dr. Schuller is a visit with him long before his enormous church (the Crystal Cathedral in California) was ever begun. He described it in such precise detail that I commented admiringly that the church was already built, for in effect, he was imaging it into being, which was consistent with his creative attitude.

One thing I like about New York is big league baseball. I have always been a dedicated fan. I watched some of the greatest pitchers in action: Christy Mathewson, Walter Johnson, and others, including Carl Erskine of a later era. He is my special favorite. One unforgettable pitcher was Cy Young, whose record of games won and strikeouts was formidable indeed.

In his later years, Cy Young was given the job of curator of the Museum of Honored Battle Flags in the rotunda of the Ohio statehouse in Columbus. I encountered him there one day and was awed that I was actually conversing with one of the athletic heroes of my youth. "Mr. Young," I said, "it is a great privilege for me to meet you, one of the greatest pitchers. I have watched you with such admiration."

"One of the greatest?" he echoed. "Not one of, but *the* greatest. And if you will look up my lifetime record, you will know that is no idle boast." Later I verified that his seemingly immodest statement was pretty well substantiated by the facts. Though he was perhaps somewhat too forceful and opinionated, nevertheless he was a thoroughly likable man.

Cy Young was cryptic and wise in the comments he made to me in the several visits I had with him. In answer to my question as to how current baseball players equated with the old-timers, his reply was, "Pretty good in general, but actually they are sissies compared to us. Take pitchers, for example. Nowadays they seldom let them go a full game. Guess they want to pamper 'em. And they pitch one day and rest for three or four. Why, in our time we might pitch several days hands running. We were tougher—a lot tougher." So ran his gusty appraisal.

I remember another of his remarks that surely applies not only to baseball but to life's problems in general: "Take the soft and easy way they handle a pitcher today," he growled. "When he gets into trouble, the manager comes walking out to the mound and takes him out and calls a replacement from the bullpen. But in our day when a pitcher got into trouble, the manager knew he had it in him to get back into the groove and he was left in and expected to pitch his way out of trouble." I have always been grateful that I got the famous old pitcher Cy Young to talking so that he came up with that marvelous bit of insight, for I have found that I, too, in my own way have had to stay right in there and keep pitching.

I found I had to pitch my way out of trouble when I got myself into one of the most difficult situations I have ever experienced. It occurred in the autumn of 1960 during the presidential election when John F. Kennedy defeated Richard Nixon. Traditionally being a sort of independent Republican and Nixon being a longtime acquaintance, naturally I was for him. But I have never taken any part in politics, holding strongly to the opinion that a minister of the Gospel should not become politically involved. So in no sense did I give any support to Mr. Nixon as a candidate. Nor did I even think of being against Senator Kennedy and certainly not because he happened to be a Catholic.

There was no bigotry in my upbringing. Quite the contrary, we were taught as children to respect Jews and Catholics, and to honor their religious faiths as our own. When I was growing up in Cincinnati, my playmates and schoolmates were black as well as white, and Jewish and Catholic as well as Protestant, and everyone was all the same to us.

I recall a conversation with Dale Carnegie in which we fell to discussing the dumb things we had done, how stupid can you get, and so on. Dale said that sometime he thought he might write a book entitled *Dumb Things I Have Done*. With a laugh, I commented that if I undertook to write on that subject, a series of books would be required. This was proved by a situation in which, to my consternation and bewilderment, I got myself embroiled.

A meeting on religious freedom was scheduled to be held in

Washington, D.C., on a day following my return from a European holiday, and I had no plan to attend the gathering to which, I imagine, many ministers were routinely invited. Reverend Dr. Daniel A. Poling telephoned me saying that as editor of the *Christian Herald,* he expected to "look into the meeting," and would I go with him? He said we had not visited for a long while and we could come back the next morning and generally have a good time together. I let myself be persuaded, but Dan's prophecy of a good time turned out to be a horrendously bad time.

As he and I sat in the meeting, it turned out that the appointed chairman had been detained, so someone nominated me as temporary chairman until he appeared. Stupidly I went to the platform to preside. I had no information as to what the program was, but simply introduced the persons whose names were handed me. Several rather scholarly and historical dissertations were given on the general subject of religious freedom. And I do not recall that there were any political overtones.

The mistake was that the meeting was held in the nation's capital in the heat of a presidential election when one of the candidates happened to be a communicant of the Catholic Church (not the first Catholic to run for President, Alfred E. Smith having been the first some years before). In any case, the press labeled this meeting "the Peale group," though I had no part in its formulation. They immediately assumed the intent of the meeting was anti-Kennedy, and, to my astonishment, I was made the center of a great hue-and-cry. This so embarrassed me, being counter to my lifetime attitudes, that I at once felt I had brought my church into disrepute. Accordingly, I sent my resignation to the chairman of the church board. I planned to preach a farewell sermon before my congregation the following Sunday.

When Sunday came, I walked into the pulpit to face the usual full house, when to my astonishment the congregation rose en masse, expressing their support and love. It was an unforgettable moment. The church board unanimously rejected my resignation, insisting that I remain as their minister. I had been writing a newspaper column and several papers cancelled it, but ultimately most returned.

Later I had a pleasant friendship with Senator Robert Kennedy who told me "to forget it," that everyone knew of "my spirit and respected me." I told him that my grandfather had been a Catholic in Ireland. With a grin, he replied that I "should have taken after Grandpa." So the painful experience passed. But I have no doubt that when I die, this horrible incident will be raked up and printed despite all I have tried to do to advance the ecumenical spirit. But, alas, such is life.

CHAPTER EIGHTEEN

Some Politicians

PREACHING AND POLITICS are seldom compatible. I recall my only foray into politics, quite a minor one, long before I entered the ministry. It was when John Joseph and I got involved in a presidential campaign. John was one of my closest friends at Ohio Wesleyan. Later prominent in the affairs of the Ohio Bell Telephone Company and a distinguished attorney, in college he was a favorite of all the students, though the dean of men was perhaps a bit less enthusiastic about him because of John's tendency always to "be getting into something," which brought the dean's admonition upon him. And I must confess that John was not alone. I was right there with him. These were all fun things, like putting a horse in the chapel choir loft. But all is now forgiven, for John has long been an honored and sedate life member of the university's board of trustees.

But one year a presidential election was coming on and the preconvention campaign was heating up. Senator Warren G. Harding was seeking the support of the Ohio delegation to the Republican National Convention, as were several others, including a then-popular military figure, Major General Leonard Wood. John and I had many talks as to whom we would "throw our support." This was determined for us when, for some reason, the two of us were invited to come to the Leonard Wood headquarters in the old Neil House in Columbus. There we were rather surreptitiously taken into a back room, where a fat man in shirt-sleeves sat behind a table. "Sit down, gentlemen," he said. That "gentlemen" salutation went over big with us.

"Now," continued the fat man, "you two have been recommended as popular leaders on your college campus and, of course, being bright and progressive men, you are for Leonard Wood for President of our great country. You agree with us that the historic general is the man of the hour. We want to show to the electorate of this great state that all educated and intelligent people are for our candidate. What we would like you to do is to set up a straw vote at Ohio Wesleyan and carry it overwhelmingly for General Wood. Then it will be publicized all over the state. And," he added, "a month from today the candidate is to speak at a big rally in Memorial Hall. We hope you two gentlemen will honor us by sitting on the stage that night, with the general himself."

That we were honored is to put it mildly, for we were enthusiastic partisans of General Leonard Wood. I still believe he would have made a great President because of his outstanding talents as an administrator. Incidentally I believe he is the only physician ever to run for President. He had a distinguished career as a surgeon with the U.S. Army during the expedition to capture Geronimo for which he was awarded the Congressional Medal of Honor.

Wood was born in 1860 in Winchester, New Hampshire. After graduating from Harvard Medical School in 1884, he joined the Army Medical Corps. Later, as a colonel, he commanded the Rough Riders, the famous volunteer regiment in which Theodore Roosevelt also served during the Spanish-American War. While he was military governor of Cuba from 1899 to 1902, he prepared the island for independence. He built roads and schools and helped stamp out yellow fever by cleaning up swamps and mosquito-ridden areas. General Wood commanded the United States forces in the Philippines from 1906 to 1908, and served as Chief of Staff, U.S. Army, from 1910 to 1914. Wood was governor general of the Philippines from 1921 until his death in 1927.

But to get back to our political adventure—we were greatly

impressed. John and I nodded importantly and graciously accepted the invitation.

"Of course," continued our political collaborator (as by this time we felt very much on the "in") "you will need some money to put over this straw vote for the general. How much do you think will do it?"

I started murmuring that we would do it for nothing, when John kicked me under the table. The fat man reached in a drawer and pulled out the biggest wad of bills John and I had ever seen. Our eyes popped at the sight of so much cash. Impressively the man counted out two piles of five-dollar bills, dropping each bill alternately one after the other and then handed fifty dollars to each of us. "Stick that in your pockets and keep it quiet," he said in a hush-hush tone.

Like conspirators, we were ushered out through a side door into an alley. Hands in pockets, clutching our political money, we emerged onto High Street opposite the statehouse, talking in awed tones about "that wad which would choke a horse."

As a matter of fact, we used all that money on posters and other costs and carried the university student body for Leonard Wood by a big majority. This poll result made many newspapers in the state. At this point John began calling me "Senator" and I called him "Governor," and visions of a spectacular political future gleamed in our eyes.

On the night of the candidate's great rally in Columbus, General Wood was tumultuously received as he marched victoriously down the main aisle to the stage. There he sat, flanked on one side by John and on the other by me, separated, I must admit, by several dignitaries in between. In fact, John was on one end of the long row and I on the other. But we bowed to the applause and waved just as the candidate did. At the subsequent national convention in Chicago, I am sad to say our candidate was snowed under by Warren G. Harding. But if the managers of the Wood campaign had had the wisdom to take John and me to the Chicago convention, there is no doubt at all that Leonard Wood would have become President of the United States instead of Warren G. Harding!

Well, as I say, that was my one and only foray into politics, but later on I did have contact with some political figures.

When you think about it, life is indeed a romantic experience. In my case, a country boy from a small town in Ohio has made many friends one wouldn't think he would ever encounter. But life in America takes the most unusual turns, and even a poor American boy enjoys many privileges if he works hard and tries to do a good job. I've known people in just about every walk of life, from the humblest to the highest, and I am grateful to all of them, for they have been my friends.

One was Herbert Hoover, who became President of the United States and was a fine gentleman and a kindly friend whose memory I honor. I came to know him a long while ago when he used to spend quite a lot of time in New York after his presidency. "I would like to do something for you," he said puffing reflectively on his pipe, "because you are always doing something for so many." That he overstated my service goes without saying, but at the time I was trying to build up a rundown, almost defunct church.

So I said, "Mr. President, you are most kind, and I wonder if you would be willing to come down some night and speak to the men of my church." He said at once that he would be glad to. And so it was that out of the kindness of his heart, a former President of the United States spent an evening in a church basement giving the benefit of his experience to some churchmen. I marveled and thought that only in America perhaps could a former head of state go back to the people in this simple way. I shall never forget that night as Herbert Hoover addressed this relatively small group as he would have done had he been speaking to thousands.

Once Mr. Hoover was spending some time in San Francisco at the Mark Hopkins Hotel. During his stay there he kindly invited me to stop by to see him, as he knew that I was to be in San Francisco. I found him in his suite surrounded by books and papers. "You seem busy on a writing project," I observed.

"Yes," he replied. "I have it in mind to write about Woodrow Wilson."

"That is quite unusual," I commented. "A Republican President writing about a Democratic President."

"Ah," he replied, "but Wilson was one of our greatest Presidents, dealing with epochal events and doing so as a very great American."

241

Probably no President was so maligned and mistreated as Mr. Hoover. So on this occasion I took the opportunity to ask him how he had endured it and seemingly not let it affect him. "Well, you see, when I decided to enter politics, I knew I might have it rough, and so when these attacks came I was prepared for them. And being by profession an engineer, I was trained to take an objective view. I examined every criticism. If it was valid I tried to learn from it. If it was not valid I just ignored it and," he added, "you know I am a Quaker." While he did not elaborate on that last remark, I knew what he meant, for a basic Quaker teaching is to develop peace at the center.

Always being interested in a person's own reason for having attained success, I once asked Mr. Hoover the basic reason for his great career. His quick answer was, "I was reared among older people, being left an orphan at an early age. And I had exposure to their maturity and wisdom."

Herbert Hoover unknowingly helped me with my inferiority complex. One Sunday I preached in Christ Church on Quaker Hill, which, though a small church, has a distinguished congregation. On this particular Sunday, Herbert Hoover sat in the front pew. I have the habit of turning a speech into a sermon and a sermon into a speech to suit the occasion. I didn't feel that it went very well that morning, but afterward I heard that Mr. Hoover told a group that it was "a damn good talk." Later in the week I was backstage in a city auditorium, about to address a huge audience at a business convention, when my old inferiority complex started working on me, telling me I couldn't do it. But I remembered Mr. Hoover's remark that this was "a damn good talk." So I said to myself, "If it's good enough for a President of the United States, it ought to be O.K. for the people out in front." Thus encouraged, I laid it on with more confidence.

One night years ago I went up to West Point, having accepted an invitation to give a talk in the old Thayer Hotel to a sizable group of young men who were concerned about the country. Always I have sought to avoid participation in political gatherings, but in this instance I found myself in one for sure. These bright and enthusiastic fellows were there to plan how to recapture the White House from Franklin D. Roosevelt, then at the height of his unprecedented popularity and power. They struck me as audacious Davids, without even a slingshot, presuming they could bring down the mighty Goliath and his almost unanimously supported New Deal.

They never did succeed in their objective, but I learned that night that dedication and enthusiasm can carry one far in life. For present at that meeting among others was William Rogers, who years later became secretary of state under President Eisenhower, and Herbert Brownell, then a young assemblyman who served as attorney general in the same administration.

Also at that West Point meeting I met for the first time an eager, dynamic, and brilliant young man whose career was to lead him to the very doors of the White House. Thomas E. Dewey did spend twelve years in the governor's mansion at Albany. And Dewey was one of the greatest in the long line of distinguished men who have been governors of the Empire State.

Tom Dewey was also my Quaker Hill neighbor. His two sons, Tom, Jr., and John, grew up with our children, Margaret, John, and Elizabeth. I admired the governor tremendously. He had magnificent talents as an administrator, which he demonstrated when he was district attorney and governor, and in my judgment would have been one of our superior Presidents. I was with him the night he lost the presidency to Harry Truman after early returns indicated his victory. He took defeat philosophically. "It just was not to be. So be it," he said, and never afterward engaged in postmortems. He wanted to win but defeat never broke him.

One of his closest friends was G. Lynn Sumner, a distinguished New York advertising executive. One cold winter day, I assisted Rev. Dr. Ralph C. Lankler, pastor of Christ Church on Quaker Hill, in conducting Lynn Sumner's funeral. Dewey was a pallbearer, and as we stood in the portico of the church, there was some little delay in getting the cortege moving. In a gruff voice to hide his emotion, the governor said, "Let's get going. Lynn is in the hands of Someone Who will always take care of him."

Tom Dewey was a deeply religious man. I can see him even yet, coming into church every Sunday, walking down to a front pew preceded by Frances, his beautiful wife, and followed by his two boys. Once when I was in the minister's room, I saw the Deweys get out of their car behind the church, Frances wetting her fingers to plaster the boys' hair down as mothers have ever done.

Thomas E. Dewey was one of the most magnificent public speakers I ever heard, possessing a rare power to move a vast audience. He had a kind of strut with which he would move into an argument, working it to an impassioned climax when his great melodic voice would ring out like a silver trumpet through the huge hall, bringing the crowd to its feet in a roar.

I was present one night at "The Barn," the community meeting place on Quaker Hill, and made some remarks. Dewey spoke a bit later and referred to my statement, expressing some slight difference of opinion in his own gracious and humorous manner. Later someone told him that he had hurt my feelings. Though it was late, nearly midnight, he telephoned me. I had just gotten into bed. "I must see you at once," he said. "Are you in bed?"

"Yes," I replied, "but for you I will get up anytime."

"Well, just throw on a bathrobe. I'll be right there."

Clad in a robe, I met him at the front door. "What brings the governor to see a preacher at this hour of the night?" I asked.

He came in and sat beside me. "I'm afraid I hurt your feelings tonight, Norman," he said. "You know I wouldn't hurt a friend of a lifetime for anything. Please forgive me."

"You did not hurt my feelings," I replied. "Surely friends can express a bit of a differing view. But, Tom, I will never forget your kindness and your goodness of heart in coming to see me tonight."

We chatted awhile, then moved out to the front porch. He put his arm around my shoulder and said, "You're a great friend." So saying, he got into his car with a wave of his hand. And I stood watching the governor of New York drive away into the night. I had seen the real Tom Dewey. He was not at all the cold-blooded character writers sometimes made him out to be.

Along with several other pastors, I was once invited to meet President Truman in the Oval Office. The subject matter related to a question in which the President was interested at the time and about which he wished to talk with some clergymen. I cannot recall the details. Sometimes one's memory bank fails and this is one of those times. The conversation, however, was most delightful and I found him a strong and interesting man. He asked each of us about our children, and I informed him that my young daughter Margaret had firmly informed me that if I did not return

244

with a personal autograph from the President, there would be dire consequences. "I have a daughter Margaret also," Mr. Truman replied, as though we did not know.

"Please write it on this, Mr. President," I said, handing Mr. Truman a piece of ordinary, lined yellow paper which I had in my pocket.

"That's no kind of paper for a presidential autograph to a girl named Margaret," Harry Truman declared and proceeded to rummage in a drawer of his desk, mumbling something about "Where are those damn White House cards?" The desk drawer was actually less orderly than mine, which is saying something. Finally he located a nicely engraved card. "The President. The White House," it read. On this he wrote "To Margaret Peale. With best wishes, Harry S. Truman." "Tell her to hang on to that. It will be an heirloom sometime," he said, "and give her my love." He quite won all our hearts by his down-to-earth kindness. Margaret cherishes that card to this day, and my being able to bring it home added to her father's prestige.

J. Edgar Hoover, famous director of the Federal Bureau of Investigation, was a devout man and a strong personality. It was his policy to hold at intervals what he called the F.B.I. Academy, to which as many as perhaps two thousand police chiefs and other officers would come to Washington for refresher courses in police work. Director Hoover on two occasions invited me to speak at a commencement exercise on the last day of the academy when certificates were given to these men. It was a challenging and exciting event.

On my second visit I was seated on the stage with Director Hoover on my right. Other government dignitaries were on the far side of the large platform. A vacant chair was at my left. I wondered who was scheduled to occupy that chair, and the question was answered when the President of the United States, Dwight D. Eisenhower, came in, to the great enthusiasm of the huge audience. He greeted everyone on the platform in his characteristically affable manner, flashing the famous Eisenhower grin, and then sat in the vacant chair.

Turning to me he said, almost like an awed boy, "What do you know? I'm to receive the badge of a special agent of the F.B.I. Isn't that something?" He was absolutely delighted that he was

245

to wear the badge of such police authority. Mr. Hoover told me the President viewed this as one of the greatest honors of his life. He impressed me as just an American boy grown up a bit.

"Mr. President," I said, "I'm supposed to be the speaker here today, but when you are here no one else should speak. So I defer gladly to you."

"Not on your life," he responded. "All I want is that special F.B.I. badge and to hear one of your positive talks," he graciously added. Thus encouraged, I gave my talk, using my usual vigorous gestures and energy. The President's reaction was very generous. He said he liked a preacher "who fought bees while he preached," meaning, as I took it, an energetic and forceful style.

There is always an aura around the presidency. But Ike Eisenhower was such a delightful and enjoyable human being that one could talk to him with ease, as to an old friend. The title of his book *At Ease* is a description of how comfortable he made one feel.

I expressed surprise that after receiving his coveted medal and remaining courteously throughout my talk, he stayed on during the presentation of certificates to over two thousand men. He said that since those police officers had given a lot of time to the F.B.I. Academy, he guessed he could give an extra hour to honor them. "Besides," he added, and this completely floored me, "I am having a good time talking to you." It was not simply a polite remark. He was a straightforward and sincere man.

So for the greater part of an hour, we talked about the Christian life, about spiritual experiences, about how the Lord had guided him in various ways through some of his difficult decisions. He asked about my feeling of assurance regarding immortality and life after death; and he firmly testified to his own belief. "If the Bible says a thing is so, that is the end of it. It is so," he declared. As he revealed in that conversation Eisenhower was a convinced, Bible-believing Christian. And it was quite evident that he acquired his solid faith from his family background.

During our conversation I put a question to him. "Mr. President," I asked, "you have known all the great men of this world during your lifetime. I wonder who you would say is the greatest man you have ever known. Will you name him?" Without a second's hesitation he replied, "I sure can. But it isn't a man. It's a woman, my mother." He went on to say that his mother had never had much formal schooling, but she was highly educated just the same. "She went to school to the greatest of all books. From the Bible she acquired wisdom and insight in depth. She became intuitive and perceptive. She had profound understanding, due to her close walk with the Lord." It was a son proudly describing his mother, who obviously meant much to him.

"In this job," he said, "I have often wished that I could pick up the telephone and ask my mother what she thought of this man or that one. She knew people. She sensed what they were. And I would have relied on her thinking about a lot of things. Sometimes"—and he hesitated a bit at this—"I've actually tried to read her mind in heaven. And I feel her nearness."

He told me a story about his mother that impressed me greatly. One night in their farm home, Mrs. Eisenhower was playing a game of cards with her sons. He grinned. "Now don't get me wrong," he said. "They were not cards with kings and queens and jacks. Mother was too straight-laced for that. It was an old family game called Flinch, but it was played with cards, and hands were dealt.

"Well, Mother was the dealer and the hand she dealt me was completely impossible. I began to complain that with such a poor hand I had no chance at all. Finally Mother said, 'Put your cards down, boys. I want to give you some advice; especially you, Dwight. You are playing a friendly game here in your home with your mother and your brothers, all of whom love you. But out in the world, life will deal you plenty of bad hands and those involved may not love you at all. So the lesson is to take whatever hand is dealt you and with God's help just play it out.' I've never forgotten that advice of Mother's and I've just played out every hand and," he added, "God has helped me all along the way."

When Richard Nixon was a junior naval officer stationed in New York, he and Mrs. Nixon worshiped with us most every Sunday; and when the family lived in New York, they were frequently in one of the church pews.

Then Julie began coming to church with a likable young man, David Eisenhower, grandson of President Eisenhower. One day they came to see me with the news that they were going to be married and wanted me to perform the ceremony, which of course I was highly privileged to do. As the time for the wedding approached, Julie came to visit me at my office to discuss the ceremony, and she was carrying her own personal Bible as a help in understanding the significance of marriage. I was struck by her sincerity. Her father having just been elected President, I asked her if she did not want to wait until after the January 20 inauguration and be married in the White House. Her answer was that a wedding is a personal, religious service and she wanted to marry David in a church, in God's house.

And so it was that I joined David Eisenhower and Julie Nixon in holy matrimony at the altar of Marble Collegiate Church on December 22, 1968, with the Nixon family on one side of the center aisle and the Eisenhower family on the other. Mamie Eisenhower looked proudly at her grandson, always a favorite of Ike's. Ike, who was ill at Walter Reed Hospital in Washington, was able to watch the ceremony by means of closed-circuit television.

Sometime later, after a Sunday morning church service, Mr. Nixon told me that he was planning to hold religious services on Sunday mornings in the East Room of the White House that would be conducted by visiting ministers, priests, and rabbis. I commented that I seemed to have heard that William McKinley did something of that kind when he was President. However, it was later discovered that those gatherings were Sunday afternoon hymn sings, so President Nixon's practice was a historic innovation.

I spoke at four of these East Room services, which were attended by members of the Cabinet, the Supreme Court, the Senate, and the House of Representatives. Invitations were also extended to secretaries, cooks, maids, groundskeepers, police, and others; and they came as families. Thus, the congregation was a democratic gathering of Americans of varying statuses in life, and there a homey, spiritual fellowship was achieved.

On two of these occasions we stayed overnight in the White House. I recall that when we were about to be ushered into our quarters by President and Mrs. Nixon, the President asked whether we would rather sleep in the Lincoln Room or the Queen's Room. I was about to opt for the Lincoln Room when

Ruth asked why the other room was called the Queen's Room. The President replied that it was because of the many queens who had slept in that room and he pointed to their photographs on the walls: Queen Elizabeth II of England, the present Queen Mother, Queen Wilhelmina of the Netherlands, and others. "I'll tell you what," he said, "we have Queen Ruth with us tonight. So you sleep here." And so we did.

Always a fresh-air fiend, I crossed to the window in the Queen's Room to raise the shades, so as to open the window to the night air, but drew back when the light that always bathes the White House in its brightness suddenly silhouetted me at the window. The fence was lined with people trying to look in, even at that relatively late hour. I concluded then that being President isn't all a bed of roses and certainly privacy is at a premium. I climbed into the big four-poster bed and lay there thinking. "Do you know something, honey?" I said. "Ruth and Norman Peale, a country girl from Iowa and a country boy from Ohio, two preacher's kids from humble parsonages, are actually sleeping in the Queen's Room in the White House. Isn't that something?"

Next day I sat with the President in a very small room which in Lincoln's day had been where the telegraph instruments were set up to keep in touch with the battlefront. To this little telegraph room Abe Lincoln would come at all hours of the night for news of the armies and to know how the boys in blue were doing. Great was his heart, and here he yearned over the boys in Confederate gray also.

As a college student, I remember the nationwide consternation and feeling of disillusionment caused by the Teapot Dome oil scandal, which involved the secretary of the interior and the secretary of the navy, men close to President Harding. I have never discussed the Watergate matter with President Nixon. I regard him as a practical man of uncommon intelligence and, knowing him as I do, I find it difficult to understand how Watergate could have been allowed to occur.

Since Mr. Nixon's retirement from the presidency, the statesmanlike books he has written and the dignity he shows as a world figure have been admirable.

In 1968 at a luncheon following a service in the White House,

President Nixon said suddenly, "I want you to do a job for me."

"Certainly, Mr. President, I will be honored to serve in any way I can."

He said he wanted me to go to Vietnam on a speaking tour among our troops. It was in the very midst of the war. "I will arrange for you to speak to concentrations of men, to visit lonely posts, to see men in hospitals."

"What do you want me to talk about?" I asked.

"Just tell them the same things you tell us every Sunday in church. Preach the Gospel to them just as you do to all of us. Help them in any way that you are able."

In Vietnam I was under the supervision of Chaplain Colonel Will Hyatt who later, as a general, became chief of chaplains of the United States Army, a great personality and a delightful companion. We flew by helicopter to many outposts, to combat units, speaking to the soldiers, marines, and air force personnel about the deep things of life. I tried always to make my talks helpful to those of any faith, though never failing to present our Lord as Savior. Every consideration was extended to me by officers and men alike, and I had the honor of being a guest at a dinner given by General Creighton Abrams, the commanding officer.

Visiting hospital wards, I stopped to speak to each patient. Sometimes it was a word of prayer, in other cases I wrote a message to someone back home in my notebook. It was amazing to find that a man wounded on the battlefield could be in a well-equipped hospital within half an hour, and have the services of doctors as competent and expert as those back home. I shall never erase from my memory the small brown Vietnamese boy whose lifeblood was pulsating away through a gaping wound while young, earnest American doctors were doing their best to help him. I stood by and prayed lovingly for him. He opened his eyes in his misery and looked his thanks at me. "Why," I asked myself as I went away, "did such a fine boy have to die? Receive his clean young soul, O Lord," I prayed.

As we visited the front lines, there were always three helicopters accompanying the one in which we were flying. When I asked the reason, it seemed that a presidential emissary had the temporary status of a general and was therefore entitled to extra security. So it was that, quite unaware, I approached one of the great high points in my preaching ministry. We landed on Hill 55 where some thousand men in full battle dress were drawn up. "What do we do here?" I asked.

"You are here to conduct a memorial service for a regiment that yesterday lost eight men in battle." Then I noticed eight guns in the ground, upended, each with a helmet atop its butt. The troops sat on the ground in rows, facing a makeshift podium draped with a flag.

I looked at the young faces before me. "Why, they are only young boys," I thought. Never shall I forget the serious expressions on their youthful faces. "What shall I speak to them about?" I asked the commanding general seated beside me.

"Talk to them about their God and their country. What else is there to talk about? Some of those boys will likely be dead before the sun goes down today," he concluded solemnly.

A fine-looking black sergeant sang that inspiring hymn "How Great Thou Art." A chaplain read the Twenty-third Psalm and the fourteenth chapter of the book of John, his voice filled with tenderness as the great old words went out to the farthest row on that bleak hill, which had been swept clean of all vegetation by gunfire. The men listened in deep silence, each of them no doubt thinking long thoughts of little churches back in Ohio or Nebraska or on the sidewalks of New York. During the service we could hear bombing in the distance and actually could see planes dropping bombs.

Then it came my turn to speak. As I looked over the sea of young faces, I choked up for a minute. Then I talked of home and loved ones; of the many places from which they had come. I described their country from the rocky hillsides of New England to the lush plains of the Midwest, the beauties of the North, South, East, and West. I spoke of the freedom America gave to all men. "It's a fair land," I said. "A beautiful country of hills and plains and towering mountains, of villages with tree-shaded streets and great cities and wonderful people, our native land."

I gave thanks for the eight men who had died and committed them to God. I talked about God, their Heavenly Father, and Jesus Christ, their Savior, and urged each one who had never done so to commit himself to God. I closed with a prayer that the Lord would watch over each one, always, to the very end. A hymn followed, then taps, the benediction, and the service was ended.

I proceeded to the helicopter and looked back to see all thousand men and officers standing at the salute. It became evident that they were saluting me. I scarcely knew what to do, for as a civilian, it was hardly proper for me to return the salute. Anyway they were all-American boys, my countrymen, my boys—so I just waved to them.

Suddenly all thousand men broke the salute and waved back. And as the helicopter took off, I could see them still waving to one of their simple pastors from back home. I have to confess that I sat back in my seat and shed some tears.

A few days later, I flew with Will Hyatt in a navy plane onto the deck of the aircraft carrier USS *Kitty Hawk,* lying miles offshore in the Gulf of Tonkin. As we approached the carrier over the sea, it looked like a toy ship down there. But it quickly grew in size, and we descended to the flight deck in what to me was a thrilling landing. I occupied the captain's quarters while he was on the bridge all night. And in the evening, on the wide forecastle, I spoke to most of the five thousand men on the ship. It was a rousing evangelical service with hymns, prayers, and a sermon in which the central appeal was for commitment to the Lord. The response was most gratifying.

Though Chaplain Hyatt and I had dinner with the fleet admiral and other officers, I had a chance to go down the line where the men were being served. It warmed my heart to see the huge roasts of beef and lamb, the turkey and chicken as well as large steaks, the many kinds of fresh vegetables and fruit, and the mouth-watering pies and cakes available to the boys. And their plates were piled high! It was very satisfying to know that our government was taking care of our men in this bountiful manner.

Next morning we took off from the *Kitty Hawk* flight deck. Never in all my flying experience had I felt so powerful a thrust as when that catapult projected us into the air. After leaving *Kitty Hawk,* the aircraft slowly sank down from deck to deck of the great ship until it seemed that we would plunge into the sea. But slowly, laboriously the engines began to lift the aircraft, and it gained altitude, circled the ship, and headed for Vietnam.

During this takeoff I saw Will's lips moving. Later I asked him if he was praying at that moment, to which he replied, "What do you think?" I knew, for I was praying, too. Next day I left my friends in Vietnam with unforgettable memories and joined Ruth in Bangkok.

It so happened that my speaking schedule put me on the platform several times with the late Frank Lausche, onetime governor of Ohio, later senator. While Frank was a Democrat, he was always able to gather Republican voters in significant numbers. This was not due to any fence-straddling on his part, but rather to the fact that he was well liked personally. He had a compassionate love of people and was kind to everyone. For example, he would listen intently to my speech when we spoke together. I could hear him behind me on the platform laughing heartily at my jokes, and afterward he would say it was "a terrific speech." And he was not putting it on. He sincerely thought everyone did a good job. Perhaps a reason he was so well liked was that he helped bring out a person's best.

Frank Lausche and his lieutenant governor were in Youngstown, Ohio, late one night, and the two men sat at a lunch counter unrecognized.

Governor Lausche asked the white-capped, rather saturnine waiter behind the counter his name. The man, uninterested, replied, "Joe."

"Well, Joe," continued the governor, "you will be pleased to know that this gentleman is the lieutenant governor of Ohio." Unimpressed, Joe merely grunted. The lieutenant governor in turn said, "That isn't all of it Joe, this gentleman is the governor of Ohio." Whereupon Joe plunked both hands down on the counter and said, "Okay, let's get this straight. You are the governor and you are the lieutenant governor. That makes me the President of the United States."

I recall once years ago speaking in Allentown, Pennsylvania, at a dinner honoring Supreme Court Justice Frank Trexler. One of the speakers was the lieutenant governor of the state, who later became governor. He said that as lieutenant governor, he had to make an official trip out into the state and got on a train in the Harrisburg station. Shortly thereafter a couple of guards also boarded the train from the state mental institution (back in those days it was called the state insane asylum) with twenty men who had been committed to the institution, and they sat down all around the lieutenant governor. Before the train started, one of the guards started counting the men: "One, two, three, four, five, six, seven." Then he came to the lieutenant governor. "Who are you?" he asked.

"I am the lieutenant governor of Pennsylvania."

"Eight," the guard said, going on with the count.

Another time I was the speaker at a national drugstore convention in Chicago and was backstage when the famous longtime mayor, Richard Daley, came in. He was slated to give an official welcome to the convention, a function of all mayors. After his speech he came and sat by me, and said he looked forward to hearing my speech. "Now look, Mr. Mayor," I said, "I deeply appreciate your courtesy, but I know how terribly busy you are, so please do not take up your valuable time by staying here." And I shook his hand, sure that he would leave.

But when I finished the speech and returned to my chair, there sat Mayor Daley. To my astonished "Are you still here?," the mayor replied, "When I left home this morning I told Mama that you were speaking here and what do you think she said! 'Now look here, don't you run off as you usually do. You just stay and listen to that talk, for you need more of this positive thinking.' "

Mayor Daley was a most interesting man and deeply religious. Once in talking with me on this subject, he told me he went to Mass or stopped in a church almost every day.

Ruth and I have had all sorts of experiences across the years, some funny, some pathetic, some bizarre, others inspiring. One curious event has never ceased to puzzle me. Ruth and I were spending a few days in Manila where I was giving some talks. We were invited one evening by Mr. and Mrs. Go Puan Seng, the publisher of a Manila newspaper, to go with them to a state dinner given by President and Mrs. Marcos in the Malacañan palace, in honor of the President of the United States and Mrs. Nixon. The American President was making a state visit to the Philippines.

The two Presidents and their wives were seated up on a stage so as to view a program of Philippine folklore and music after the state dinner. Then suddenly an officer or aide, in a rather resplendent uniform, appeared at our chairs and, identifying me, said that Madame Marcos wanted Ruth and me to come to the stage to sit by her. Astonished, I replied, "You must be mistaken. I am a private citizen. Madame Marcos does not know me." I certainly did not want to experience the embarrassment of mistaken identity. He then said he had orders from her to bring us to the stage, and that we were to be seated beside her.

So we accompanied the officer to the stage, where we were pleasantly greeted and seated next to Mrs. Marcos. There was no explanation of this courteous but astonishing treatment of us, either then or later; nonetheless, we were flattered. Mr. Go and others guessed that the Philippines' First Lady had read some of my writings and wanted to show us this unusual courtesy. It was a rather remarkable experience for private citizens to be seated with two heads of state and their wives. Doubtless everyone was perplexed as to who we were.

Senator Robert Dole of Kansas and his charming wife, Elizabeth, secretary of transportation in President Reagan's Cabinet, occasionally worship in Marble Collegiate Church.

One Sunday they came into my office for a visit after services. It was shortly after Bob Dole had been defeated for Vice-President along with President Ford in the general election. Wondering how a man might feel upon having lost election to such an exalted position, I asked the senator, "I would be interested to know your inner feelings when you knew that you had lost the election to the vice-presidency." He weighed the question; no doubt I was presumptuous in asking.

But Secretary Dole quickly answered for both of them. "We have committed our lives to the Lord and always want to be in His will. We accepted the outcome on that basis and took the result as just not being in His will for us." She said this with such obvious sincerity as Bob nodded agreement that it made an unforgettable impression on me.

As a married couple they are unique in that he is a United States senator and she a Cabinet officer. Perhaps this is the first time that has ever happened.

The human quality, the down-to-earth absence of big shot-ism is something I have noticed in the truly great people I have known. When you are real, it is totally unnecessary to put on airs, and indeed such pretense would be repugnant to a truly with-it sort of person. In this connection I think of Herbert Lehman, onetime governor of New York. I remember him as one of the most approachable and delightful of men. Having appeared with him numerous times on programs of one sort or another, I got to know him quite well and he was always extraordinarily nice to me. Once, during World War II at a big meeting in the Waldorf-Astoria, I shared the platform with Governor Lehman, Postmaster General James A. Farley, and other dignitaries, each making a brief speech about war bonds, as I recall. Some members of the audience were somewhat restive about the subject matter, and a man, obviously half drunk, heckled a couple of speakers, but seemed especially to have it in for me. By some good luck I was able to soothe him with kindness, and he quieted down. Governor Lehman later spoke approvingly of my attitude. "Don't fight them, don't get mad, just love them. That's the way to do it."

"Governor," I replied, "you are Jewish, but you practice Christianity very well."

To which he replied, "Judaism teaches 'love your neighbor as yourself.' So I guess we are both on the same wavelength."

The sequel to this incident was that the heckler waited for me on the way out and said, "You're a nice fellow. Sorry I acted so badly."

"Sure," I replied, "we're friends."

To celebrate the tenth anniversary of my ministry, a church committee organized a special Sunday night service in October 1942. A number of dignitaries accepted an invitation to attend, but the committee especially wanted the governor. They did not know quite how to reach him, the number of secretaries they would have to go through, and all that.

Finally I was consulted. "Well," I said, "the governor has a telephone and so do we. Why not call him up?"

"Oh, the governor never talks on the phone like common people."

"This governor is very likely to talk. He is a regular guy," I said. "He will talk with anybody."

So I put in a call to the governor's personal secretary in Albany, saying I was Norman Peale and could I speak to Governor Lehman at his convenience?, and I would like to leave my telephone number. Quickly a voice came on the wire. "Hello, Norman. This is Herbert Lehman. Are you calling me up to pray for me? I sure do need it."

I explained about how we would be greatly honored to have him come to our celebration and started giving him an outline of it. But he broke in: "Sure, I'll be there. When is it?" He came and made a fine talk, sharing his own spiritual feelings in a sincere and unaffected manner. The congregation was captivated by him as, of course, I was, too.

Nelson Rockefeller liked people, all sorts of people, and he moved among them with his familiar "Hi-ya, fella," shaking hands and patting them on the back, and everyone loved him. The fact is that he was sincere all the way in his outgoingness. He was no phony backslapping politician out to get votes. Governor, later Vice-President, Nelson Rockefeller got the votes, plenty of them, because he was real and highly qualified.

I first knew him when we had sons in Deerfield Academy at the same time. Because he was reared, as all the Rockefeller children were, in a religious family, his faith obviously meant much to him, and from it I think he drew not a little of his motivation for public service. He was sincerely concerned about human betterment and wanted to do something about it. The personal side of his religious faith was a strong sustaining factor when he lost a son and went to faraway places futilely searching for him. He told me later that in this sad experience he "felt the reality of God. He truly helped me," he declared simply.

Nelson Rockefeller was a kindly man, and I found him to be very thoughtful of other people. The last time I saw him we were fellow speakers at the annual Rotary assembly for which the grand ballroom of the Waldorf-Astoria was filled with two thousand Rotarians from all the northeastern states. He spoke first that day, largely about his famous grandfather and his principles of constructive life. My talk followed, and, concluding, I went to the back of the platform where Governor Rockefeller was seated and sat beside him. He clapped me on the knee. "Great, fella, great," he said. He took a pen and scribbled something on his program. "Remember me with this," he said, handing it to me. It read: "To Norman Peale who has done more good for more people than any man alive." It was signed "With admiration, Nelson." I was overcome not only by the fact that he would make such a generous comment, but that such was his feeling for me. And I was touched by the friendly manner in which he performed this kindness.

At the end of our conversation I said, "Your brother, Laurance, is a dear friend of mine and I see him and Mary quite often."

He sat quietly for a moment and said, "Laurance is a saint, a wonderful, good man." Then he said he had to go. Patting my back, he said, "Be seeing ya, fella," and walked off the stage. Two weeks later he was dead.

I met President Jimmy Carter when he was governor of Georgia. Every year *Guideposts* magazine gives an award to some church, large or small, which has accomplished something innovative and outstanding. In 1974 the award went to the Church of the Exceptionals in Macon, Georgia—"Exceptionals" denoting handicapped people.

Mrs. Peale and I went to Macon to confer the award and were greeted by a capacity crowd of ten thousand in the Macon city auditorium. Four rocking chairs were placed on the stage for Governor and Mrs. Carter as well as for Ruth and me.

An altar had been prepared in front of the stage to create the effect of a church. A young man, having an acute spastic condition that made the control of his arms and legs most difficult, came forward haltingly to light the candle with a taper. The entire audience seemed to strain with this afflicted young man in an effort to help him control his gyrating hand and arm enough to apply the taper to the candle.

Governor Carter was sitting in the rocker next to me. He leaned far forward in his eagerness, and I distinctly heard him say in an earnest whispered prayer, "O Lord, please help that poor boy light that candle." When the boy accomplished the task, the face of the future President lighted up in a very relaxed smile.

Years ago I often made speeches with Jennings Randolph, and I have always considered him one of our greatest speakers. After he was elected Democratic United States Senator from West Virginia, I didn't see him so much. However, once when I had a speaking engagement in West Virginia, I was told someone would meet me at the Charlestown airport to drive me some miles to the place of the meeting. The night was wild with wind and heavy rain. Who should be awaiting me but U.S. Senator Jennings Randolph, who drove me through that inclement night to and from the meeting, where he gave me one of his great introductions. When I expressed my embarrassment that he had gone to such trouble, he replied, "Can't have an old friend come to our great and hospitable state of West Virginia and not keep him out of the rain."

Perhaps our church had a hand in helping give a start to at least one national political leader. The men's league at the church raised scholarship money to be given deserving students. One recipient of this aid was a boy named Guy Vander Jagt at Hope College in Michigan. He distinguished himself in college, and later became a United States congressman from Michigan and a leader in the House of Representatives. He says that the scholarship aid from the church made the difference whether he could get an education. I thought of this as I heard him deliver an eloquent speech nominating Ronald Reagan for President at a national political convention.

James A. Farley, onetime postmaster general, was an old friend. He is credited with helping Franklin D. Roosevelt become President. Farley was one of the most naturally friendly men I have ever met. It wasn't just being a politician that motivated his outgoingness. Once he told me with great joy on his face and in his voice, "I've become reconciled to the only two men with whom I've been on the outs. I went to each of them and we straightened out our misunderstandings, vowed to forget it, and we reestablished our once strong friendship. Now I'm at peace with every person in this world, thank God," he said, smiling.

When Ruth and I had been married twenty-five years, we gave a reception at the church that was attended by several thousand people. For those who were waiting to greet us, standing in the long, slow-moving line that hot June day must have been an ordeal. Someone came up to me and said, "Jim Farley is way back in the line."

"Tell him to leave the line. Please bring him up here now. Everyone will approve."

The man returned quickly. "Mr. Farley refuses to bypass the line. Says he would stand in line for you anytime."

When finally he reached us, I voiced my regret that he had been forced to wait so long. All he said was, "I respect you and Mrs. Peale as servants of God and as my dear friends." Jim Farley was one of the men of big soul whom I have been honored to know over the years.

Once I spoke with him at a book-and-author luncheon in Philadelphia. The people at the head table assembled in a suite upstairs. On the way down to the ballroom, I was walking with James Farley when we passed a maid beside her cart. Mr. Farley stopped, put out his hand, and said, "Hello, my name is Jim Farley. What's yours?" And passed by, leaving the girl with a big smile of surprise and happiness. He was totally unaffected and outgoing not only in his love of people but also in his esteem for everyone.

CHAPTER NINETEEN

I Like People

MY OLD EDITOR, Grove Patterson, for whom I had worked as a reporter on a Detroit newspaper, titled his autobiography *I Like People*. So do I, and I want to tell you about some I have known and liked. Of course, there are many more I could write about, but a book can be only so long.

One man whom I thought had a very exciting personality was a poor boy from Columbus, Ohio, who became an authentic American hero and the developer of a large airline. His name was Captain Eddie Rickenbacker, one of the unforgettable men this country has produced.

He told me once of the poverty in which he was reared and how in his family, clothing was handed down, getting more ragged as it passed from child to child. I noticed that the incident in the hand-me-down process that really got to Eddie was when he had to wear an older sister's shoes. They were of the old-fashioned high-button type. "Think of a guy like me wearing my sister's shoes. I pulled my pants as low as they would go trying to hide them." After forty years this episode still rankled in Eddie's memory. He determined savagely that he was going to rise out of poverty.

He idolized his mother. "Every night all us kids knelt by our beds and said our prayers. Then she kissed us good-night and stroked our cheeks with her toilworn hands, hands that I knew were once soft and pretty." And his hatred of poverty came through as he said this.

Years later Eddie was in an airplane accident that almost took his life, and ever afterward he had a game leg. Once when I was with him, he asked me, since because of his leg he could hardly kneel down to say his prayers, "Would it be O.K. if I sat while I prayed?" Despite my assurance that he could do so properly, it was evident that it was hard to overcome his childhood training to kneel.

In the story of aviation, the name of Eddie Rickenbacker looms large. He flew when pilots did so, as he put it, "by the seat of their pants and the great radio beam." He was ever a positive thinker. As an automobile racer, he believed he could bring a car in with the power of his mind no matter what might happen to it mechanically. An indomitable daredevil, deeply patriotic, he became the American flying ace of World War I, shooting down enemy aircraft, often flying back to the base on one shattered wing but on an unshattered prayer of faith. At least, so he said, giving you a look as if he would punch you if you expressed doubt.

He had enormous faith in prayer, seemingly having no doubt at all about its efficacy. Adrift without food in the Pacific Ocean with his aircraft crew, Eddie prayed. Shortly afterward a gull alighted on his head. It provided just enough food to sustain them. This story was widely printed in the United States and discounted by a few ministers who were disposed of by Rickenbacker as being "far-out, left-wing so-and-sos." "I was there," he declared. "I prayed to my Heavenly Father Who watches over us all, and He sent that bird to save our lives, and that is all there is to it." And he concluded with a few expletives that had better be left out of this narrative.

Once during the war I went with Eddie to an air force rehabilitation center and hospital that had been set up in Trinity-Pawling School under supervision of my friend the celebrated Dr. Howard Rusk. Looking at the injured and suffering airmen who had been shot up in the war, Rickenbacker talked to them like a father of his love for them and his admiration of their service to their country. After he finished his talk, he was given a thunderous ovation, for he was the idol of every flyer present. Then he held up his hand for silence, and with a choke in his voice, the old hero said, "And listen, fellows, one thing more and take it from me for I know what you have been through and have had to face. I've been down the same road myself. Pray to God and our Lord Jesus Christ. And listen, you guys, if you have never had a deep spiritual experience, for God's sake get yourself one." The ovation he received after those remarks far outdid the other. Tears glistening in his eyes, he said, "Come on, Norman. Let's go. I can't take it any longer. What great guys they are."

As we walked down the corridor, I said, "Believe it or not, Eddie, you're a great guy yourself."

Eddie Rickenbacker finally gave up to his old enemy, death. They wanted me to conduct his funeral at my church. I was in Europe, and so Lowell Thomas and my old friend Dr. Daniel A. Poling took the service. But had I been there, I would have told the overflow audience of admirers of the time in Rickenbacker's office when a delivery boy came into the outer office with a package just as I was on my way out. Looking into the inner office, he saw Eddie. Eyes popping with awe, he asked, "Is that Captain Eddie?"

"It sure is, son," I replied. "Want to meet him?"

"I'd give anything just to shake his hand," he replied.

"Eddie, this young fellow wants to shake your hand."

He rose, took the boy's hand, and must have seen the adoration in his eyes. "Son, always be a good American and have faith in God."

Outside in the hall the boy said, "I will remember this all my life."

As I look back over the crowded years and start counting up all the people I have known, I realize how very much I have learned from them. There was Amos Sulka, for example, who came to New York penniless a long time ago and became a prominent haberdasher with expensive shops in New York, Paris, and other places. He was a fellow member of the Rotary

Club of New York. I was asked to speak at his funeral service and pay tribute to this man whose story was in the great old American tradition.

Once Amos said to me, "To do a good job with anything, you've got to know all there is to know about it. Then do the best you can, study, trust God, be honest, give value received, have good merchandise, treat people right, and hold your own when you know you are right." He told me about the time he met William Randolph Hearst. Hearst owned the *New York American* and other newspapers. At that time he was probably one of the greatest newspapermen in the world. He was said to be a tyrant, very set in his ways, and imperious. I met him once, and he was impressive in the stern manner in which he looked at you. He was very assertive; he ordered everybody around and was accustomed to being obeyed.

One day, when Hearst was well along in years, he came into Sulka's shop, according to Amos. A clerk, failing to recognize him, asked, "May I help you, sir?"

Hearst snapped, "I want to see Sulka!"

"But," said the clerk, "he is the owner and does not usually wait on the trade."

"I am William Randolph Hearst and I want to see Sulka."

So Sulka came out and said politely, "Welcome, Mr. Hearst, what can I do for you?"

"I want some new collars just like the one I'm wearing," said Mr. Hearst. This was in the days of separate collars that fastened onto the shirt. "I want two dozen of them."

"Mr. Hearst, I am Mr. Sulka, the greatest haberdasher in the world, and I am now speaking to Mr. Hearst, the greatest newspaperman in the world. I must tell you that the collar you're wearing doesn't suit you at all. I just cannot sell you that collar."

Hearst bristled. "Look here, Sulka, I have worn collars of this kind for years. I know what collar to wear. Either you give me this collar or you don't sell me anything."

Sulka replied quietly, "I would rather sell you nothing than sell you that collar. I do not want the great William Randolph Hearst to be seen in an incongruous, out-of-date collar."

The eyes of the two men met, both of them knowing their

business, both strong men; and finally Hearst said, "All right, you old egotist, what collar do you want me to wear?"

I asked, "Did you sell him your choice of collar, Amos?"

"Of course I did, and year after year he came back for more. Hearst was big enough to admit when he was wrong."

Amos Sulka *knew* his business and therefore had confidence. He was an excellent salesman.

Ruth and I were among the guests at dinner in the White House when DeWitt and Lila Wallace were honored as great Americans. The President of the United States presented them both—for they were ever a team—with the Medal of Freedom, the highest honor the President can bestow upon civilians. When Mr. Wallace stood to acknowledge this great honor, he said, "I am supposed to be shy and tongue-tied but . . ." Then he proceeded to make a moving and thought-provoking statement about his love of country and the opportunity it offers to all.

This remarkable man, always a reader and thinker, had a simple but unique idea that none before him had ever had or at least had never implemented. This was to digest interesting articles from every source and publish them in magazine form. He sent a prototype to ten of the largest publishers in New York, and every one turned him down. William Randolph Hearst told him the idea could never succeed. Undaunted, he launched out on his own with six hundred dollars from his father and his brother. The idea did succeed; the *Reader's Digest* became the most successful magazine in history with a monthly circulation of eighteen million copies in the United States and another thirteen million abroad.

As has been said before, six words determine the success of any enterprise: "Find a need and fill it." The need in this case was man's enduring desire to improve himself. Mr. Wallace filled his magazine with articles that helped the reader find more fulfillment in life. He made an incredible contribution in his lifetime. He believed in certain basic things—in God, America, and human values.

Wally was a quiet, rather shy man of impressive stature, and even in old age never looked old. Always there was the touch of enduring youth about him. He was a sturdy Christian and an equally sturdy American. He never put himself forward and, despite his fame, always maintained a simple profile.

When DeWitt Wallace died at age ninety-one, I conducted the memorial service. It was attended by a distinguished company of friends and co-workers of the *Digest,* and was held in Wally and Lila's beautiful home, "High Winds," set upon a hilltop in Westchester County. As I rose to speak, I heard the wind sighing around the house. I let a silence fall so that all might hear the sound. "Listen to the wind," I said. "Nature is joining us in mourning the passage from the human scene of one of the greatest and gentlest spirits we shall ever know. . . ."

John Galbreath was a country boy from Mount Sterling, Ohio. His father, an impoverished farmer, eked out a precarious living from twenty acres of land. The family were good religious people, and John grew up with the positive idea that America offered opportunity to a young person of faith and character who would work, think, treat people right, and practice honesty and frugality, all Horatio Alger principles. He was gifted with a charming personality and the ability always to be the same lovable down-to-earth person even when he became the possessor of great wealth.

John, a leader in real estate, has restored a large and decaying section of Columbus. He has also built Mei Foo, an astonishing residential development in Hong Kong housing some eighty thousand persons. He is the owner of the Pittsburgh Pirates National League baseball club. As a raiser of fine racehorses, he has won several Kentucky Derbies. Through a common interest in horses, he became a friend of Queen Elizabeth II. But despite all this achievement and distinction, John Galbreath has remained an Ohio country boy who loves the land and the old American ways.

I recall the night when he and his wife, Dorothy, drove us to a speaking engagement at an evangelistic church service held in a restored barn. The old time hymns and the Gospel brought tears to John's eyes, as they did to mine. Through a torrential, at times blinding, rainstorm, with John at the wheel we made it back to Darby Dan Farm, where we ate a bowl of cornflakes in the kitchen, less than fifty miles from the twenty-acre plot where he was born. From his own airport John's jet plane often takes off over the dusty country lane along which he trudged as a boy.

Some years ago I was a frequent guest on Art Linkletter's popular TV programs. I have spoken with him at many a sales rally or convention. Once he came all the way from the West Coast just to emcee a dinner given for Ruth and me in the Waldorf Astoria grand ballroom.

As a public speaker, Art has an extraordinary genius for winning an audience. I have watched the process many times and always with admiration, and I must say I have learned much by listening to him. To begin with, the audience is electrified by his name, for it has gone deeply into American consciousness and is universally honored. Then this big, fine-looking fellow walks unhurriedly across the platform to the podium and stands with that great smile of his as the people give him—inevitably—a standing ovation before he even begins his speech. He projects the fact that he likes people, then he just proceeds to talk to them like a friend. As a speaker he has the rare ability to be relaxed, so he puts an audience at ease and unconsciously people react to that. Art must be one of the best-liked men in America. And one of the most respected, too, for all know that in tragic experience he is supported by a sturdy faith. He illustrates the truth that if you like people, they will like you back.

For many years a romantic cowboy and cowgirl, Roy and Dale Rogers, rode into the hearts of millions of American children and adults, too. During their annual Madison Square Garden engagements, they would always be in church on Sundays. On these occasions crowds would line up to shake their hands. To them, Roy and Dale were the personification of America.

These two people are such dedicated Christians that they always give a witness. Roy, astride his famous horse Trigger during a thrilling performance, might pause to say a good word for Jesus Christ and advise his huge audience of kids to live right. Once when a timorous sponsor warned Roy that he might terminate their contract because of this brief injection of religion, Roy did not hesitate to say that his loyalty to the Lord was more important to him than money. The sponsor, impressed by such strength of character, did not pursue his threat. He just might also have been impressed by the huge crowds thronging the Garden to see their favorites, Roy and Dale Rogers.

Another man who has long been an associate is W. Clement Stone, founder of the Combined Insurance Company of America, a sales expert, and an outstanding philanthropist. Clem, the son of a widowed mother, sold newspapers on the South Side of Chicago to help her eke out a living. He would go into a restaurant and peddle his papers from table to table to businessmen who lunched there. If the proprietor threw him out, which often happened, he would come back in through a side door. Finally the patrons, impressed by the boy's persistence, asked the proprietor to let him sell his papers. Eventually the newsboy came to be worth, so they say, a third of a billion dollars. He is one of those wealthy men who have money but by no means does money have them.

Clem gives away millions and always in ways that benefit poor boys and girls or people who are trying to make something worthwhile of their lives. He has a big heart and always wants to motivate people to find new opportunities for themselves. Over the years he has probably given two million dollars to the work of our Institutes of Religion and Health, of which he was chairman. His picture hangs in an honored place on the walls of the Institutes alongside that of the founder, Dr. Smiley Blanton, and mine. His benefactions are too numerous to mention here, but it is significant that Dr. Arnaud C. Marts, the acknowledged authority in the field of benevolent giving and author of the classic *The Generosity of Americans,* stated that "Clem Stone is the most generous man I have ever known."

Clem is also one of the world's great positive thinkers, having popularized a system which he called P.M.A. (Positive Mental Attitude). He always had a strong compulsion to teach positive attitudes to everyone. With Napoleon Hill he wrote several books, one of the most popular being *The Success System That Never Fails.* He founded the magazine *Success.* To Clem, life is terrific, opportunity is terrific—and in my opinion *he* is terrific.

I telephoned him once about some difficulty that had developed in the Institutes of Religion and Health. "Clem," I said, "we have a problem."

"Congratulations!" he shouted over the telephone.

"But it's a very tough problem," I explained.

"Then double congratulations," was his reply. After listening to the details of the difficulty, he came up with one of his great positive insights: "To every disadvantage there is always a corresponding advantage."

From boyhood John Walton, Bert as he was called, had a dominating inferiority complex. Convinced that he had only an ordinary mind, he proceded to act on that negative assumption with the result that he flunked out of several schools to which his moderately well-off father was able to send him. Finally graduating at the minimum level of academic work, he secured a job only to have his long-developed failure pattern appear once again. Then he lost several jobs in succession for the same reason. Not surprisingly, his work performance did not exceed the low competency level at which he viewed himself.

Presently he secured a minor job with an American corporation doing business in Australia, where Bert lived. He started well, for his attractive personality commended him, but it was not long before the old failure pattern began once again to assert itself. About that time an executive from the home office in the States came to Sydney. Having a special interest in the young people of the organization, this official held several meetings at which he talked about the potential built into personality. He stressed the idea that "you can if you think you can," pointing out that as one cultivates positive thinking, the failure pattern gradually becomes eradicated.

Bert had never before been exposed to this type of thinking. At first he was surprised to realize that by merely changing one's thoughts and attitudes a dramatic reversal could take place within one's nature. Surprise gave way to excitement and excitement to belief, which was followed by all-out acceptance of the positive thinking philosophy. For the first time in his troubled young life, he began to believe in himself and to entertain an enhanced respect for talents he never imagined he possessed. Still, he was tortured by the feeling that he had only an ordinary mind and therefore faced a limited future.

The official had taken a special liking to the young man, accurately sensing his locked-up potential. He countered the "ordinary mind" obsession with the concept that he could actually become an extraordinary person by developing a positive instead of a negative thought pattern, and by the cultivation of an additional principle called imaging.

He explained a powerful truth that I have often written and spoken of: a deep tendency to become precisely what you habitually imagine or image yourself to be. Such a mental picture when held long and persistently tends to reproduce itself in fact. Visualize yourself as inferior, and the net result is likely to be inferiority. See yourself as sick or weak or incompetent, and those characteristics are thereby encouraged to develop. On the other hand, positive images produce positive results.

The company executive then did something which started the young man upon what ultimately became a distinguished business career. "Bert, come with me," he said. He took him to the third floor and down a hall, stopping to look through a window where a gray-haired man sat behind a desk. "That is Mr. ——, manager of our company locally. He will retire in three years. Someone will succeed him. It can be you. If you are interested, I suggest that you see or image yourself in that chair. But to arrive there you will have to think right, work hard, in fact, give your present job all you have, and you have plenty."

Bert responded as outlined. In time, he became one of the most effective employees of the company, eventually occupying the imaged managerial position. Ultimately he was appointed head of the company for all of Australia. Always he carried in his pocket a small plastic ball in which was imbedded a mustard seed to remind him of the Scripture statement "If you have faith as a grain of mustard seed . . . nothing shall be impossible unto you." (Matthew 17:20) And came the day in London when Queen Elizabeth II dubbed him Sir John Walton. All of this seems to underscore the old and valid truth that a person can do incredible things with himself or herself by the persistent application of the positive principle.

* * *

In all investigations of this phenomenon, certain accompanying principles are usually present, such as a strong adherence to ideals of belief and conduct. A loyalty to moral concepts is likely to be involved as well as enthusiastic positive commitments.

All these principles appear in the case of the late Branch Rickey, one of the few greatest baseball executives in the history of the sport and head, successively, of the St. Louis Cardinals, the old Brooklyn Dodgers, and the Pittsburgh Pirates. Mr. Rickey's achievements were numerous and inspiring. Advancing years did not dull his consummate enthusiasm for the game. At a dinner to celebrate his fifty years of leadership, a reporter asked, "What has been your greatest thrill in fifty years in baseball?" Quick as a flash, Rickey answered, "I haven't had it yet." Needless to say, Branch was a positive thinker. He led scores of players to be positive also, and they went on to athletic immortality.

His adherence to moral and Christian principles was marked by his breaking of the color barrier in baseball when he brought Jackie Robinson into the Brooklyn club. He taught the fiery player to exercise control when bigotry was violently turned loose against him. Rickey's advice to Jackie when he hired him was to read and reread the New Testament and to pattern himself after Jesus when he was spat upon. Robinson's ability to follow this wise counsel made the first black big-league player not only an athletic tradition but a very great man as well.

When doubts were expressed about bringing black players into baseball and that "it wouldn't work," Branch Rickey was heard to say, "It has to work. And I am positive it will work. It's right and the right always works." It's a matter of historical record that Rickey's unqualified positive thinking on this moral question made it work.

Mr. Rickey was once in a tough negotiating session at the Union League Club in New York. The matter at issue was the rental of old Ebbets Field for pro football. The negotiations finally drew close to a settlement in which Mr. Rickey's baseball club stood to make a substantial gain.

Suddenly Rickey shifted his cigar to the corner of his mouth and clamped down hard on it. He threw his pencil down on the table. "The deal is off," he growled. "No dice." All looked at him in surprise.

"Why, we have just about reached agreement. How come you suddenly say the deal's off?" asked the head of the organization seeking to rent the baseball park.

"Because I don't like the way you keep talking about a friend of mine," replied the stocky, formidable Rickey. "I don't have to listen to it and I don't care a damn about the money."

"But I don't understand. I haven't said anything about any friend of yours. What friend?"

To which Rickey answered, "You keep saying Jesus Christ this and Jesus Christ that. He is my friend."

The other man sat stock-still. Silence sang in the room. "I get you, Mr. Rickey. He is my friend, too. I belong to the Holy Name Society. I won't do it again, I assure you."

At a later session of the negotiating group, Branch had a seizure, which could have been a heart attack, and he was put to bed in the club. A doctor attended him, and as his pastor I came and offered prayer. The man who had offended Rickey was also in the room, and I walked out with him. With tears in his eyes, he nodded his head toward the bedroom. "That fellow," he said brokenly, "is the greatest man I ever knew. He is a real man in my book." It was not a heart attack and Rickey recovered, but the above incident conveyed to all involved something of the rugged nature of a true positive thinker in action.

John Glossinger, a tall, gray-haired man with a big kindly face, was a personnel consultant whom businesses called on for help in dealing with employment problems. He referred to himself as a kind of doctor for sick companies that were not doing well in management-employee relations. He was low-key and had an enviable record for ironing out difficulties. He seemed to have a way about him that all was going to be o.k. "So just believe in good outcomes," he would say reassuringly. And he had an effect on situations, nothing spectacular or dramatic, but conditions always improved.

Perhaps one reason for his success was his positive approach to problems and to people. Because he believed in people, he had a way of bringing out qualities in them that had never appeared before.

Take the case of a young man in a shipping department. He did his routine job efficiently, seemed to like what he was doing, and got the merchandise out in good time and in good order. Glossinger noticed that the young man, Jack, was liked by everyone and could always be depended upon to get full cooperation. Even under pressure he was relaxed and seemed always to believe things could be well handled.

Glossinger came to his department one day and, sitting on an empty crate, said, "Jack, ever think of becoming a salesman on the road for the company?"

"Oh, no, sir. I am comfortable here in the shipping department." But Glossinger saw in this man the makings of an outstanding sales representative, and he was resolved to take him out of his secure but dead-end niche and gently but forcibly start him up on his way to a higher level.

Against Jack's protestations, Glossinger transferred him to sales, giving him a West Virginia territory, and said, "I'm going on the road with you for a few days to help you get started." John Glossinger was a highly competent salesperson, and Jack, being bright and observant, learned quickly. Finally Glossinger said, "Tomorrow morning I'm leaving you on your own. You are perfectly able to do this job."

"Oh," said Jack, "as long as I'm with you, Mr. Glossinger, I have confidence, but when I'm alone . . ."

"You're never alone," Glossinger interrupted. "Every day affirm the following: I am never alone. I know how to do this job. With God's help I will do it well. I will serve my customers for their best interest. I see myself getting maximum results. I am a positive thinker at all times."

John Glossinger related this story about Jack some years later after a dinner honoring the young man for achieving the highest sales record not only in his company but industry wide. When John Glossinger left Jack on the railroad platform that day in Wheeling, he started a young fellow with a positive attitude on the road to a successful career.

It is the custom of my church to have the minister's portrait painted. The artist selected to do mine was Howard Chandler Christy, then at the apex of his illustrious career.

Mr. Christy was a spiritually minded man with an inspiring

personality. He was a robust and gutsy person. Even in the dead of winter he would appear in the streets near Central Park West, hatless and coatless, his face ruddy in the cold wind, and greet you with a great shout and laugh.

One day while I was sitting for him and thinking of a sermon for the upcoming Sunday on the subject of worry, I asked him, "Howard, did you ever worry?"

"Not on your life. I don't believe in it."

"But haven't you ever worried?" I asked.

"Oh," he responded with a laugh, "only once and that was because everyone seemed to be worrying and I thought I must be missing something. So I decided to set aside one day on which to worry. I had a good night's sleep and a big breakfast, for I figured one should not try to worry on an empty stomach. Then I started worrying, but about ten o'clock in the morning I couldn't make head or tail of it and gave it up as a bad job. And I have never worried since."

"But how can you say that you have worried only once and for only a brief time?" I asked wonderingly.

The answer in his own zestful style was, "You see, every morning I spend fifteen minutes filling my mind full of God and so there is no room left for worry."

One can see Arthur Rubloff, the name of a top real-estate builder and developer, all over Chicago. One of his creations is the "Magnificent Mile," a glittering section of world-famous Michigan Avenue. Benefactor of the arts, collector, and public-minded citizen, he must be watched lest he give you the coat off his back.

On one rather warm May 31, my birthday, he and I visited his great Evergreen Plaza Shopping Center. I was hatless and wearing only a suit, while he was adorned in a derby and topcoat. Mr. Rubloff said, "You need a coat."

"I don't," I replied. "It's too warm."

"Winter is coming," he growled as he led me into a men's shop. "Give Dr. Peale an overcoat, a real stylish one."

He paid no attention to my objections, and I walked out clad in a classy topcoat with velvet collar, a stylish hat, and a dozen neckties. I watched Arthur as he moved along, gold-headed cane in hand. Admiringly I said, "Quite a cane you have there, Arthur."

He thrust it into my hand. "Glad you like it. It's yours."

"But I don't want a cane. I've never carried a cane."

"Time you did," said the now-caneless Mr. Rubloff. I tried to carry it with his style. Whenever I hear of someone being called big-hearted, I think of Arthur Rubloff, a poor boy who became another of America's Horatio Algers.

At one time I shared quite a number of speaking engagements with Millard Bennett. We gave our joint talks before large sales rallies in cities across the country and in Canada. Mr. Bennett is a great speaker with a rare power to move and motivate an audience. He possesses the gift of persuasiveness to a high degree.

At one meeting, Millard Bennett gave one of the best definitions of salesmanship I ever heard. "Salesmanship," he said, "is a process of persuasion by which another person is induced to walk a road of agreement with you." I liked that definition, for according to it, I, a preacher and writer, may also qualify as a salesman, since I try to persuade people to walk a road of agreement about the Gospel and positive thinking.

CHAPTER TWENTY

Health, Energy, and Long Life

A NEWSPAPER REPORTER after listening to one of my forty-minute speeches, accompanied by the usual forceful gestures, asked the source of what he called "my unusual energy."

The answer, I told him, is in the following quotation: "They that wait upon the Lord shall renew their strength; they shall mount up with wings as eagles; they shall run, and not be weary; and they shall walk, and not faint." "Hey, that's good!" he exclaimed. "Who said that?" He was surprised to learn it is taken from Isaiah, chapter 40, verse 31.

Frankly, I do not know why I am able to do more work in my mid-eighties than I could when I was half that age. I have asked many people who have lived a long life to tell me the secret of their longevity. One man said, "Because I have never smoked." Another told me it was because he had smoked cigars since his youth. Others say they have always eaten lightly. Yet others claim their great age is due to eating everything in sight. Some say they reduced their workload as they grew older, but some declare they have worked hard all their lives. Perhaps an overpreoccupation with advancing age may possibly have something to do with accelerating the aging process.

I give little or no thought to how old I am, but go about my business as always. If I were to remind myself constantly of my age, I might be persuaded to make no more speeches, write no more books, and take no more trips. But that would not be my way. I do endeavor to regulate my activities more carefully than in earlier years. Formerly, when I went out on a speaking engagement, I would let a committee meet me, show me around town, and set up a dinner; and after the speech, I would often shake hands with several hundred persons and top off the day by attending a reception.

But no more. If I must attend a dinner, my arrival at the ballroom is timed to coincide with the dessert. And after the talk, through prearrangement, I am escorted out of the ballroom or hall, and I go to my hotel room. I am far from being antisocial and I enjoy talking with people, but I have learned that socializing, shaking hands, and especially autographing, draw off energy more than the actual speaking.

When I was in my early fifties, I wrote in *The Power of Positive Thinking:* "The longer I live the more I am convinced that neither age nor circumstance needs to deprive us of energy and vitality. . . . The conservation of energy depends upon getting your personality speed synchronized with the rate of God's movement. . . . When we become attuned to God's rhythm we develop a normal tempo within ourselves and energy flows freely."

I sleep about eight to ten hours every night, going to bed as early as possible and rising early. I do not smoke and I eat moderately. My working day starts when I arise and ends when I go to bed. On trips Ruth and I inevitably take work along. We swim in the summer and walk a mile or two every day.

While eating and exercise programs are no doubt important for a long life and the continuity of energy, of greater importance is mental attitude, especially about other people. I can honestly say there is no one I dislike, certainly no person I hate or about whom I am angry or resentful—nor am I jealous of anyone. I believe that resentment, ill will, jealousy, hate, and kindred reactions produce illness and reduce energy. I once knew a doctor who told me that one of his patients actually died of "grudge-itis," as he termed it. This man's long-held grudge toward a former friend with whom he had fallen out made him ill and finally caused his death.

My basic rule for health, energy, and long life is to keep your thoughts healthy and positive in nature. I subscribe to a statement by Ralph Waldo Trine in *In Tune with the Infinite:* "Would you remain always young, and would you carry all the joyousness and buoyancy of youth into your maturer years? Then have care concerning but one thing—how you live in your thought world."

Of course, it helps to have good doctors. I have had the best of medical supervision by Dr. Louis Faugeres Bishop of New York City, Dr. Milnor B. Morrison, Jr., of Pawling, Dr. John C. Carson and Dr. Z. T. Bercovitz, both of La Jolla, California.

I have worked all my life and still work, only now more than ever. My scheduled daily habits or life-style can hardly account for my good health at this age. And Ruth, younger than I, has as much or more energy and health.

During our annual holidays in the Swiss Alps, Ernst Zingg, a manufacturer of processed Swiss cheese, and Max Schwab, a Swiss American businessman, taught us scientific walking and breathing exercises that have greatly contributed not only to our pleasure, but to our well-being too.

In these walks both men taught us to take two long breaths in and two long breaths out, while maintaining a relatively slow but always rhythmic pace. This practice is especially important on upgrades, of which there are many in the Swiss mountains. Nor does the true walker engage in conversation but proceeds silently, breathing in the prescribed fashion. At intervals, walkers stop to rest or admire the ever-changing and magnificent scenery, at which time talking is of course permitted. This disciplined walking has, I am sure, had much to do with our health. At home in New York City and on the farm, we walk two to three miles daily, and in the Swiss mountains, at least twice that distance.

Over the years I have greatly benefited from taking up walking as a daily priority. For one thing I feel sure it has helped in deterring the aging process. In his "Notes on Walking," Ralph Waldo Emerson says, "It's one of the secrets for dodging old age." Perhaps Thomas Jefferson had this benefit in mind when he said, "Of all exercises walking is the best."

I have taken many walks along Dutchess County roads with my friend Frank Wangeman, for many years the popular general manager of the Waldorf-Astoria Hotel in New York. Frank gave me a book, *The Magic of Walking*, by Ruth Goode and Aaron Sussman, which he inscribed "With affectionate esteem and in anticipation of many happy walks together." Goode and Sussman appraise walking as "a good medicine" and declare: "As we walk, our muscles literally milk the blood back to the heart." They further assert: "When we walk . . . the circulation speeds up and the heart rate and blood pressure go down." Well, having walked regularly for many years, I'm going as strong as ever and enjoying excellent health, so there must exist some logical relationship between the practice and the result.

Since I first became a positive thinker, I have naturally benefited immensely from never thinking negatively about myself. I constantly think health, never sickness. I have mentally repudiated physical, mental, and spiritual decline and disability.

One rather minor but interesting illustration of the power of positive thinking as it affects health is that many years ago I would always develop a horrendous cold in February. It would start with a sore throat, sniffling, aching—all the classic cold symptoms. Inevitably my vocal chords would end up being affected so that I could talk only in a croak. Then I was plunged into a crisis of whether or not I could fill contracted speaking engagements or preach in church on Sunday. Year after year this defeatist situation went on until one day I decided it was irrational and decided to stop it. I realized that there was no sense in the assumption that I must have a cold in February or indeed anytime. Accordingly I began to think positively that I need not have such a cold and that I could get through the winter season and never lose my voice, as had been my custom.

From the minute I took that firm decision, I have never had another cold, at least, never one that could inhibit activity. Even so, you must watch negativism like a hawk. Once when I was surrounded by people coughing and sniffling and talking about having colds, I forgot to think positively and began to join the chorus of snifflers. Quickly I caught myself, turned the positive thinking back on, and have never once missed a speaking engagement due to a cold. And I have never again been unable to use my voice.

I believe that any normally healthy person can determine creatively his or her state of well-being and maintain it at a high level with a strongly held positive self-attitude. Grove Patterson kept well by his positive view toward his own health. Once I walked into his office and asked how he was. "Terrific," he replied. "Terrific, and that's the way it's going to be. Besides, if I felt badly I wouldn't tell you for that would only be affirming a condition which I deny." Always deny an adverse condition. Deny that it can have any power over you.

Also I apply to my health and age the positive power of imaging. In human nature there is a strong tendency to become precisely what you strongly visualize yourself as being or becoming. See yourself as declining, and decline will inevitably set in. See yourself as sick, weak, or infirm, and these conditions will tend to reproduce themselves. See yourself as a feeble, confused old woman or old man, this self-image will actually make you as visualized.

An eighty-seven-year-old friend, Frank Bering, ran a big hotel in Chicago, the Sherman House. On one occasion I was at the hotel to speak to a luncheon meeting of some three thousand members of a convention of the National Standard Parts Association. Frank was directing this huge affair with his usual calmness and efficiency, and I watched him with admiration. "Frank," I asked, "how old are you anyway?"

He turned a cold stare on me. "What's the matter? Isn't your room all right? Is something lacking in our service?"

"Oh, no," I hastened to add. "It's just that you do everything so well and I was simply curious. Besides," I continued, "I know your age, for you went to high school with my mother."

"Well, since you know, why bring it up?" he growled.

Then he punched me in the chest. "Listen, son, live your life and forget your age." He explained. "When I look in the mirror, I don't see Frank Bering as an old man. Instead I see him as he has always been, an excited, happy young fellow. So the years have never been able to make me old because I won't let them."

James A. Farley was always vigorous and interested in everything, even in his later years. I asked him once, "Jim, how come you never get any older?"

His reply straight off was, "I never think any old thoughts. It's oldish thoughts that make a person old."

One day I ran into another old friend, Bishop Fulton J. Sheen, when he was along in years, and I was struck anew by his dynamic quality. "My, but you look good!" I exclaimed.

Whereupon he asked with amusement, "Did you ever hear the three ages of man?"

"What are they?" I asked.

"Youth, middle age, and my, but you look good." Bishop Sheen's secret was that he was always fascinated by the world, and he loved people and kept up his good humor.

From my own personal experience, and that of others as well, I became convinced that there definitely is both psychological and physical creative power in thought and in faith. This power depends upon the intensity of the belief of the individual.

In his healthy and vigorous old age, I became well acquainted with William H. Danforth, head of Ralston Purina Company. He was an enthusiast about health and exercise. Once when I was having a vegetable and cottage cheese lunch with him in a St. Louis hotel coffee shop, he expounded upon the value of a daily exercise program, and continued to describe the program after lunch as we were crossing the lobby. Suddenly he stopped. "I'll show you now," he said. Taking off his coat, he insisted I get down with him on the floor, and then and there he instructed me in push-ups and various other body-building exercises with particular emphasis upon reduction of the waistline. That a crowd was gathering bothered him not at all. He was widely known and respected, and I noted that this, shall we say, eccentricity further endeared him to his fellow St. Louisans.

Mr. Danforth's little book, *I Dare You,* is a gem of wisdom and motivation and has benefited me greatly in connection with my own health and positive attitudes. In the book he tells of his frail health and sickliness as a child. It was his good fortune to have a teacher in an early grade who was a "health freak." He believed that a sickly boy could become healthy, vigorous, and strong, and his method for dealing with young Bill Danforth was direct and forthright. "I dare you to become the strongest, healthiest boy in the class. You can do it. I dare you." Mr. Danforth told me that "dare" got to him and motivated him. "And," he chuckled, "I've outlived all my classmates, and I'm still stronger and healthier than most men I know." He was well along in years when he said this.

As I walked up the street with this vital man, I resolved to emulate his spirit, his philosophy, and his health regimen, which was: Think health, eat sparingly, exercise regularly, walk a lot, think positively about yourself, keep your thoughts and your actions clean, ask God Who made you to keep on remaking you. As we separated that day, he said, "I dare you to be healthy and live to a great age but never think age. Only think long life." Well, I took the dare. And incidentally some years ago in Taiwan, I bought a pair of gold cufflinks having on them a Chinese character for long life. I wear them much of the time, but do not really need them to remind me that long life has long since been carved into my consciousness.

I learned another attitude from Mort Cheshire, at one time the most famous player of the bones on the old vaudeville circuit. He was still healthy and vigorous at 102 years of age. "Mort, how do you account for your long life?" I asked.

He replied simply, "It's the Lord's will. I'm in His hands. He will give me life until He takes me home." The Lord did so when Mort was 103. Humbly, like Mort Cheshire, I have put my own life in the Lord's hands. He gave life. It is His to take when He deems the time has come.

While I was on a West Coast engagement my secretary, Doris Phillips, telephoned from New York to say that the White House had just called to notify me that I was to receive the Presidential Medal of Freedom from President Reagan at a White House luncheon on Monday, March 26, 1984.

Naturally this came as a great surprise. I sat in partial shock that I was to be so honored. I knew that the Presidential Medal of Freedom is the highest award the President of the United States can confer on a civilian and that it ranks with the Congressional Medal of Honor. My reaction as we talked of it, just Ruth and I together in our hotel room, was an emotional one. My first thought at that moment was of my mother and father, how in their straitened circumstances they scrimped and saved and denied themselves to put their boys through school and prepare them for life. How proud they would be that a son of theirs was actually to receive this great honor from the President himself.

The luncheon was a brilliant affair. President and Mrs. Reagan graciously received all the recipients and their families. Then the President presented the medals, saying a few words of commendation to each. It was an impressive and memorable moment in my life, and my heart was full, for never had this country boy from Ohio expected such recognition as this from the President.

I issued the following statement: "For me to be awarded the Presidential Medal of Freedom is the surprise and honor of a lifetime. If I have done anything to justify this distinguished award I am grateful. Like every American I owe so much to my country. I only hope I can give something to it."

Perhaps my continued participation in active life accounts for some of the surprising honors I have received lately.

We have lived in Pawling, New York, for over forty years, having a home there as well as an apartment in New York City. The Pawling Chamber of Commerce joined with the Pawling Rotary Club to give Ruth and me a testimonial dinner soon after the presentation of the Presidential Medal of Freedom.

The largest hall in town, the Holiday Hills YMCA dining room, was filled by a capacity crowd of friends and neighbors for the dinner on April 19, 1984, with Dr. James L. Stoner, president of Pawling Rotary, and Richard Novik, president of the Pawling Chamber of Commerce, jointly presiding. Speeches were made by John and Elizabeth Allen, my son-in-law and daughter. Their subject was "We're Proud of You, Dad." Ruth described our visit to the White House. Village, town, and county officials presented awards. The New York State Assembly presented a Legislative Resolution. The Town of Pawling changed the longtime logo of the town to "Pride of the Harlem Valley and Home of Positive Thinking." This pleased me immensely as did another award, the Rotary International Presidential Citation for 1983–84, the highest award of Rotary International.

My reply to all these distinguished encomiums was deeply appreciative but brief: "After this memorable occasion I fear I shall have difficulty getting my ego back into shape considering all the honor and love shown me tonight! I love Pawling. It is my home-town. I think it is the best village in the world with the greatest and kindliest people."

Sometimes I am asked if I have any plans for retiring. In reply I have to ask, "From what?" Actually I have at least six jobs at which I work currently: *Guideposts* magazine, the Foundation for Christian Living, the church, writing books, radio programs, speaking engagements. Almost any one of them could be a full-time occupation. I enjoy work. It has always been my life. The idea of retirement has no attraction for me. I think perhaps I will go right on with most of my present activities as long as the Lord continues to give me health and energy.

CHAPTER TWENTY-ONE

Help in Time of Sorrow

LIKE EVERY MINISTER, I have been involved in the sorrows of many persons. I have prayed with people in times of illness, comforted them in hours of grief, and stood by their side at the grave when death had taken a loved one. Always my purpose is to strengthen their faith and their assurance of God's love. To have had this privilege is certainly one of the great honors and deep experiences of life. The healing, comforting, and sustaining function of the ministry gives one a respect and a compassion and a feeling for people that would surely be difficult to surpass in any other occupation.

I recall the woman who asked me to come to the hospital. Standing by her bed, I asked, "How are you, Helen?" Her answer was strong and wise, unforgettable. "How am I? Well, my physical body is about to die, but I, Helen, am very much alive and ready for the future. You have helped me to conquer the fear of life and now the fear of death." Then she added, "As my pastor and our longtime friend, please stay close to Joe [her husband]. I've watched over him always. Strong guy that he is, he really is dependent. Let him lean on you for a while until he gets steadied up after I've gone." I saluted her as a great lady, and I think I was able to help big, old, pathetic Joe. This is an important part of the work of a minister, the comforting of grieving people, supporting them by the power of love and faith along with rational thinking and understanding.

In the course of years of ministering to the dying and as a result of my close association with death, I have gradually evolved an absolute conviction that physical death is by no means the end and that enhanced life continues after mortal life is concluded. And it is my unequivocal belief that life on the other side is of much higher grade than on this side. If we look upon mortal life as an incredible miracle, what an even more incredible experience will be that higher-level existence we call eternal life.

For many years at services commemorating those who have been translated from mortality to immortality, I have used a parable, the truth of which I personally believe to be unassailable. I think this idea came to me from something written years ago by Leslie Weatherhead of London. Let us suppose that an unborn infant in its mother's womb is able to reason and express itself. Suppose also that someone says to it, "Soon you will die out of this present state in which you are living or, as we in life call the process, you will be born."

The infant might protest, "But I like it here. I am fed, warmed, loved, and cared for. It is so pleasant and I am very comfortable. I don't want to die out of this place or be what you call born."

However, the change is inevitable and the moment comes when the infant does "die," or finish its appointed time in the womb, and it is born. Then what? The baby looks up into a beautiful face and into eyes looking down upon it in love. The infant is cuddled in loving arms, and is astonished by the wonder of the thing that has happened. The child soon discovers that all it has to do to get anything he or she wants is to cry or coo. Everyone loves the baby and runs to do its bidding. So quite soon the infant says, "Why, this is wonderful. This place they call earth and what they describe as mortal life is so much better than where I came from. This life is a great improvement over the former one."

And so the years of happy childhood pass, and the child becomes a youth, then moves into the exciting and creative years of young adulthood, and on into full maturity. He (or she) marries, and his children in turn experience the joys of parenthood and family. He knows the excitement of achievements and enjoys the rewards and engages in the struggles; solves the problems and knows the tears and laughter of life.

Then he begins to grow old, and perhaps the infirmities common to age come to him. One day the thought of death comes menacingly.

Again he is told, or more likely he tells himself, "I cannot stay here. I will pass away. I am going to die." And, as before, he protests, "But I don't want to die. I love it here. I do not want to leave this place. This has been my home for so long. I love life, the mystery of the dawn, the glory of sunset, the loveliness of the changing seasons. I love to feel the crunch of snow under my feet on a winter's night and to smell the rain on a summer's day and view the beauty of faraway hills half lost in their haze of blue. I don't want to leave those I love. I don't want to die."

But nature again takes its course. He does die. Now what happens? May we not rationally believe that he does not die, but instead is born once more? He looks up into a face more beautiful than that of his mother. Loving eyes look down upon him and underneath him are the everlasting arms. Again the law of development and growth proceeds—this time in a land, as the old hymn has it, that is "fairer than day."

Is God suddenly going to change His nature from one of love to one of cruel destruction? Is He unpredictably about to violate His own laws and plunge His creation into oblivion? Could He so treat him who is created in His own image? Such a concept does not make sense. It runs counter to the Creator's own rationality. Since He is "the same yesterday, and to day, and for ever," we can be certain not only spiritually but rationally that this mortal existence is but a temporary event in total life—and that it leads to its goal by the birth, death, and rebirth cycle to life that is immortal and eternal.

By every means of communication, I have hammered hundreds of times on the foregoing argument, which I sincerely believe to be the truth, the sure truth, and I have been rewarded time and time again by scholars and by the humble wise, who have given testimony that this reasoning has answered for them that old haunting question "What is death?" The simple answer is, it is the continuance of the responsible, normal, natural laws of God which He set in motion in the first place.

I have been particularly impressed by the number of scientific and practical people to whom this line of thinking has been mentally satisfying. Mrs. Thomas A. Edison told me that when her husband was dying it was evident that he wanted very much to speak. Bending low, the physician distinctly heard the great scientist say, "It is very beautiful over there." Edison never reported as fact something he did not believe or see. He was not a dreamer or a poet but an exact scientist.

In another book, *The Positive Power of Jesus Christ,* I tell of two practical men to whom these thoughts were profoundly helpful and convincing.

One day I received a telephone message that Mr. Alfred P. Sloan, the industrialist who had much to do with the creation of the General Motors Corporation and who was then its president, "desperately" wanted to see me. This seemed strange, since I had never met Mr. Sloan. It was explained that his wife of fifty years, to whom he was utterly devoted, had died, and he was desolated. No one had been able to give him any peace or comfort, and, being a reader of my books, he had now turned to me for help. He was so depressed that he was not leaving his house; the caller asked if I would be good enough to call upon him at his home in New York City.

Mr. Sloan was an impressive figure and had a dominant personality. He had a rather stern facial expression and a direct, businesslike manner. Fixing a cool, direct gaze on me, looking at me with eyes that brooked no evasiveness, he said, "I want to ask you a simple question and I don't want any weasel answer or philosophical discussion. I want a straightforward, unequivocal yes or no. I want an answer, and if you don't know it, say so." I gave him as straight and firm a look as he leveled at me. "O.K., you ask a straight question and I will give you a straight answer," I said.

"Here's what I want to know. My wife recently died. I loved my wife and depended upon her. When I die, will I be with my wife again? Now," he continued, "I called in a curate from a nearby church and put this question to him. He gave me a lot of inconclusive gobbledygook and actually came up with a sort of muttering that we take a more educated and modern look at such things as immortality in this enlightened day and age. I got rid of him as soon as I could. He was a not-dry-behind-the-ears kind of guy. Now, what's *your* answer?"

"The answer is yes."

"How sure are you?"

"Absolutely, positively one hundred percent sure."

In a sense I was amazed by Mr. Sloan's almost childlike quality, though outwardly he gave an impression of dominance and power. He explained that his wife had possessed a great mind and an intuitive knowledge of people plus the ability to reason. "I bounced all my ideas off her mind," he said, "and she came up with remarkable insights." He struggled with his emotion. "She was my life. To her I came home every evening. She was my home. Whatever will I do without her?" Tears stood in his eyes; his voice trembled. But he shook off the emotion. "So you're absolutely sure? Why?"

I proceeded to tell him the parable of the reluctant unborn infant, and that the reason for my certainty was that the Bible clearly teaches life after death for those who love the Lord and have experienced His grace. I quoted such passages as "Because I live, ye shall live also," and again, "I am the resurrection and the life: he that believeth in me, though he were dead, yet shall he live: And whosoever liveth and believeth in me shall never die." I reminded him of how Jesus appeared to many and that His own resurrection had impeccable proof. I also reminded him that "in him we live, and move, and have our being." I gave him every biblical assurance that came to mind at the moment.

Then I added, "Mr. Sloan, to be sure that you will meet your wife in eternal life, that quality of life must be in you. Tell me, then, your identification with the verse of Scripture: 'And this is the record, that God hath given to us eternal life, and this life is in his Son. He that hath the Son hath life; and he that hath not the Son of God hath not life. These things have I written unto you that believe on the name of the Son of God; that ye may know that ye have eternal life, and that ye may believe on the name of the Son of God." (I John 5:11–13).

He looked me straight in the eye. "I believe and I do have the Son of God."

"Also, do you subscribe to the following? 'If thou shalt confess with thy mouth the Lord Jesus, and shalt believe in thine heart that God hath raised him from the dead, thou shalt be saved." (Romans 10:9)

Again he affirmed his faith. "I do so confess."

I shared with him my own deep spiritual experiences in my personal times of bereavement and sorrow, and I told him how, through prayer and faith, I had received the divine assurance that somewhere, somehow, we would meet again. "You *are* a believer, aren't you?" he said. "And thank you, for you have strengthened my own faith. May I say that I, too, believe. I'm comforted. I, too, am sure." And he added, "I like a minister who believes, knows why he believes, and does not hesitate to witness to his belief."

Mr. Sloan himself has now moved on from this world to the other side, and that his faith and mine have been verified I have no doubt whatsoever.

Another rugged character was Lord Thomson of Fleet. Roy Thomson was one of the few great newspapermen of our era. At one time he owned and operated many newspapers in England, Scotland, Canada, and the United States. Eventually he owned the London *Times, The Sunday Times* of London, and the *Scotsman* of Edinburgh. He had a reputation for buying and selling newspaper businesses, and his enjoyment of this career was a byword throughout the English-speaking world. Born poor in Canada, Roy Thomson was created finally a peer of the realm—Lord Thomson of Fleet.

One day he invited me to be his guest at a luncheon in the sumptuous dining room of *The Sunday Times*. The company about the table consisted of the distinguished editors and writers of *The Sunday Times* as well as prominent London businessmen. The table conversation ranged over many themes: world affairs; politics, British and American; and the prospects for world peace. Suddenly, in the midst of general conversation, Lord Thomson said, "Dr. Peale, I would like to propound a question. I am becoming an old man, and one of these days I'm going to die." Silence fell in the room. "What I want to know is this: Is there an afterlife, do you believe in it, and if so, why? Tell me, for I really want to know."

Prior to this time there had been much humor and good-natured banter, but now the conversation took a serious tone. I wasn't sure that he wasn't pulling my leg a bit. Then I sensed that the question was indeed on his mind, that he was really serious. All those present listened intently.

"Well, Lord Thomson," I said, "I am no great scholar, only a practical sort of preacher, but I am a committed Christian and believe in the promises in the Holy Bible. I believe in immortality, in life after death, in the Christian plan of salvation for time and eternity. I am a believer, sir, and say to you that if you are in Christ you will be with Him in paradise." I stated to him the same biblical truths I had to Mr. Sloan.

"But even beyond the biblical, my Lord, is the evidence of intelligence and common sense. You are a man of rational, intelligent mind and you appreciate that which makes sense."

Then I went on to tell him and the others my parable of the unborn baby and noted not only his Lordship's profound interest but that of the entire luncheon company.

"Does this not make sense?" I concluded, suddenly realizing that I had talked too long. A deep silence hung over the table. Men coughed. Some brushed tears from their eyes. Lord Thomson sighed. "It does indeed make sense," he said. "I will never forget that parable. It has helped me by answering questions that have haunted me for years."

Then suddenly his mood changed. "Do you think I will like it over there?" he asked.

"Of course you will, for it will be exciting, and you've always been an exciting man."

"What do you think I will do there?" he asked with a grin.

"Knowing you, I think you may perhaps buy and sell newspapers!" A laugh went around the table as the luncheon party broke up.

On the way to the elevator, Lord Thomson put his arm around my shoulder. "I have always thought of you as a teacher of positive thinking," he said. "You know something, my friend? You are also a man of God. And I like you for both!"

Since then, Lord Thomson has gone on into the life beyond. I think God must be taking care of this gifted man, judging by the affirmative way he responded to the faith and the power.

This biblically oriented faith is, I believe, related to exact natural law, which may be defined as divine law. If, as I believe, God is the Creator, then it follows that He is the Author of all natural law. And natural law is the methodology by which everything works according to formula.

For centuries man slowly began to understand laws which had existed for all time but which he did not perceive or understand or use. Then the scientific era began and human beings developed a spectacular series of inventions. Invention is only the discovery of how to use natural forces, materials, and processes. An illustration might be Alexander Graham Bell's discovery of how the human voice could be transmitted over a wire. Then Guglielmo Marconi, Thomas Edison, and others discovered how it could be transmitted over radio waves without wires; later it would actually be accompanied by a picture of the persons speaking or singing.

We were astonished and awed at first by these discoveries and adaptations of law, but now, being satiated by wonders, we accept new ones not without interest but rather nonchalantly as normal and routine.

There is another area which we, like primitive man, think of as miraculous or outside natural law. And in referring to it, we use such terms as "mysterious," "psychical," "extrasensory perception," or "beyond sense." We even call it clairvoyance or, at its worst, phony. People who dabble in it are in danger of being considered oddballs or dreamy-eyed. But along have come a few adventurers in thinking like Steinmetz, Edison, Einstein, McDougall, Rhine, and others, notable scientific scholars who lend credibility to a vast body of truth that obviously exists but remains practically unexplored. No one would have visualized the conquest of air that followed the primitive experiments of the Wright brothers on the sands of Kitty Hawk. Men smiled tolerantly; it would never amount to anything.

But now we remember Steinmetz's prophecies of future scientific demonstrations in the realm of the spiritual, and Einstein's belief that intuition is an amazing avenue to knowledge, and McDougall and Rhine's demonstration of a real world beyond our traditional concepts of the universe.

For example, to the ancients heaven was up somewhere in the sky. But men fly routinely to 35,000 feet and have not encountered heaven, and even to the moon and have not come upon it.

This fact leads thinkers to a different concept of space, one that perceives the afterlife as occupying the same space in which we live, though in a higher frequency, an enlarged dimension. Stewart Edward White in *The Unobstructed Universe* uses a simple example of an electric fan as an illustration of this truth. When the fan is not on, one cannot, of course, see through its thick metal blades; but when the electric current is turned to high speed, one is able to see through the blades clearly. The stepped-up frequency enhances sight.

In similar fashion, though in a much more sophisticated way, the higher elevation of spiritual insights may now and then penetrate the barrier between this side and the other and provide glimpses or intuitions or some sort of perceptions or flashing illuminations of that heaven which does more truly than ever imagined lie beyond. And it is to this superimposed state of life, this heaven, that our deceased loved ones have gone and to which we, in our time, shall pass through a gate we call death but which more accurately is the entrance to a higher life.

I came to this view of life and death and enhanced life gradually over the years both through study and certain personal experiences. I had heard reliable persons tell of similar experiences, though always reluctantly through fear of being considered a bit "touched." Although I had read extensively about communication with those who had crossed to the other side, I approached such literature cautiously and with a scientific attitude. A literal-minded boy from Ohio, I was dubious about anything I had not experienced myself.

Then one night my mother died after a joyful evening we had spent together in the family home at Canisteo, New York. I had taken a midnight train to New York. Scarcely had I arrived at our apartment when the telephone rang. It was my wife, Ruth, who gently gave me the news that Mother had just died. Naturally I was shocked and stricken with grief and loss. At sixes and sevens, I went to the church and sat in my chair in the pulpit. She had always told me that whenever I went into the pulpit, she would be right there with me. I sat awhile, thinking of her and trying to feel her presence. But I believe generally the first shock of the death of a loved one makes us feel temporarily alone in the world.

Still distraught, I went to my study in the church, the windows of which face Fifth Avenue. On the desk was a Bible Mother had given me many years before. It is my custom every Sunday, just before going into the main sanctuary to preach, to put my hands on that Bible and offer a prayer. So at this moment instinctively I placed my hands on the Bible, looking unseeingly at the avenue beyond the window. Suddenly, I seemed to feel two cupped hands resting lightly but distinctly upon my head.

At once my scientifically trained mind, my modern speculative rational intellect, began to dismiss the reality of the amazing experience. Despite my doubts and so-called educated reasoning, some other part of me "knew" that a realization of Mother's actual presence was valid. I heard no voice. I saw nothing. I only felt the hands, and unmistakably they were her own, comforting me. Alone in my sorrow and reaching out, did I attain for one fleeting second the higher frequency, and did she, reaching back, cause mother and son to make a quick but unmistakable contact between time and eternity? Despite all mental questioning, I cannot abandon the conviction that she was actually there spiritually saying in effect, "I am all right. I love you." I view it as a bridging of the unobstructed universe.

Some years later on a Saturday, Ruth and I went to Ocean Grove, New Jersey, where I was scheduled to speak the next day in the large auditorium. Methodist Bishop Arthur J. Moore, one of the outstanding preachers of his time, was to share the platform. On Saturday afternoon Ruth, the bishop, and I were strolling on the boardwalk at Asbury Park, when we came across an auction where furnishings were being sold that came from the nearby summer White House of the late President Woodrow Wilson, which was called "Shadow Lawn." The bishop was an insatiable auctiongoer, so we went in. Presently a beautiful pair of crystal hurricane lamps were put up which the auctioneer said President Wilson especially prized.

To my astonishment I put in a bid, a quite low one. Several people raised it. My competitive instincts aroused, I topped each one, though alarmed at what the cost was becoming. Suddenly, the others dropped out and I was the buyer. I could see that Ruth was pleased.

Monday morning we packed them in the trunk of the car and headed for New York and home. But having been raised close to the poverty line, I have a strongly developed frugal streak, and as I drove along, I was much concerned that I had spent too much for the lamps. We stopped for a lunch at a Howard Johnson's restaurant and, perched at the counter, had hot dogs. When we emerged from the restaurant into the bright sunlight in the parking lot, Mother's presence suddenly seemed to materialize and said to me distinctly, "Stop worrying about those hurricane lamps. Ruth is a wonderful girl. Nothing is too good for her." And she was gone. Tears started rolling down my face. Ruth was aghast. "What is the matter?" she asked, deeply concerned. It was miles up the road before I could answer, "I'll tell you sometime."

I could not but wonder what there is in the rules of the unobstructed and sensitive universe that would bring a mother to her son so unexpectedly in the mundane atmosphere of a restaurant parking lot. I recalled James Russell Lowell's line "Love can never lose its own." But while understanding is dim, reality is not. I can see those lovely hurricane lamps as I write today. They have a special meaning quite apart from their beauty.

Why these mystical events and three others, which I shall relate, happened to me I cannot say. But as I have told of them in talks and writings, people—and very rational people at that—have told me of similar happenings. All this seems to confirm our thesis that there is in existence a body of law that is spiritual but factual in nature.

And it is, I believe, quite rational and realistic to expect that we will sometime attain a more exact understanding and knowledge of what we now view as mystical and mysterious. Where now we apprehend primarily by faith, such apprehending may ultimately be aided by a greater understanding of God's laws of the eternal life processes. For it seems reasonable to assume that the natural laws that lift the tides and regulate seed time and harvest are also operative in the realm of life and death and the life beyond this earthly phase. Even as eternity is indivisible, existing now as well as later, so the Creator's laws also govern the mortal and immortal life He created.

That those who have gone to the other side live and continue to grow and develop is a legitimate postulate of both faith and reason. Scripture tells us: "In my Father's house are many mansions: I go to prepare a place for you . . . that where I am, ye may be also." (John 14:2-3) This could mean not only a heavenly home, but also many levels of understanding and spiritual growth to which we may attain after we graduate from the primary grades of life on earth. The real and advanced schooling is, on the other side, the main side, of our lives. And the Lord has prepared that place and will be there with us and we with Him.

I have had three experiences in which I read the law of development and growth. In the first I was seated on the platform of a large auditorium in Sea Island, Georgia. Some ten thousand persons filled the building. They were singing hymns. Again I was with Bishop Moore, who was presiding. He called upon all the preachers present to come forward and form a choir "and show all these people how to sing." I watched them, seemingly several hundred, come streaming down the aisles, singing that old hymn "At the Cross, at the Cross." Then I "saw" him, my father who had died at age eighty-five long before. He came striding down the aisle, singing. He appeared to be about forty years old, in the prime of life, no more arthritis, no sign of stroke or enfeebled body. He was vigorous and obviously happy, and gave every evidence of enjoying life.

I was spellbound, completely lost in what I was "seeing." The huge audience faded away. I was only with him. Getting closer, he smiled that great old smile of his and raised his arm in the old-time familiar gesture as he moved strongly forward on spritely step. I arose from the chair, advanced to the edge of the platform, reaching for him. Then he was gone, leaving me shaken, somewhat embarrassed by my actions but happy at the same time.

However the phenomenon may be rationalized I felt we had been together. The bishop, puzzled by what I had done, asked if I was all right. I nodded. Later, when I told him of the incident, he said something about "the communion of the saints," adding, "Why shouldn't we believe your father was here? He would like a meeting like this, wouldn't he?" The line of a poem came to mind: "Spirit with spirit can meet." And so it can in an unobstructed universe governed by God's unmistakable laws of eternal life.

Not long after that experience, I stood on the sidewalk in front of one of my boyhood homes on a quiet tree-shaded street in

Norwood, Ohio. Roger Ferger, then publisher of the *Cincinnati Enquirer,* had driven me around Norwood. My family had lived in three different houses during our years in this beautiful town in the Cincinnati area, and that day we had stopped briefly before each old home. At the one on Madison Avenue, I left the car and was standing on the sidewalk when the profound mystical experience and vision occurred.

It seemed that I was removed from worldly reality and was once again a small boy standing on that sidewalk, holding the hand of my little brother Bob. The two of us were dressed up as children were in those days. We were waiting for Mother and Father. Then the door opened, and they came down the steps. Mother was wearing an old-fashioned dress that reached her shoetops. The dress seemed to be made of a lacelike material with a full skirt and a narrow waist, and a high collar giving a choker effect. Her hair was piled high and a hat added grace and charm. She seemed about thirty-five years of age. Father appeared to be about forty and was dressed in a suit of a dark blue serge, a derby hat atop his head. He took Mother's arm, and with his accustomed vigor and old-style courtesy, was escorting her down the steps. They were smiling at us.

The experience was so completely real and I was so lost in it that I started to rush forward to them. That broke the spell and the vision vanished. But the reality to me was unmistakable. I was very happy, but the joy turned to sadness when I realized that they walk the ways of earth no more. The emotion showed as I returned to the car. Telling Roger about it, he sat in silence for a moment, then said with conviction, "They were there! You were with them." I, too, think that it was so, for perhaps we live in an unobstructed universe where those we have loved long ago and lost for a while may now and then brush our lives with their loving presence. And perhaps such a gracious experience is meant to say, "We shall meet again," as an old hymn expressed it, "in the sweet bye-and-bye."

Similar to the foregoing was a time when I was speaking at the weekly prayer fellowship attended by the employees of the Foundation for Christian Living in Pawling. My brother Dr. Robert Clifford Peale had died a few weeks before at age sixty-nine. He was a physician and surgeon practicing in Pawling, and was a strong believer and a man of faith. He was compassionate and used his medical education and skills to help people. Before his death he was enfeebled and physically ravaged by the disease that took his life.

This day while I was speaking, suddenly I no longer saw the audience, I only "saw" my brother Bob. He was in a plaza outside the building. Two walls, that of the room and the outside building wall, which lay across a wide corridor, separated the meeting room from the plaza. But Bob was striding across the open space vigorously and full of life. He was young and zestful, exuding joy and enthusiasm. He, too, had his arm raised in a gesture characteristic of him, and his old charming smile was evident. He seemed to say, "It's O.K., Deacon," using a nickname only he had ever applied to me, "it's all O.K." Then he vanished. I had stopped talking while this experience, lasting only a second or two, took place. But I was so affected by its reality that it was necessary to discontinue my talk, and the meeting was dismissed.

However, this strange happening served to deepen my conviction about four facts: (1) Our loved ones who "have died in the Lord" are not dead; (2) they live and grow and are well and happy; (3) their love for us continues; (4) they are near. And though they live in another and higher dimension, at rare times they may break through the barrier. But if they do not reach you as others have been reached by their loved ones, the relationships continue to exist, awaiting your acceptance of them.

Just why I had these experiences is a matter for speculation. It could be that my need was acute. I like to think they happened because I am a spiritual teacher, and therefore had to learn and be convinced so that I might be of more adequate help to those in sorrow. You can hardly teach conviction unless you are yourself convinced. And I am convinced that Almighty God wants us to know that He is the same yesterday and today and forever. And on that basis, since He gave us life here and blessed us, He will give us life over there, and bless us still. His laws are not administered according to whim, nor are they changeable. You can count upon God and His laws, which He formed, as being the same always. In life or death, He loves us and will take care of us. And of that message I have not the slightest doubt whatsoever.